MOUNTAIN EXPERIENCE

MOUNTAIN EXPERIENCE

The Psychology and Sociology of Adventure

RICHARD G. MITCHELL, JR.

With a Foreword by Gerald Suttles

The University of Chicago Press
Chicago and London

Richard G. Mitchell, Jr., is assistant professor of sociology at Oregon State University. He has climbed peaks in the Sierra Nevada and Cascade ranges, in Switzerland, and in British Columbia. He has taught courses in basic mountaineering for the Sierra Club and in climbing and survival skills at colleges in California and Oregon.

The University of Chicago Press, Chicago 60637
The University of Chicago Press, Ltd., London

© 1983 by The University of Chicago
All rights reserved. Published 1983
Printed in the United States of America
90 89 88 87 86 85 84 83   5 4 3 2 1

Library of Congress Cataloging in Publication Data

Mitchell, Richard G., Jr.
  Mountain experience.

  Bibliography: p.
  Includes index.
  1. Mountaineering—Social aspects. 2. Mountaineering
—Psychological aspects. I. Title.
GV200.M57 1983   796.5'2201'9   83-6454
ISBN 0-226-53224-0

This book is dedicated to Dan, who pushed,
and Eleen, who held the rope.

Contents

Foreword

Why do men climb mountains? The question has been asked so often that it has acquired classical—that is, repeatable—answers. But as this book makes clear, the question itself is almost as interesting as mountaineering itself. Others want to know if it is sheer bravery, vanity, phallic worship, a sense of overadequacy, or escapism that drives climbers to high places. These are the standard answers for the standard question; both questions and answers fit an individualistic scheme in which motivation is explanation.

Mountaineering, like life, is more complicated than that. To say why people climb mountains means to say something about why they do anything at all. Some may be able to sit at a desk all day and find that engrossing; others abandon every guarantee of security when possessed by "summit fever"; and still others manage to give themselves up to chance and monotony altogether. Mountaineering is a figurative experience, a metaphor in actual motion and concrete hardship. To put the matter too simply, it is a captivating experience in which, at least for long stretches of time, movement and intention are so confined that one loses the distinction between means and ends or, in Mead's terms, between the "I" and the "me." It brings back into awareness, at least retrospectively, the large part that intrinsic reward can play in getting us through the day. Mountaineering is not the sole way one can experience these intrinsic rewards, but as Mitchell makes clear it is especially tailored to do so. For substantial periods of time the coordination of attention, muscle, and eye is so desperately focused that they flow together with unambiguous purpose.

Ordinary daily experience is often so clouded with detail and distraction that it is difficult to find in it the skeletal outlines of intrinsic purpose. Even the overriding importance of extrinsic rewards—their ultimate necessity—may distract us from what is intrinsically engrossing. Thus, to a large extent we must create occasions, games, or sports in which these distractions are temporarily held in abeyance. Mountain climbing may be one of the most demanding and purest examples of the intrinsically engrossing, for it literally makes its accomplishment a life-and-death matter. Mathematical puzzles, jogging, or writing a well-honed paragraph may suffice for some, but in mountaineering engrossment is what keeps one (not always, but often) from making a fatal misstep.

Is mountaineering, then, a form of escapism, a way of getting away from it all? It is, to some extent, and Mitchell documents how people do find in mountaineering what they cannot find but still want in their workaday life. But I think that his central argument is more complex and subtle. Engrossing activity, and especially mountaineering, revivifies for us a primordial experience of intrinsic gratification and sets a standard against which other experiences can be judged. Those who experience this engrossment know the shortcomings of many of the other things they do. To some extent such an experience relieves them from the "artificiality" of public standards and restores to us a private and seemingly more "real" basis of evaluation.

Knowing the shortcomings of unengrossing activity, we are more able to judge it for what it is; to do it perhaps, but to want something better. In this respect it seems to me that mountaineering or other engrossing activities tend to create or sustain some of the independent spirit that Mitchell finds so pervasive among his mountaineers. To know with confidence what is intrinsically rewarding is emancipating because it provides one with an independent standpoint for evaluating extrinsic rewards. Thus I find it rather expectable that mountaineers are a bit more than usually dissatisfied with their occupational life; that they regard even their own public symbols of mountaineering success with a wry humor; or that they view the outer forms of urban and industrial life with misgiving. Perhaps, they are only being "realistic." That is, they have a private reality against which they may compare that social reality steadily defended in the public marketplace.

Nor is it surprising that mountaineering is popular in the West, for it is in the West that individualism has been tolerated or extolled. For better or worse, this sort of individuality, the secure knowledge of what is intrinsically rewarding, has been allowed in the West. At first sight it may seem trivial to say that mountaineering or other sports are a refuge in which individuality can be grounded in experience. But in the West, sports and recreation are exceptionally developed despite a grudging unwillingness to consider them "serious" activity. True, as Mitchell points out, many of these activities, even mountaineering, can be corrupted by commercializing them or making them subject only to extrinsic rewards. But the serious possibility of discovering the intrinsic value of engrossment remains at the periphery of commercialization and perennially recreates the opportunity for individual knowing. Perhaps that is why we call it "re-creation."

Of course the objective inner experience of mountaineering is not all there is to it. Mountaineering, like other sports or recreations, is embedded in a large organization. Sometimes this organization threatens the inner experience itself, overwhelming it with public signs of verified accomplishment, measures levels of difficulty, and groupings that serve as audiences ready to give appropriate amounts of applause. Some people give in to these external signs of accomplishment, as in the case of "summit baggers" who climb mountains only to count them. And mountaineering is also subject to a substantial degree of commercialization with clothing, equipment, and color slides serving to advertise products as well as awe the masses. Its own stratification system and audience appeal threaten to turn it into only a performance, something done rather than felt.

This kind of corrosion has taken a heavy toll in other forms of recreation, especially the professionalized ones where extrinsic rewards and ulterior purposes have come to govern the smallest details of performance. The Olympics have become a show of national feeling, and Monday night football probably provides more of a sense of recreation for the audience than for the players—and not much for either. Mountaineering, however, has largely escaped this sort of externalization. It takes place in remote places away from the TV cameras and other audiences. The level of difficulty alone is sufficient to dissuade the more opportunistic. And it seems especially to attract the independent-minded with a kernel of skepticism about the exhaustive validity of public standards. Wanting to "get away from it all" in their case may be less a form of escapism than a search for something with experiential validity.

Even where the encasing organization of mountaineering threatens to turn the activity into mere role playing, its practitioners often manage to wiggle out of these constraints. As Mitchell points out, mountaineering clubs have created a stratification system which is sometimes so detailed that one can evaluate practically every movement upwards according to difficulty. By comparison, the NORC or Duncan ratings of occupations are extremely crude and incomplete. Seemingly, one could rank almost every mountaineer from the most accomplished to the least able in a finely graduated series of steps, top to bottom. But mountaineers do not use their stratification system exactly that way, and this is something we need to take to heart in the general study of stratification. For the devotee, at least, all of these ratings and past accomplishments are essentially standardized descriptions of different climbs that permit the climber to know what to do to avoid a "routine ascent." Some do it by altering the route from a known one to a less known one, some by using less enabling equipment than a climber ordinarily takes along. It seems perverse, but others may increase the level of difficulty by steadfastly remaining out of physical condition. Of course the ultimate experience is to climb a virgin peak, where there are no prior standards to guide one. The important thing, says Mitchell, is to maintain a ratio between one's ability and the level of difficulty. One makes an easy climb difficult by deliberately putting obstacles in one's way or one makes a difficult route easier by accepting a variety of mechanical devices. In practice, then, one subverts the entire stratification system, bringing easy and hard climbs into one's orbit of ability while still testing that ability.

I do not mean to suggest by this that mountaineers, or anyone else for that matter, are indifferent to their general ranking or to how others see them. Mitchell rightly says that this is a big part of mountaineering and documents the variety of insignia and signs of accomplishment which are often bandied about. For the most part, however, that occurs after the climb, at club meetings or mountain lodges. These extrinsic rewards are desired, and even when they are not desired (for example, by those hardy solo climbers) they are necessary for substantiating the standards. But if these public acknowledgments are essential in one way or another, they are not what gets one up a mountain. The experience of mobility in some system of social ranking is a relatively rare event in practically any realm of life, sometimes taking years of effort before there is anything public to point to. Even if we give all due respect to the human capacity to defer gratification, mobility itself cannot always be the proximate aim that keeps one trudging along, either up a mountain side or almost anywhere else. For that matter, most people reach the top of their profession or occupation relatively early in life, and if they are to continue to find interest in what they are doing, they must play with their stratification system. Finding a new route to the same place, putting obstacles in one's way, even being underprepared, add to one's sense of accomplishment when public acknowledgment is remote or nothing new is accomplished.

This business of playing with one's stratification system is, I think, something that deserves more of our attention. The means-ends scheme so heartily embraced by sociologists makes all of us seem designing. Primitive rebels are revolutionaries; schoolchildren are investing in their human capital; college professors are playing the "status game." Nobody is having any fun. This image, I suspect, is vastly overdrawn. People still play with externally imposed stratification systems and institutionalized routines. That is one reason they are able to do what they do and to get as far as they do. Indeed, one might advance the hypothesis that the person who is a grind, someone who adheres to accepted practice with unfailing devotion, is unlikely to win the long-term acclaim that he is said to be heading for. He will expire of boredom beforehand. Style and self-esteem, then, are as essential as the incentive of ultimate social acclaim.

None of this denies that many roles, especially work roles, give little latitude for playing with one's stratification system—for what some people call "creativity." One thing that Mitchell presses on us is the fact that many mountaineers have sought and failed to find in their work lives the intrinsic gratifications they do find in mountaineering. Despite the "white-collar revolution," the diminishing presence of assembly lines, and the widening availability of "flex-time," it seems to me that Mitchell is putting his finger on a sensitive spot in American life. Undoubtedly our standards for what work should provide have risen; the number of college-educated in the labor force alone would suggest as much, as would the often vacuous publicity about the many occupations that offer a veritable universe for creativity and self-expression. Such expectations are perhaps excessive and unrealistic. But at the same time there is another trend in sociology and managerial ideology which says that work should be hard and earnest. An earlier tendency to talk about the "joy of work" has been discredited as a smokescreen for exploitation. What workers want is the money, the power. Maybe so. In any case there seems to be a new crop of MBAs, armed with the rhetoric of Weber and Milton Friedman, for whom the work place is only figures on a piece of paper: wages and profits. Meanwhile, in the personnel department, the industrial psychologists are promising self-expression and autonomy. The trouble is, of course, that people want everything: extrinsic and intrinsic rewards. Knowing the limits and possibilities is especially hard. To get some perspective on this, it may help to climb a mountain. Certainly one is impressed with the renewed strength of American participation in sports, at least some of which provide their own private experience.

There is a good deal more to Mitchell's study than its timely examination of athletic re-creation. It captures especially well the persistent tension between the essential social organization for supporting mountaineering and its tendency to erode the inner experience of the devoted practitioner. This seems to be one of the generic dilemmas of social life, though it is fair to say that some activities, such as mountaineering, survive it far better than others—say downhill skiing or Monday night football. We can appreciate it here as a primordial drama just as we enjoy the dramas of playwrights who put together new works on old themes. Also, for those of us who still find in the written word a more effective way of vicariously joining in someone else's world, this book brings a part of mountaineering into our own ken. It is a vivid portrayal, both appreciative and analytical. One's only misgiving is that those who read it may add to the overcrowding of America's peaks and ridges. At least they will have learned their ethics from a sensitive practitioner.

GERALD SUTTLES

Preface

This is a book about mountains and the people who climb them, a book about mountaineering. While other books recount climbing's history and significant achievements, or outline climbing techniques, this volume examines what it is like to be a mountaineer as the occupant of a role and the participant in a relationship. Its special focus is on the experience. The perspective is sociological. From this point of view, the climber's world is composed first and foremost of people. How these people interact literally and symbolically, how they share, cooperate, compete, assist, judge, criticize, encourage, and otherwise influence each other, is what this book is about.

Mountain climbing is a technical process with a social meaning and morality of its own. Understanding the experience of climbing requires attention to the social context in which it occurs. Without an investigation of the social component of the climber's world, mountaineering is reduced to makeshift engineering, to a manipulation of tools for no purpose. No climber would long tolerate such a reduction. Climbing is least of all simply getting to the top of mountains and other awkward locales. It is, most centrally, a social event, a deed done usually with others and always with others in mind.

The vital importance of social definitions in mountaineering is made clear when one considers that the awesome importance ascribed to mountains is largely a social construction. Topographically speaking, mountains are not particularly noteworthy. The earth's surface is relatively smooth. On some imagined giant globe of our planet, equal in diameter to the height of a 36-story skyscraper, the greatest mountain on earth, Everest, would rise less than 1 inch above the Indian Ocean, only infinitesimally higher than her sister peaks on the Himalayan plateau. In spite of this relative insignificance in scale, people have strong feelings about mountains. Everest, for example, is worshiped by Asian Buddhists as Chomolungma, Goddess Mother of the World. For Western mountaineers, ascending Mount Everest has been one of the great climbing challenges for more than a century. Millions of dollars and dozens of lives have been spent in efforts to place a handful of humans on that special summit.

For some, mountaineering symbolizes certain quintessential human qualities—plucky striving and courage in the face of adversity and danger; achievement, conquest, self-actualization. For others, it is the epitome of foolishness and waste, a dim-witted, plodding exercise that ends in dreadful falls. Whether mountains become objects of religious veneration or consummate challenges, whether climbing is seen as an exercise in absurdity or as a higher calling, depends upon the ways in which people choose to act toward the mountain and the mountaineer.

The material upon which this book is based comes from a wide range of sources. First and most important is seven years of participant observation within the Southern California climbing community. This included my taking, assisting with, and, finally, teaching courses in basic mountaineering sponsored by a local chapter of the Sierra Club. I have also taught courses in climbing and survival skills in colleges in California and Oregon. During the past ten years I have had the opportunity to ascend over fifty peaks in the Sierra Nevada and Cascade ranges in the company of various climbers and climbing groups with and without formal club affiliation. Special skill-seminars and advanced sessions in rock climbing and snow and ice travel were also attended. A brief summer period of climbing, observation, and interviewing in Zermatt, Switzerland, provided valuable additional material, as did two month-long expeditions in the coast range of British Columbia.

Mountaineering has a literature of its own. I read a small but important sampling of this writing, including roughly sixty volumes of climbing history and lore, as background material, along with a half-dozen "how to" books on mountaineering techniques. Information on a sample of Southern California Sierra Club climbers was obtained by questionnaire. In a nationwide sample, projective techniques were employed to elicit public opinion on mountaineering. A sample of mountain-top summit registers was analyzed and offered a nonreactive indication of the background and experience of climbers. In sum, methods were selected with regard to their suitability to the questions being asked. As this inquiry covers a broad spectrum of issues, diverse methods were appropriate and utilized.

The sociological study of mountaineering is important. It complements the sociologist's perennial concern for work and vocations with additional knowledge of a rapidly increasing aspect of American social life—leisure. More time is now spent in leisure pursuits than in any other social activity, including family and personal care and employment. During the past two decades, life expectancy has increased,[1] the age at which people retire has decreased,[2] health has improved,[3] and paid vacations for career plant and office workers have more than doubled in number and increased in length.[4] A larger share of consumer dollars is now expended for leisure pursuits.[5] People have more time,[6] energy,

money, and inclination to participate in leisure activities. Social scientists
are only beginning to recognize this rapid shift in priorities. A look at
introductory sociology texts reveals a predominant concern with the
conditions, rewards, and consequences of work, while little notice is
taken of events in the avocational social world. For sociology to retain its
utility and relevance, understanding the ways in which leisure activity is
selected and the gratifications and challenges it offers is of vital importance. This book is a step in that direction.

Sociology benefits in another, perhaps more important, way. Heretofore, most studies of this sort have been deductive applications of established sociological principle *to* sport and leisure. Here I have attempted to
reverse that trend and generate *from* the study of mountaineering new
insights about human behavior that are applicable in broader spheres of
social experience.

This book is organized around three major questions. Part 1 examines
climbing action in addressing the question, "What is mountain climbing?" Mountaineering is shown as a series of interrelated tasks through
which climbing ventures are initiated, planned, and executed. Part 2
looks at "What is a mountain climber?" This part turns to the issue of the
climber's identity and the ways in which reputations are earned and
enhanced in the climber's social world. The techniques of mountaineering impression management are discussed, and the role that formal clubs
and organizations play in this process is examined. Finally, Part 3 shifts
attention from identity to motive. "Why do people climb mountains"
becomes the central question. The historical accounts, psychological rewards, and social pressures experienced by the climber all contribute to
the answer.

This book is more concerned with typical climbers than it is with
extraordinary elites. The heroes of expeditionary extravaganzas and specialists in rock-climbing firsts are mentioned and admired throughout,
but my central concern is climbers with more common abilities and
achievements. These have often been my companions and confidants in
the mountains. It is their world I am trying to understand and share.
While the deeds of typical climbers are less dramatic than could be
imagined, they are honest and fulfilling adventures, satisfying to tens of
thousands of weekend and holiday climbers, novices and veterans alike.
Mountaineering journalism has disproportionately reported on the
avant-garde in climbing, on those who push back the limits of the possible. As a sociologist I am more concerned and content with reporting the
qualities and experiences of conventional, representative participants.

Many have contributed in various ways to the writing of this book.
For the generous willingness of Gerald Suttles to prepare the Foreword I
am especially grateful. Herbert Blumer and Tom Lasswell provided detailed commentary on the manuscript as did John Johnson and Carol

Warren. Ruth Dyer Mendenhall, Jim Lester, and Larry Hamilton helped clarify numerous technical issues of mountaineering throughout the text. Both the published works and personal correspondence of Mihalyi Csikszentmihalyi inspired and sharpened the discussion of climber motive. Robert N. Wilson and Allen Guttmann offered refinements to my treatment of leisure in modern society. Others offered further critical review: Robert Harlow, James Haehn, Ed Finegan, and Clark Molstad. Special thanks is due to the friends who introduced me to the mountains and with whom I shared climbing adventures: Lynn and Cresson, Sig and Gabe, Gerard, Steve, Rosalind, and others in the Angeles Chapter of the Sierra Club. Christina Pyle's assistance in typing the manuscript is gratefully acknowledged. With the considerable aid these persons have offered, the book no doubt has been improved. The errors that remain are my own.

I also wish to acknowledge permission to use material from my article "The Benefits of Leisure Stress," which appeared in the *Journal of Physical Education, Recreation, and Dance* (October 1982).

This work is dedicated to two people. For seven years Daniel Glaser provided guidance, personal encouragement, and unflagging enthusiasm, from original inception of the project through many drafts. Eleen Baumann began as my companion on the rope a decade ago. We now share much more of our lives.

In an era of research dominated by sophisticated quantitative investigations of pressing social problems, writing what amounts to an ethnography about mountain climbing is not easy or perhaps even wise for the serious social scientist. This project, like climbing itself, is best described in Styles's (1967, 263) words:

The thing is useless, like poetry, and dangerous, like lovemaking.

___⋀___
Part One
What Is Mountain Climbing?

INTRODUCTION

The expedition members scaling such lofty giants as Mount Everest are clearly engaged in climbing a mountain, but in other instances the distinction is not always clear. Is the ascent of 6,800-foot Strawberry Peak in the San Gabriel range near Los Angeles mountain climbing? Are the wintertime skiers who ascend Mount Whitney, California's highest peak, mountain climbing? Are the rock gymnasts inching their way up some vertical face in the Yosemite Valley mountain climbing?

Participants themselves are often quite outspoken in defining what they consider to be "true" mountaineering. Depending on their interests, some climbers may demean others as "rock engineers," "peak baggers," "skiers," "hill walkers" (a British understatement), or "ice freaks." Mountaineering as an activity is related to backpacking, cross-country skiing, wilderness exploration, rock climbing, and physical fitness programs. Each of these elements may be a part of the mountaineering experience but none is a substitute for it. In order to avoid definitional arguments as much as possible and to separate mountaineering from its cousins, I suggest that mountaineering be viewed as having seven separate but interdependent parts.

The seven components of mountaineering endeavors are: planning, equipment, companions, conditioning, travel, technical climbing, talk, and debriefing. The time devoted to each of these elements is not well correlated with the interest or concern participants and lay people alike show for them. Actors and onlookers often show the greatest attention to one component, technical climbing, as the definitive and central phenomenon of mountaineering. Debates on ethics and style focus on technical climbing issues. When participants congratulate or compare themselves, it is often a technical climbing event or record that is highlighted. The uninitiated may see mountaineering narrowly, as only a technical climbing experience. This emphasis is out of proportion to the amount of technical climbing which in fact goes on in the mountaineering process. Like sex in a relationship between two people, technical climbing provides more spice than actual substance to the venture.

This emphasis on technical climbing should not overshadow the importance of the other elements—conditioning, travel, etc.—which make up mountaineering. As each is considered in turn, other subdivisions will develop and other kinds of distinctions will be made. Not all types of climbing are mountaineering. Neither are all forms of debriefing, planning, and so on a part of climbing. It is a particular emphasis, approach, or perspective brought to these seven elements that renders them consitutent parts of the mountaineering process. This combination of parts into a cohesive, identifiable activity is a tenuous and elusive merging. Any of the components may become an end in itself, as in the world of the cross-country runner, hill walker, wilderness skier, equestrian, sports-car buff, or professional lecturer. They also may combine with subtle changes in emphasis and give rise to mountaineering's close cousins—rock climbing, backpacking, trekking, and so forth. These acts are discussed in the order they might typically have in the planning and execution of some mountaineering venture, with the recognition that many variations are possible.

1
Planning

When a mountaineer decides to climb, he foresees everything possible to foresee, organizes the smallest details of his ascent precisely. . . . Those who do not proceed thus are mental cases who need a psychoanalyst and generally won't live long.

Maurice Herzog, *Annapurna*

An analytically distinct activity pursued by all mountaineers is that of planning and preparing for future trips. This may at first sound like a phase common to all action, but for climbers it has special properties. Planning is both a creation and a calculation. Planning is the process of fantasy and dream, of imaginatively constructing future and potential experience; it is also the careful enumeration of possible outcomes attendant on some action, of assigning probabilities to those outcomes, and of preparation for those contingencies. This second phase of planning sets mountaineering preparations apart from those associated with other sports, since the climber's comfort, well-being, and even life may depend on these plans. Planning to travel and climb in the mountains is a joyous task, with serious implications.

Planning involves two stages. Inspiration and goals define the project, information collection gives it substance and direction.

Inspiration and Goals

Picking a mountain to climb is the first task of a person who decides to go mountaineering. This is seldom an on-the-spot, spontaneous decision but one involving considerable interaction with self and, usually, with others. Climbers are unlikely to stroll along mountain pathways, suddenly exclaim "There's a nice one!" and rush straight off for the summit. True, possible peaks and routes may be discovered while in the mountains, especially in expeditionary-type ventures in which advance scouting trips are part of the planning process, but the actual climb may not follow this early reconnoitering until weeks, months, or even years have passed. The typical West Coast climber journeying to the Sierra Nevada or Cascades selects the peak well in advance of departure from home. How are these selections made?

One source of inspiration and goals is the past experience of the climber. A peak glimpsed in the distance from the summit of one mountain becomes the object of a later climb. Clarence King, while working with the first geological survey of California, under Josiah Whitney's direction, attempted to climb what he believed to be the highest point in the Sierra, Mount Tyndall. When he reached the summit, new climbing challenges emerged.

> To our surprise, upon sweeping the horizon with my level, there appeared two peaks equal in height with us, and two rising even higher. That which looked highest of all was a clearly cut helmet of granite upon the same ridge with Mt. Tyndall, lying about six miles south. . . . Mount Whitney, as we afterwards called it in honor of our chief, is probably the highest land within the United States. (King [1872] 1970, 76)

It was to take King three tries over a span of ten years to reach that distant summit.

Mountaineering literature sometimes stimulates interest in climbing in some little-known area. A series of articles published in *Mountain* focused attention on the climbing potential of the high mountains in Pakistan.

> The Karakoram Range has everything for the ambitious climber; high mountains, virgin summits, appealing granite spires, elegant snow and ice problems, reasonable weather and limitless potential. . . . Now that the middle stage of exploration has been reached on the accessible peaks of Nepal, the latter part of the decade will probably see greater attention being paid to the Karakoram. . . . In this special feature we have drawn together much interesting though loosely related material that has resulted from the renewed activity that has occurred since the Karakoram again became accessible in 1974. . . . Malcolm Howells casts a searching eye over the tempting possibilities in the Biafo area. . . . and it is hoped that the whole feature will add up to a useful preface to what looks like being an exciting new chapter in mountaineering history. (*Mountain Magazine* 1979, 18)

Guidebooks, a typical example of which is *The Climber's Guide to the High Sierra* (Roper 1976), published by the Sierra Club, provide catalogs of peaks and routes described in some detail, along with information about approaches and technical difficulties. These guidebooks provide such a wealth of information, in fact, that they are claimed by some to reduce much of the uncertainty in mountaineering and are decried as ethical intrusions. More will be said about this below and in the discussion on record keeping in Chapter 8.

The climber interacts with a community of fellow mountaineering enthusiasts who have experience and knowledge of their own. They share (or jealously guard) discoveries, ideas, and information at club meetings and other social occasions. An anecdote about the climbing adventures of Tom Patey, renowned Scottish climber, illustrates how this knowledge may be provided to friends and denied others.

> Tom's Black Book was legendary. It was handled with reverence and spoken of with awe by those privileged few permitted to see it. A large black ledger . . . , it contained all of Tom's far-reaching research into potential new routes in the Alpine areas which tickled his fancy. It bulged with photographs, sketches, "topos" [maps], foreign press reports and clippings from climbing magazines from all over the world. We had just been stormed off one of the Black Book's secret lines . . . and sitting over a brew in our Val Veny campsite, Tom produced the Book again. "Ah know of a great wee line on the [Aiguille du] Plan," he confided. "Ah canna think why nobody's seen it before . . . ." It was dark when Tom came rushing into camp. "Damn Bonnington," he cried, "he's back from the Vercors and what's more he's already carried off and away up our route! Left this afternoon with Lito, that American manny, and planned to bivouac at the bottom. Ah should never have shown him ma book!" Rusty gave a grunt of disapproval at so base an action. Obviously the spirit of friendly rivalry had been overdone. (Cleare 1975, 36–37)

Knowledge is more likely to be shared with those who follow than with those who intend to precede, particularly if the objective is a highly prized "first ascent."

Some climb experiences are "made-to-order" in the form of organization-sponsored trips, such as those offered by mountaineering clubs, and commercial tour groups, such as Mountain Travel, Inc. Individually guided climbs of standard routes in well-known climbing areas are also available, notably in the Pennine Alps and the Mont Blanc massif in Europe, and to a much lesser extent in the United States (e.g., in the Palisades in the Sierra Nevada, the Wyoming Tetons, Washington's Mount Rainier, and Alaska's Mount McKinley). These ready-made trips represent a distinct departure from other forms of mountaineering in their explicit recognition of two levels of expertise, leader or guide and follower or client. Planning goes on within such groups as well, but often the activities which concern us here are the more experienced person's unilateral responsibilities.

These professionally guided trips vary in difficulty, cost, and number according to the group sponsoring them. In Southern California, most of the trips of this kind are offered by the Angeles Chapter of the Sierra Club through its various suborganizations, principally the Sierra Peaks, Desert Peaks, and Rock Climbing sections. These trips are announced in the tri-annual *Sierra Club Schedule* sent free to club members and sold at modest cost in sporting goods and mountaineering shops throughout the area. Trips sponsored by the Sierra Club are free and open to all who meet the trip requirements. As an illustration:

> June 17–19, Fri–Sun, Sierra Peaks. Mt. Ritter (13,157'), Banner Pk. (12,945'): Hike Fri. to camp at Ediza Lake (9 mi, 2000' gain). Sat. climb Mt. Ritter and Banner Pk. (class 3 rock and glacier, 4500' gain, 4 mi. rt.). Possible optional climb Fri. or Sun. of Mt. Davis (class 1, 3000' gain, 8 mi rt. from Ediza). Ice axe, crampons mandatory. Group limit 15. Send . . . resume of recent climbing, ice axe and cramponing experience to Leader: Meridee Muell. Asst Dennis Lantz. (Sierra Club, Angeles Chapter 1977, 90)

While this particular trip stipulated an upper limit of fifteen, typical parties may involve as many as twenty-five people. Such groups, by their size and sharp division of skills, are limited in the climbing difficulty that can be attempted but do offer a wide variety of intermediate-level experiences. How many people are involved in these trips is suggested by the bulletin listings. As an example, the offerings for the month of August 1981 included thirty-six separate trips attempting sixty-eight peaks, three additional rock climbs, and potentially involving over 850 participants.

At the other extreme are guided group-trips involving multi-day technical ascents of an expeditionary character in distant mountain ranges throughout the world, at a cost commensurate with the difficulty. An example is the Aconcagua expedition of 1977.

> Climbing the highest peak outside Asia. As the highest summit in the Western Hemisphere, Aconcagua is of intense interest to many mountaineers. There is still some debate as to the exact height of this massive mountain, Argentina's "stone sentinel," but most people now agree 6970 meters or slightly under 23,000 ft.
>
> Our ascent of this Andean giant will be via the Polish route . . . first climbed in 1934. This route involves some 1800 ft. of technical ice climbing, which can present serious difficulties depending on weather and acclimatization. The itinerary will be the same as for our successful 1975 expedition, but we have scheduled four extra days on the mountain to allow for the possibility of Aconcagua's sudden and furious storms. This trip is open to those with at least six years of solid experience.

ACONCAGUA
DATES   January 1977   About 30 days
LEADER   John Fischer   Grade F
LAND COST $1705
FROM MIAMI via BRANIFF
TOTAL COST $2515
(Mountain Travel, Inc. 1976, 31)

Such trips seldom involve more than ten paying participants and thus represent an ideal, if rare, guided climb. Many aspire to but few actually participate in this sort of trip.

The cyclical and episodic nature of climbing activity should be noted here. It is often the last phase of a climb, debriefing, that provides interaction with other climbers and stimulates new ideas, inspiring the planning of another trip. By whatever means a climbing objective is selected—prior personal experience, the suggestion of friends, periodicals or other literature, or, to a lesser extent, ready-made opportunities—that selection is followed by a search for specific additional knowledge.

Collection of Information

What is known about a particular climb varies enormously. On popular rock climbs in the United States and Europe, guidebooks offer more than just a catalog of climbs. They may detail climbing routes to the extent of outlining the difficulty of each rope length or "pitch," enumerating specific moves and special difficulties:

> Route 4. Venusian Blind Arete. III 5.5. . . . Climb the lefthand snowfield for 150–200 feet until a snow-covered ledge leads horizontally left about 350 feet to the left side of the base of the 200-foot-high sweeping slab. This slab is the farthest visible to the left; it is not the minor slab which begins the third rib. Climb an open book for 100 feet. The next pitch stays close to the left side of the slab and then moves onto the prow above the slab. Move up through a ceiling; then climb a class 4 pitch. This is followed by a 10-foot notch and a 100-foot tower on the right. From the top of this tower move immediately onto the major tower of the arete and climb it in three pitches. Above, one long pitch over gendarmes leads to the base of the next pillar. This is 160 feet high. The remainder of the climb is easy and involves notches, gendarmes, and chocks. This section takes one to the talus slopes on the east side of Temple Crag. (Roper 1976, 207)

The extreme of foreknowledge is found on some rock climbs in popular areas so frequently repeated that it is possible to determine from inspection below where one's hands and feet should be placed on the climb. Black rubber marks the rock from the passages of numerous climbing shoes and white stains remain where holds have been powdered by climbers using gymnasts' chalk on their hands for greater friction. In such areas it is sometimes joked that all one needs are numbers to indicate which of these black and white spots are for the left or the right hand or foot.[1] While on some climbs almost everything is known in advance, others are almost total mysteries at their onset.

In the record of the first ascent of Annapurna, the first of the great 8,000-meter Himalayan giants to be climbed, Maurice Herzog, the expedition leader, recalls the following exchange among team members. It should be noted that they are discussing the tenth highest mountain in the world—26,502 feet high.

> "But where the devil *is* Annapurna?" asked Ichac.
> "It's almost certainly behind that handsome triangular peak, over there—look to the right, in the distance."
> "I'm not so sure," said Ichac.
> "Nor am I," said Rebuffat.
> "And the Tilicho pass—where's that?" went on Ichac.
> "At the far end of the plateau, on the other side of the lake. It must overlook the Manangbhat valley, which lies just beyond."
> "[There's] no sign of a lake on the map! And it's at least four miles long." (Herzog 1953, 75–76)

Both of these examples are atypical of mountaineering experiences. Most mountains are not climbed "by the numbers," nor are they totally unknown entities; they are somewhere in between.

In planning a typical weekend climb the mountaineer needs to know how difficult the proposed objective may prove to be, how long it might take to complete, and the best way to get to and from the peak. This knowledge will guide the selection of gear, companions, and the provision of adequate time. Climbing guidebooks have been mentioned as a potential source of such information. Other publications describe trail and pass systems useful to climbers in their approaches; some discuss ski tours to the bases of peaks; still others detail rock climbs in popular areas. These publications are supplemented by articles on specific climbs and climbing areas in mountaineering journals and magazines.

This information, however, is not universally available. A certain sophistication is required to learn of these and related data sources. The novice climber may lack that sophistication. The first and ultimate source of information remains fellow climbers. As hinted above, climbers more readily reveal past experience than future plans. This limitation aside, other climbers are still an important source of firsthand knowledge (as well as of hearsay, myth, and rumor). Friends, or even strangers, may be queried for details of their experience.

It is common for persons setting out on a semi-exploratory climb to ask for and receive considerable information from individuals who have gone before them, as scientists working in a new area of inquiry may correspond and share their discoveries with each other (while guarding some details until publication). It has often been noted in mountaineering circles that the British success in climbing Mount Everest in 1953 was a direct result of the lessons learned by the Swiss in their two 1952 attempts on the mountain and generously shared by them. The leader of the British team describes the Swiss assistance:

> I was naturally anxious to meet with the Swiss team as soon as possible after their return from Nepal. A meeting was arranged in Zurich on January 25th, and Charles Evans came with me on a twenty-four-hour visit to that city. We were most kindly received by Dr. Feuz of the Foundation for Alpine Research, and there met Dr. Chevalley, leader of their autumn expedition, Raymond Lambert, who had climbed so high with Tenzing in the spring of the previous year, and other members of their expedition. We were shown all their equipment and received a very frank and generous "hand over" of their knowledge and experience . . . for our ascent was linked at almost every step with their attempt. (Hunt 1954, 51, 226)

In general, the less that is known about a particular climbing area, the more one is held responsible for sharing a personal knowledge of that area with fellow climbers. To withhold knowledge of particular objective hazards which would not be otherwise noticeable to a competent mountaineer is distinctly untoward behavior. Information need not be volunteered, however. The latter point is underscored by Ed La Chapelle in his recounting of the circumstances surrounding the deaths of three avalanche victims.[2]

> On the other hand, the survivors advanced the interpretation that the responsible camp leader should have been advised in regard to the recognition of avalanche danger and of the rescue organization without having to ask. This interpretation runs counter to reality and is to be rejected. No native of an area can be expected to offer guests unsolicited advice about possible danger of the area, not the least reason being that such a warning more often than not encounters ingratitude. It is the elementary obligation of the camp organization to seek clarification of questions regarding avalanche danger from trustworthy residents. (La Chapelle 1970, 53)

Climbs of an expeditionary character are often carefully documented in considerable detail with films, slides, and often a book. These materials serve as sources of information to others who subsequently journey to these areas.

Two other information sources commonly utilized are weather forecasts and topographic maps. Weather predictions may be of critical importance in mountaineering. Two feet of fresh powder snow over ice-glazed rock, low temperatures, and high winds imply a radically different sort of climbing experience than dry, sun-warmed rock, T-shirt conditions, and gentle breezes. Hypothermia, commonly referred to as "exposure" by the media, has claimed victims unprepared for wind and rain on high alpine slopes where, a few hours earlier, warm sunshine and clear skies prevailed. On the British Everest climb in 1953, special arrangements were made with the Indian Meteorological Service to broadcast via All-India Radio and the BBC daily reports of expected conditions in the Everest area. These forecasts were received at base camp and radioed to climbers higher up the mountain. For the weekend climber, preparations are usually not quite as elaborate.[3] Newspaper weather reports can be scrutinized daily and calls can be made to the Weather Bureau, which may be able to provide special forecasts of a particular local climbing area on request. During the late 70s, "Dr. George" Fishbeck's dynamic and amusing nightly weather prognosis on ABC television in the Los Angeles region became popular viewing for mountaineers preparing for trips to Southern California areas. Whatever the source, predictions are combined with the climber's own past experiences and with the expertise of others gleaned from texts and articles (e.g., "Mountain Weather" in Ferber 1974, 428–40) to construct a composite picture of what may be forthcoming climatically.

Maps have been mentioned and maligned above. In general, excellent and detailed maps are available to the climber in most of the popular climbing areas. For the mountain ranges of the United States, topographic maps produced by the U.S. Geographical Survey provide an abstract picture of the ups and downs of terrain to be traversed on the approach to one's intended climb. These maps may be more fully utilized by the many climbers who also carry a compass for pinpointing and identifying distant landmarks and the climber's own position. The sport of "orienteering" is pursued by some as an end in itself. Orienteers, using map and compass, attempt to locate markers placed in advance on a course in varied and sometimes mountainous terrain. The object is to follow directions from one marker to the next around the entire course of perhaps several miles in the shortest possible time. Thus, the orienteer experiences the navigational problems faced by the mountaineer in a structured and miniaturized context. Although orienteering is not widespread in the United States at the present time, it serves to illustrate one activity related to, and sometimes confused with, mountaineering. While the orienteer may travel through mountainous terrain, even from summit to summit, his purpose in being there is only tangential to that of the climber. They share a common setting, along with the backpacker, wilderness skiier, and others, but the mountaineer's motive and perspective remain separate and unique.

In summary, planning is the first step toward the mountain top. It takes place well in advance of actually setting forth on the climb. Climbing goals may be inspired by past experience, other climbers, literature, or even commercial offerings. Once a goal has been selected, further information is sought concerning the conditions likely to be encountered on the trip. At this stage, guidebooks, journals, weather reports, and, most important, other climbers are consulted. The sharing of information between climbers is a normatively governed but uneven process. If asked, climbers are expected to provide as much information as they have that might contribute to another climber's safety. They are not, however, expected to volunteer this information. Knowledge that might lead to a successful climb of some as yet unclimbed route or peak may be jealously guarded or generously shared according to the chivalry of the climbers involved, the significance of the proposed objective, and the probability that the information provided will influence the outcome of the climb.

After goals are set and information gathered, climbers turn their attention to another concern, companions. Mountaineers do not often go alone to the mountains. Who accompanies them requires and receives careful thought.

2
Companions

For the most part climbers climb together and there is a communication which transpires between them, an immutable
mutuality of experience.

Michael Tobias, "The Anthropology of Ascent"

Independence and Interdependence

Mountain climbing is a social activity. With notable exceptions, it is
seldom a solitary endeavor.[1] Rather, it is a companionate and often
collective act. The intimacy and interdependence between climbers is,
however, variable.

At one extreme we find the loose-knit conglomerate of hikers who
join together on a trip sponsored by a local climbing-club, perhaps one of
the many such trips offered by the Sierra Club in Southern California.
Their prior knowledge of each other and of the trip leaders is circumstan-
tial and incidental. They come together because of the leadership offered,
the opportunity for logistical coordination, car pooling, sharing of stoves
and tents, etc., and for the confidence provided by "safety in numbers."
Should the need arise, they can divide the contents of an exhausted
climber's pack and lend him or her assistance in clearing the mountain,
fetch mountain rescue personnel, or render first aid. Participants in such
groups need not know or be particularly predisposed toward each other
beyond basic acceptance of another human being in relatively close
company for a day or two. Knowledge of one's companions is desirable
only for the gregarious or the lonely. The success and safety of the
climbing venture rests elsewhere—in the judgment and motivational
skills of the leader.[2]

At the other extreme is the climbing "rope"—usually two climbers
joined together in one of life's most intimate and fateful embraces. As
they proceed up the mountain, each, in turn, places his or her life in the
hands of the other in the faith that the other's skill and attention will not
betray that trust.[3]

This dichotomy between independent and interdependent climbers
has, at its roots, the activity in which the climbers are engaged. Hiking
and camping generate less intimacy than technical climbing. Mutual need

is present or absent as the circumstances of any climbing trip change. When two skilled technical climbers stroll along a mountain path on their way to base camp or when they attend to the housekeeping chores of putting up tents, finding water, cooking, and the like, they need count on each other for little more than companionship and a helping hand. The next day's climb may find them roped together for many hours on a difficult ascent where they must continually safeguard each other's progress.

Similarly, while the loose-knit group on a club trip scrambles over easy boulders to the summit of some readily accessible peak, its members need share perhaps no more than the view and the exercise. But when a sudden storm engulfs this party on the mountain top, the rocks so easily ascended on the way up become a difficult, ice-encrusted barrier requiring the utmost in delicacy and care on the way down. Under such circumstances, the trip leader might well safeguard party members passing this obstacle by use of a rope belay, a precaution that had not previously been necessary.

The difference in interdependence between the technical rope team in action and the club group encountering unexpected difficulties is both of frequency and duration. The rope-team members lend each other reciprocal and repeated assistance throughout their climb while in the more casual collective of club-type trips the leaders' technical climbing help is reserved for unusual circumstances. Regardless of the direction and frequency of aid extended between fellow climbers, trustworthiness and at least a modicum of technical skill are requisite components of all climbing parties, if not of individual climbers.

Collective skill and experience influence the selection of a suitable objective. Two novices, if they were wise, would not undertake a winter climb of difficult Mount Humphreys in the Sierra Nevada. Such a trip would pose hazards and challenges beyond the beginner's scope. However, if these same two novices were invited to accompany another pair of more experienced climbers on a less demanding endeavor, such as a summertime ascent of the relatively simple "Mountaineers Route" on Mount Whitney, the enterprise might well be feasible. But technical skills are not the only necessary feature of climbing companions or, sometimes, even the most important one.

Time, Money, and Energy

Companions must be chosen on more than the basis of their mountaineering know-how and experience. Climbers are enmeshed in a larger social framework of jobs, families, and other commitments which place time and scheduling restrictions on their availability as climbing companions. Some climbers may be endowed with considerable physical strength and endurance while others are less powerful or indefatigable. Quite independent of either of these factors but equally important is the material well-being of potential companions. While a few climbers may have the finest gear and can afford airline tickets and bush-pilot fees to reach distant climbing areas, others may be less well equipped and financially endowed, even without ready means of traveling to the local ranges. These pragmatic requirements of availability, physical strength, and material resources are also factors in selecting companions. In turn, these factors interact with the technical ability and experience of the participants to determine the form and outcome of climbing ventures.

Remarks to a diminutive would-be climbing-party member illustrate considerations of physical strength and endurance: "If Gerard and Cresson come on the trip, you can come too. They are both strong and can break trail" (Field notes, November 1976). What is implied is that the two strong climbers would be able to forge a path through the early winter snow with relative ease. Without the aid of these two, however, the smaller climber would be required to assume equal responsibility for this arduous chore, a task which would probably prove exhausting and thus prohibitive. Without the aid of the first two robust climbers, other companions or less tiring challenges must be found.

The money, equipment, transportation, and time available to party members influence the climbing objective and the companions who will be included. The following comments illustrate these interrelations:

> Tom can't get off [work] 'til 5:00 on Friday and we need his truck to carry the packs and skis. Why don't you take John in your car on Thursday and I'll bring E.B. in ours and we can go to the roadhead on Thursday. Then Tom can pick up Lynn at work and meet us there. If John and Tom go but Lynn is still sick they can use "San Simeon" [a spare tent]. (Field notes, March 1978)

Equipment and schedules are juggled to meet the requirements of a trip in planning, and the objective of the trip, in turn, is altered to suit the time and gear available. Talent and experience in actual climbing will further modify the choice of companions. Thus the composition of a typical weekend climbing party may involve considerable compromise in participants and, in turn, in objectives. Not so, however, on longer trips or ones of an expeditionary nature.

Expedition Companions

When trips are long, when routes and conditions are uncertain or unknown, when the objective is beyond normal scope in prestige and challenge, and especially in the case of large-scale expeditions, then the selection of companions takes on a different character. While some participating climbers may still be unable to cover their own transportation and related costs, these expenses may be absorbed by expedition sponsors for party members who are selected. Expeditions and extended trips are often planned months or even years in advance, thus allowing considerable lead time in the scheduling of business, family, and other affairs. On these trips, companions are less often excluded or included on the basis of equipment available, finances, or short-term time commitments. With time, transportation, and sufficient supplies reasonably assured, other factors take precedence.

There are differences in the talents of the climbers chosen. As in all other sports, there are a few superstars at the apex of the climbing world who may be included on the team roster. Certainly the inclusion of well-known climbers with records of past expedition success will lend energy to fund raising and equipment solicitation efforts, a necessary activity in financing large expeditions. Further, these superstars may be able to perform extraordinary technical feats that affect the outcome of the expedition. Their capacity to endure and excel under adverse conditions may spell the difference between success or failure. But, talent, even extraordinary talent, is not everything. The presence of superstars is no guarantee that the venture will succeed.

Consider major Himalayan climbs for a moment. With few exceptions, expedition team members all represent an exceptionally high standard of expertise, experience, and physical ability. Himalayan expeditions, because of their cost, are few, while talented climbers are many. Superstars are but the cream of a very rich milk. For most climbers, participating in a large expedition poses a more severe test than simply a measure of their technical ability or physical strength. Expeditions reveal with painful certainty the individual climbers who are emotionally as well as physically adept. It is often required that participants abandon the traditional mountaineer's privilege of relatively independent action to work collectively toward a common goal. The larger and more complex the expeditionary undertaking, the more important cooperation and disciplined teamwork become. Making this transaction from independent actor to team member is not easy to do. Western climbers are a keenly individualistic sort with strong attachments to personal volition. They do not readily subjugate their own desires and decision-making prerogatives to the orders of an expedition leader. Yet those who can dampen their usual independence and shift their orientation to a more cooperative frame may be the most valued companions. The necessity for this increased cooperation is a function of the expeditionary climbing process.

Expeditionary climbing is like pyramid construction. A broad base of material and labor is required so that a few may enjoy long-term recognition. The expedition's task is to establish a series of camps up the mountain, a day's climbing apart. As these camps are established. they must continually be provisioned from below so that the work of pushing the route higher can continue. When full siege tactics are employed, the repeated relay of loads from below is often facilitated by the installation of thousands of feet of handrail-type fixed ropes and other devices to make the porterage safer and easier.

In major Himalayan expeditions much of the load carrying is performed by hired porters while establishing new camps is the climbers' responsibility. But the subdivision of tasks is more complex than that. Some climbers may enjoy the challenge and prestige of being "out in front," pushing the route upward, establishing new camps, while others assume the equally arduous and necessary but less glorifying jobs of maintaining the fixed ropes between camps in good repair, escorting porters, and carrying loads themselves in support of climbers higher up. In this way the labor of perhaps hundreds of lowland porters, scores of high-altitude porters, and a dozen or more climbers combine to make possible the summit bid of perhaps a single pair of climbers. All this activity may be directed with military-like precision through daily radio orders to all climbers and other personnel, issued from the expedition leader in his or her headquarters at base camp.[4]

Each person-day of gear and supplies carried to high camp from which the summit may be reached is earned at the price of shuttling tedious tons of material upward from the camps below. Thus, it is not logistically feasible to offer all climbers a chance to reach the top. Those in best physical form and position on the mountain, when the final push comes, are most likely to be chosen. Yet this is another dilemma for the climber. Those who contribute the greatest efforts in stocking and establishing camps may no longer have the necessary resources of strength required to reach the summit. Those who ensure the success of the venture by their own efforts may likewise guarantee that their own role in the final success will be a minor one. As a result of this acute and necessary interdependence, team members are quick to point out the cooperative and collective nature of their enterprise and to deemphasize individual accomplishments. Doug Scott, who reached the summit of Everest by the difficult South West Face, comments on being one of the climbers chosen to go for the top:

> It has taken the combined efforts of forty Sherpas, and sixteen climbers, together with Chris' [the expedition leader] planning, to get the two of us into this position. We know how lucky we were being the representative of such a team and to be given the chance to put the finishing touches on all our efforts. (Quoted in Bonnington 1976, 157–85)[5]

Smaller expeditions and extended climbing trips may lack the task differentiations of Himalayan extravaganzas. All team members are usually expected to take their turns at hauling loads, leading, and other duties and privileges. All participants may not only desire but reasonably expect to reach the summit. Nonetheless, the willingness to work in cooperation with other team members remains a prime requisite in selecting companions if these smaller undertakings are to be successful. As group size is reduced, the importance of individual affability increases. Companions, particularly in small groups on major climbs, find that their interdependence during long planning periods and on the mountain itself cements casual acquaintances into firm and lasting bonds. Team success supersedes the search for individual recognition. Maintaining team unity is even more important. Jim States tells of a medical emergency that forced the early return of a group member from a small-scale attempt on the Himalayan giant Nanda Devi, and of the trauma that separation brought to the other climbers:

> It's emotionally destructive to go home and yet it's medically destructive, potentially, to go higher. . . . We all needed sort of a mental space after having Marty leave because here you're a team, welded in spirit in a sense before you leave, and one person is left behind and it's just like taking an arm when that person leaves. (Field notes)

So, companions are selected for the practical considerations of experience, schedules, and material resources on shorter trips and for talent and cooperative discipline on larger and longer ventures. These generalizations are fine as far as they go but they place undue emphasis on the functional requirements of successfully climbing the mountain. Tom's truck, Cresson's strong legs, and Chris's careful planning are all important factors in eventually reaching the summit. But more important are Tom and Cresson and Chris as persons with whom the climbing experience itself may be shared. As will be seen in Part 3, the joy of mountaineering lies not so much in reaching the summit as in the many small successes along the way—picking a better route for the next few feet above, completing a difficult move, safely reaching the next ledge. These moment-by-moment accomplishments are what makes climbing worthwhile, yet they can only be adequately shared with one's immediate climbing companions. So climbers join in numerous small and intimate conspiracies to rejoice among themselves at the creation of upward motion in an awkward and sometimes hostile environment.

Companions in an Emergency

The need for companions is perhaps less clear when events go smoothly, when objectives come easily to hand and are overcome—when all is

well—than in the face of problems. With unexpected difficulty, the worth
of companions becomes immediately apparent. One does not look for
them in adverse circumstances, but one often finds them there. From my
diary come notes of one such occasion, an accident on the South Face of
Mount Winchell in the Sierras. This account provides a glimpse of the
hazards which frame and stimulate relationships with mountaineering
companions and, I hope, makes understandable, in another way, the
quality and importance of climbing partners.

Memorial Day weekend, May 30, 1976, 11 a.m., 13,500+ feet on
the South Face of Mt. Winchell (13,768).
    Things have taken on a different tone. Right foot on a three-
foot by three-foot-by-eight-inch slab of beautiful white granite,
only to discover that it was not a permanent part of the ledge
upon which it rests. The slab and I slip off together, unroped,
falling. The chute is steep here and near-vertical below. I turn on
my side, trying to avoid the falling stone. To get caught between
that rock and the mountain is sure to result in crushed something. Upside down now, the rock over me, but I shouldn't
worry. It won't stop there. It probably didn't stop for a long way.
The Sill glacier is 2,000 feet below. Other rock debris in the chute
begins to slide. People all over the mountain hear the roar of rock
fall. All I think of is that slab and how to avoid it. As I somersault
faster, air and mountain whirl by. My helmeted head hits another
projecting stone splinter. I claw at the mountainside with hands
and feet and get mostly air and bruises. The bruises began to add
up. People who fall off of mountains don't die all at once. They
are beaten to death, one broken bone, concussion, contusion,
and abrasion at a time. In between you think about the next
contact with the rock and how to stop your fall. Most never do, of
course, but you try. Bam! The mountain hits me again, but this
time I get lucky. Right foot on a ledge, projecting rock. Thirty feet
of fall onto the arch of one foot. A lucky fall. The steel shank in the
bottom of my heavy mountaineering boot imprints itself on the
sole of one foot, through a half-inch of stiff leather. Left hand
clutching, nothing, something—scraping, clinging right hand,
shoulder torn from an earlier grab, grasps again. Collapsing,
slower now, onto the ledge. One foot wide, three feet long.
Stopped.
    Breathing, sight come first, then pain, voices from above,
getting closer. Eleen is beside me. "Are you all right?" she asks.
"Take a picture!" I reply. "I mean it, take a picture! I'm not going
to go through this without some record. I paid my dues." That's
honestly what I said, and that is what Eleen did. Then we took
inventory. Right foot hurts, moves, doesn't feel broken. Right
hip, lower back, neck, head, all hurt, not broken. By the greatest
of luck I had managed to distribute the impact of the fall over a

half-dozen spots, all slightly damaged, and stop in thirty feet
what rightly should have been a nonstop move to the bottom of
the mountain.

People watched me fall. Sig and Gabe, Gerard, Eleen all
stood above, feeling helpless they said. Slow motion? Perhaps.
Things that are unexpected, dramatic may be recalled in slow
motion, but they don't take place that way. They happen fast. It
takes less than two seconds for a human body to fall thirty
feet—that's counting the bouncing off various projections. That
is fast. But the watchers have time to remember afterwards and
imagine what they might have done to help, what it would have
been like to fall themselves, what would happen if the ledge
hadn't been there.

The faller, too, remembers, through constant pain, the fright-
ened reassurances of friends, the sickness and exhaustion of the
walk back to camp, and the sleepless night in a wind blown tent
at 11,800 feet beside a frozen lake. He remembers the eight-mile
walk to the roadhead. Down into the valley—shorts and T-shirts
are substituted for down jackets and wool pants. It's hot. I'm still
cold. Feeling is being lost in the second and third fingers of my
right hand. Gerard and I are finishing the last leg of the walk back
to Glacier Lodge. Gerard, bearded and dusty, plods under the
combined weight of two full packs, his and mine, one lashed
upon the other. We are tired, introspective, we talk about the
accident of the day before. Seeing it happen to someone you
know, right before you, is not like reading about it in the books.
"I didn't want to go on to the top," he says. "I wanted to quit
climbing." "I wanted to help and couldn't." But now he does
help. Carrying perhaps a hundred pounds of gear and all the
while asking how I am, if the pace is right, apologizing when the
trail gets rough. I wear a sling on my right arm now. Fingers on
both hands are splinted crudely with bits of bloodstained card-
board box and tape. I carry Gerard's long ice-axe as a sort of cane.
Stepping heavily on the left foot, with a painful light clumsiness
on the right, trying to accomplish the impossible, to walk on one
foot alone and give those bruises a rest. Bipeds don't work that
way. I shuffle, wince, talk, and remember. We pass a toothless
motorcyclist beside the dirt road. He sees us coming a long way
off. We travel slowly. He surveys the stream slipping through the
valley below. "How's the fishing, boys?" he asks, when we come
abreast. How is the fishing. Later a camper near the lodge jokes,
"It must have been a mighty big fish to do that to you." Gerard
and I walk on.

Remembering at the hospital in Lone Pine, in the X-ray
room—nothing broken. "See a specialist when you get back
home." With the family doctor, "The specialist will have to look
at your X-rays." Remember. Less than two seconds. Friends on
the mountain rally to assist. They carry my gear down, provide

medical advice, offer bandages. These are real offers of needed
assistance from people who care. In the city we can say, "If there
is anything I can do, be sure and call me," and be reasonably sure
nobody will take us seriously. In the mountains it isn't like that. A
man or a woman says, "Let me help." And then they do. Carry
many pounds of gear on top of their own loads down to the cars.
Give expensive and irreplaceable medicines, food, extra warm
clothing. It is a frontier of sorts up there. Social contacts are few
but the worth of another person is great. Home again. When it's
all over, they remember too. Telephone calls. "How did it work
out?" "Glad you are O.K." "No permanent damage?" Nobody
says, "If I can do anything, be sure and give me a call."

Summary

Climbers may be independent or interdependent, according to the particular mountaineering task they face at the moment. Companions are
selected on the basis of both their objective and subjective qualities. In
picking someone with whom to go mountaineering, climbers take into
account such pragmatic features as technical climbing skill, strength and
endurance, financial resources, and time availability. The more elusive
qualities of willingness to work cooperatively toward a common goal and
to provide affable company are also important in selecting companions,
especially on expeditionary climbs where talent, time, and resources
abound. Finally, companions are selected to be the persons with whom
the experience of climbing itself can be shared, in moments of success and
in emergencies.

Climbers for the most part do not go to the mountains alone. Nor do
they go empty-handed. For some obvious practical reasons and some not
so obvious ethical ones, the equipment they take with them is of special
concern.

3
Equipment

The equipment that climbers take with them on their mountain adventures is second in importance only to the persons who accompany them in ensuring the enjoyment, safety, and success of their enterprise. The few items the mountaineer includes in his or her kit must serve many functions.

Gear must provide protection from storms and extreme cold and from the searing heat of high-altitude solar radiation in sun-crisped snow bowls. The thin atmosphere of higher elevations allows the sun to shine with full force onto snow fields and glacial cirques from which it is reflected in all directions. Such intense radiation has caused many a climber to have even the roof of his or her mouth burned by the high concentration of ultraviolet rays bounced off the snow surface while the mountaineer pants for breath in upward journeying. In spring climbs in the Sierras, still air temperatures may exceed 90 degrees Fahrenheit during the day. At night they may plummet to 10 or 20 degrees below zero. These nighttime temperatures, when combined with a wind of only 15 miles per hour, a gentle zephyr by Sierra storm standards, can combine to produce a wind-chill factor of 60 degrees below zero. At this point exposed flesh of the face or uncovered hands may freeze within 60 seconds and frostbite becomes a serious concern (Lathrop 1975, 6–7). The climber needs both shelter and clothing that permit travel and work in extremes of temperature, wind, and precipitation.

Climbers require food and the cooking utensils in which it may be prepared in the oxygen-poor environment of high altitudes. At a base camp of 10,000 feet, typical for the Sierra climber, water boils at 193 degrees Fahrenheit. A "3-minute" egg would require over 11 minutes of cooking. A medium-sized potato which takes 35 minutes to cook at sea level would not be done for more than 2 hours at 10,000 feet and that same potato at the 20,000-foot-high camp of the Himalayan expedition climber would take more than 7 hours to cook. Thus mountaineers must depend upon "instant" foods which require little or no cooking, or, in extremes, use a sort of portable pressure cooker on the camp stove.

Some of the climber's other needs include navigation instruments to guide his steps in the proper direction through mists and snow and at night. Gaining purchase, maintaining one's balance, and safely progress-ing over steep rock-, snow-, and ice-faces require yet additional gear. The mountaineer must provide for mundane needs as well—toilet articles, reading matter for stormbound days in tents, glasses, watches, and other personal effects. The climber must be prepared to repair items of equip-ment, darn socks, fix torn tents or trousers, replace shoelaces, straighten bent tent poles, fabricate equipment that has been destroyed by some calamity or was not included, manufacture snowshoes, dig a snow cave. Then there are the requirements of a medical emergency. Equipment and medications must be carried to treat a wide range of serious injuries or illnesses, which may occur many miles and perhaps several days from the nearest professional medical care.

It is a tribute to modern technology that we may imagine most of these needs being met with the contents of a well-stocked mobile home or travel trailer, but the climber does not enjoy even these sorts of facilities. He or she must make do with far less. Climbers transport their equipment up the mountain at least in part with energies of leg and lung alone, their provisions and equipment all in backpacks they must carry themselves. Given this combination of dependence upon one's gear for the reliable performance of basic functions and the strictures of energy requirements to move that gear toward the peaks, it is no wonder that each item of equipment is selected with the utmost attention to utility, durability, and weight.

Testing

In preparation for a major expedition equipment selection may involve field testing and comparison. The British, prior to their successful 1953 climb of Mount Everest, spent a period of time in the Swiss Alps in midwinter.

> We were testing a variety of clothing, boots, tents, bedding, food, and cooking stoves. . . . For instance, we each had no less than eight different designs of high-altitude boot. We had first to discard a few of these out of hand and then to wear one type of boot on each foot during each day. As for clothing, while the models and materials were also varied, we had fewer suits available; we had, therefore, to exchange windproofs each day and compare notes at the end of the period. In the same way we changed from one tent and sleeping bag into another. (Hunt 1954, 48)

Conscientious equipment-manufacturers make their own efforts to evaluate the gear they sell through field testing-programs. This process

usually involves the provision of gratis equipment to experienced mountaineers and other wilderness travelers for their own use on extended
trips or expeditions. In return for this free gear the users are expected to
offer suggestions concerning ways in which the donated items might be
improved. For example, a few years ago I was provided with two models
of a new type of backpack and specialized climber's raingear being mar-
keted by Kelty Pack, Inc., for my use on an extended climbing trip in the
Sierra Nevada. In return I provided a number of observations for use in
refining the design of these products, and several photos for publicity
purposes. Requests for free equipment are received with considerable
frequency by major manufacturers from would-be expeditioners on a
budget. The manufacturers, in turn, do sponsor a number of such trips
whenever they feel that the experience of the gear in use or the publicity
their equipment may receive warrants the cost.

While the full-blown expedition field-tests its own equipment prior to
actual use, the average climber depends upon the integrity of manufacturers and the evaluations of more active climbers to make sure the gear is
functional and enduring. This dependence upon others' opinions is not
complete. The typical weekend climber also conducts pretests of sorts.
New tents are set up in the backyard, new boots are broken in by wearing
them on errands around town or on short local hikes. The new wind
parka or down jacket is worn about town on cool evenings. Mountain
recipes may be tried out at home where failures can be passed on to the
appreciative family dog rather than to one's hungry and disgruntled tent
mates on an actual climb.

Historical Comparisons

The climber attempts to maximize the utility and strength of the items in
his or her kit and to minimize weight, but there is another priority. The
contemporary American climber, while seeking ever-increasing challenges in the experience of mountain travel, depends less now than ever
before upon the mountain environment to provide for his or her needs.
Increasing concern for environmental impact discourages the climber
from fashioning tree-bough beds and lean-tos or warming oneself and
preparing food with bonfires. State law as well as conservation-con-
sciousness regulate or prohibit the killing of game for food, a common
practice in earlier times. The additional needs created by this separation
from natural resources have been met in part by an increasingly sophisticated cadre of equipment manufacturers producing freeze-dried foods;
nylon, goose-down, and synthetic-fiber garments and sleeping bags;
nylon and aluminum tents; and lightweight, efficient gas stoves.

Comparison of a few items of contemporary equipment with those
used on the first ascent of the Matterhorn in 1865 illustrates the extent of

these technological improvements. Edward Whymper, the driving force behind the Matterhorn ascent, carried a then modern ice axe of wrought iron and hickory which weighed 4 pounds and he slept in a tent of his own design that weighed "only" 23 pounds. Today's climber has available such exotic tools as ice axes of titanium and aluminum that weigh 19 ounces and two-person tents of Mylar and polyester fabric with aircraft aluminum tubing that weigh a gossamer 28 ounces. While these items are not yet part of the typical climber's equipment, being both expensive and in limited supply, they nonetheless indicate the quality of gear available for the serious or well-to-do climber.

Most significant perhaps are the differences between ropes available today and those used earlier, rope being the key to safe progress on the mountain. Formerly, ropes were made of natural fibers—manila or hemp. At best these were heavy, cumbersome, and ironlike when frozen; they could not be relied upon to arrest a serious fall. Such ropes were in use from the sport's beginnings in Europe in the early 1800s to the onset of World War II. With the war came the development of nylon ropes of layed construction and later the sophisticated sheath-and-core variety kernmantle ropes. These nylon ropes offered lightness, flexibility even when frozen, and an unprecedented level of security. Modern climbers may purchase a rope of a kind tested by the impartial international climbing organization the Union Internationale des Associations d'Alpinisme (UIAA). In these tests, under carefully controlled laboratory conditions, the rope is subjected to the most severe sort of fall theoretically possible. Such circumstances seldom occur in actual climbing, but when they do the mountaineer may be confident that a new rope of the approved type will hold not one but a minimum of five or more such falls. Some may hold many more. Of course, wear and abuse render even these fine ropes weaker than their original design potential, so continued vigilance is required to protect against and inspect for damage occurring in use. Unlike the ultralight ice axe or tent, the highest-quality rope is a basic requirement of even the most impecunious climber. Economy in this area of gear is considered foolish, not frugal, and only the uninitiated will undertake anything more daring than the hanging of freshly washed socks on inadequate cordage.

Preparation Rituals

In getting their equipment ready, climbers go through their own ritual preparations before a climb. These rituals reflect the personalities as much as the necessities of the people involved. One climber with considerable experience with whom I am acquainted does almost nothing by way of preparation. Upon returning from a climb, he gives his dirty clothes to his wife. She tosses them into the washer and gives them back. They are then returned to their accustomed places in the pack where everything else has remained. Toilet paper, suntan lotion, and insect repellant are replaced as needed. When the next trip comes up, food is added, ice axe, crampons, and an extra sweater, as appropriate for the season, and off he goes. Others spend considerable periods preparing for each trip. Another climber weighs various pairs of sock combinations in order to determine the lightest possible set. He puts his pack together several weeks before a proposed climb and continually juggles the contents as expectations about conditions to be encountered shift with the acquisition of new information on weather, route difficulty, and companions. Some endeavor to be prepared for all circumstances, others to be perfectly prepared for a limited set of circumstances. For some, preparation serves as an end in itself; for others, it is a bothersome but important and necessary chore.

Some of my rituals are illustrative of these processes. Boots are sealed by rubbing a warmed wax compound into leather and seams to keep out snow and water. Map lining involves drawing parallel vertical lines on new maps if they are to be used with a compass. The declination, the difference between true and magnetic north, does not change much from one area of the Sierras or Cascades to another, so I seldom relocate the taped arrow on the bottom of my compass, indicating magnetic north, but I do check it each trip. I also check flashlight batteries and bulbs before departing. Older-style waterproof rainwear requires that the seams be sealed periodically to prevent moisture from penetrating the stitching holes. All packs and clothing are examined for tears, loose stitching, or other damage and repairs are carried out accordingly. Actual climbing equipment is subjected to particular scrutiny. Ropes are inspected foot by foot for abrasion, cuts, or signs of internal damage. Nylon sling material is similarly examined. Crampons and ice-climbing tools are sharpened. Hardware is selected according to the anticipated requirements of the forthcoming climb. An annual ritual is the end-of-the-season wash day. Both down and synthetic sleeping bags and garments require washing. So, too, do climbing ropes. Because this process requires special care, large commercial washers, and a long drying-time for down products— up to 5 hours—an entire day and several machines are taken up at the local laundromat. The sight of bright-colored ropes and sleeping bags tumbling in washers and dryers customarily occupied by socks and underwear sometimes leaves the nonclimbing clientele considerably puzzled.

Rituals of equipment selection and preparation are not limited to at-home activities but may be extended into the actual trip itself. Gear is continually being sorted and reorganized, checked and repaired, chosen or rejected for particular use whenever time allows or the situation requires. From the account of a climbing party high on Mount Kenya in Africa:

> Our day of rest and preparations passed in a flash. Washing, darning, mending, checking over ropes and crampons, putting on spare hobnails into the soles of our boots which had lost a lot of them owing to the continuous wading, oiling boots, and other odds and ends took a lot of time. (Benuzzi 1952, 163)

Preparation of medical equipment and supplies is also required for climbing. The climber needs to be well-versed in both first aid and "second" aid. This entails both immediate emergency procedures and the longer-term care made necessary by the extended period of time mountain rescues and evacuation often require. Without a personal and sympathetic physician, however, it is sometimes difficult to obtain necessary prescription drugs. The motives of student-aged climbers may be misconstrued and a few are forced into considerable subterfuge and machination to obtain vital medications. Codeine is obtained from the dentist for relief of pain from dental work but is retained for mountain emergencies. The unused portion of antibiotic prescriptions are gleaned from friends' medicine chests. In at least one instance a student-climber was forced to obtain the analgesic Demerol by purchasing illicit street heroin and then confronting his physician with it accompanied by the argument that the doctor could either provide a Demerol prescription or he would be forced to depend upon the medically impure and illegal alternative.

Food

Climbers, like Caesar's armies, march first and foremost on their stomachs. The famous early Everest explorer H. W. Tilman notes the ever-present concern for food among his climbing companions. "Like Dr. Johnson we minded our bellies very strenuously. For 'I take it,' says the sage, 'that he who will not mind his belly will scarcely mind anything else' " (Tilman 1975, 62).

Freeze-drying
     Modern mountain menu planning is greatly aided by the availability of freeze-dried food of all sorts. The freeze-drying process allows quick-frozen fruits, vegetables, meats, and other perishables to be dehydrated in a near-vacuum. When these items are rehydrated, they regain much of their original texture and taste and retain a considerable portion of their original food value. The weight of superfluous water and packaging are

thus reduced to a minimum and the pack lightened with little sacrifice in variety or nutrition. Other sacrifices, however, are required of those who use freeze-dried foods.

These foods are, in a word, expensive. For example, by combining several monetary gifts with money set aside over a two-month period, I was able to provide one complete freeze-dried dinner as a special treat during a week-long climbing trip. The ingredients and cost of that repast are illustrative of the possibilities of freeze-dried products and the economic burden they impose on their users.

Shrimp cocktail	$ 5.99
Pork chops	14.07
Green beans	1.79
Corn	2.78
Strawberries	2.39
Applesauce	1.60
Viennese coffee	.70
Total	$29.32

This meal fed my partner and me adequately—and deliciously—when augmented by small amounts of cheese and condiments from our regular food supply and with a few wild onions picked from beside a nearby stream.

Freeze-dried food manufacturers try to disguise the high cost of their products by grossly overestimating the number of persons that can be fed from a given packet. Corn indicated as sufficient for "six to eight servings" was consumed almost instantly by the two of us. Six pork chops may sound like a great deal until it is realized that the chops in question average no more than 2.5 inches in circumference and three eighth inches thick. The quantity of strawberries which could be consumed is limited almost exclusively by budget; a $2.39 package makes 1 ounce—one-eighth of a cup—of the rehydrated product.

While such meals represent an economic burden of the first order, it should be noted that this entire banquet for two, exclusive of the onions and condiments, weighed just over 1 pound net before rehydration.

Fresh Food
     Beyond the strictures of the wallet lies another impediment to the use of these miraculous foodstuffs. At high altitudes or when one progresses too rapidly upward and incurs altitude sickness, the appetite is depressed. In order to ensure as near the required calorie intake as possible under these circumstances, fresh foods are sometimes included. The weight of these items is compensated at least in part by their increased palatability, even over freeze-dried products. Major expeditions to high-altitude peaks endeavor to augment their packaged rations with local fresh fruit and produce whenever possible. Tilman provides an in-

triguing—although extreme—example of such efforts to provide as much fresh provision as possible, even during the rigors of the 1938 Everest attempt.

> Eggs could be got on the march, and by eggs I mean half a dozen or so a man, fewer are not much good, but for use on the mountain we had six hundred eggs preserved in waterglass, so that every morning, even on the North Col, we had the English breakfast fetish of bacon and eggs. As far as Camp III (21,500 feet) we ate normal food like meat, potatoes, rice, lentils, the meat being either freshly killed sheep or yak, or failing that, dried mutton which in Tibet is a staple commodity. (Tilman 1975, 63)

The weekend climber selects a larder which incorporates both fresh and freeze-dried ingredients. The resulting mountain cuisine is usually a compromise. A few freeze-dried delicacies are combined with less delectable but more affordable standbys—dried fruit, nuts, salami, cheese, and chocolate. The piece of fresh fruit is carried to camp or even higher as a rare and special treat. How special such a commonplace foodstuff can be is difficult to understand when one is snug at home with a supermarket a few blocks away. But try to see it from a climber's perspective.

After about a week of climbing and camp life above 12,500 feet in the Sierras one summer, I was made aware of how important even a tiny bit of fresh fruit or produce can become. It was late in the season of a dry year. My partner and I sat on the arid, rocky, windblown summit of California's second highest peak, Mount Williamson (14,395 feet). Listlessly but dutifully we chewed stale peanuts and slightly rancid cheese, and drank the little remaining tepid, metal-flavored canteen water. The body may be able to eke some sustenance from this sort of fare but our spirits certainly could not. Another party had also chosen that day to climb the peak. They were seated a little way off to the south. As the last of our pitiful lunch was disappearing, one of the other climbing-group members got up and walked over the rocks to us. Pleasantries were exchanged and then occurred what seemed at the time as one of the greatest expressions of human kindness and generosity. The stranger looked down at the remains of our miserable repast, then reached into his rucksack, and with a mumbled "Ya like this?" offered us no less than a whole, juicy, cool fresh peach! We still retain a photo in our slide collection of that kind donor and his wonderful gift. As a measure of his generous spirit, it should be noted that that peach had to be carried up 15 miles of trail and mountain side and 8,000 feet of vertical gain before it could be shared.

Unusual and Popular Items

Personal idiosyncrasy is clearly noted in the climber's food selection for shorter trips. Strenuous exercise and rapid ascents to high altitude often combine to produce a loss of appetite and even nausea. As the continued outpouring of energy required by the climb demands a high calorie intake, mountaineers will carry unusual food combinations that their experience has shown to be palatable on the summit, if not in the valley. Individual tastes and reactions to altitude vary considerably so that what is delicious to one person may be disgusting to another. For example, I am inordinately fond of grease or fat in any form, particularly in cold weather, and often carry a tube of margarine which is eaten directly or smeared on other foods: salami and margarine, breakfast bars and margarine, cheese and margarine. While such quantities of fat are shunned by others, they will, with equal enthusiasm, consume dozens of candy bars in a day—an absolute abhorrence to me since I personally dislike more than a taste of sugar while in the mountains. A well-known Sierra Club trip leader carries turnips to mountain tops where, with Fritos, they constitute the core of his daytime snacks. Taking his lead, my climbing companion has developed a penchant for weekends of Almond Roca and Fritos. Another Sierra Club leader in the Snow Touring Sections provisions for weekend jaunts by stopping at a convenient Kentucky Fried Chicken outlet for a bucket or barrel of its product.

Some specialized foods have developed a world-wide renown among climbers. In the Swiss Alps a special type of oily but mild sausage is often carried by mountaineers. The British contributed the famous confection Kendal Mint Cake, immortalized by Edmund Hillary: "We sat on the snow and looked at the country far below us. . . . We nibbled Kendal Mint Cake." This important nibbling took place on May 29, 1953, at the summit of Mount Everest. Since that time Kendal Mint Cake has become a common item in the commissary of many an expedition.

Resistance to Change

Something is missing from this review of equipment, perhaps even misleading. The notion that the climber's gear is in a constant and rapid state of change has been implied. That view must be tempered with caution and qualification. One might even argue that in spite of the foregoing discussion the essential items of equipment used by climbers are not new at all. The ice axe and rope, two key elements in the mountaineer's equipment, have been in use for more than a hundred years. Persons have sought means of survival, shelter, and sustenance in the wilderness since the origins of the human species. While the equipment serving these purposes has been diversified and improved immensely in recent years, the basic tools have remained relatively constant.

The reception given by the climbing community to improvements in these basic tools is more important than the improvements themselves. Thus far the focus has been on the multiplicity of technological innovations influencing the climber's gear. Newness, space-age materials, sophisticated design, and safety testing have been emphasized as if these features were joyfully embraced by climbers. After all, American climbers are being discussed here for the most part, and is America not the land of better mouse traps, where gadgets abound to serve (and create) every need? In fact, these innovations are not always as readily assimilated by the climber as one might suspect. Nor is this reluctance entirely a function of product availability or financial restrictions. Modest cost and easy access will not guarantee the adoption of some item of equipment into the climbing community. Other barriers must be overcome. These are the inhibitions of tradition and ethics.

Tradition

Tradition as a factor in the selection of mountain climbing equipment is evident in two ways. First, resistance to change is motivated by the crucial importance of the climber's gear to his or her well-being. When one's dependence upon a piece of equipment is as complete as in the case of the climber, new gear and procedures are contemplated with understandable caution. "Traditional" comes to mean trustworthy. In the words of Reinhold Messner, perhaps the foremost solo mountaineer to emerge in recent years, "In our technological age, being a little behind the times implies progress and safety" (Messner 1974, 92). Tradition inhibits the adoption of new items in a second way. The equipment preferences of well-known persons within the climbing community and of the leaders on club and guided trips may be emulated. These models and authorities are in a potent position to influence the selection of gear by other climbers, but for an important reason they are slow to change the gear they use.

Equipment serves more than utilitarian functions. It is an important prop in the identity-management efforts of the mountaineer. Equipment with the greatest potency for image enhancement is that which shows extensive signs of prior use. Thus, the worn, tattered, and much-patched garment or other article is more valuable in conveying an impression that the wearer or user has considerable experience than is its new, unblemished counterpart. Better-known climbers and trip leaders are most likely to be sensitive to this distinction and therefore least likely to adopt "new and improved" gear with its taint of inexperience. In this way persons of influence passively avoid, if they do not actively reject, the new item or innovation as a latent function of their own impression-management efforts.

As might be imagined, a reluctance to adopt new equipment is a nightmare to equipment manufacturers and purveyors, who make continual efforts to overcome the "old-is-beautiful" image. The equipment testing mentioned above may be used as a public relations ploy. Internationally known climbers are provided free samples for "testing" and are

hired nominally as technical advisors or "design consultants" in order
that their names and accomplishments may be used in advertising. Tes-
timonials as to the relative merits of this or that item abound in climbing
periodicals. Companies that can illustrate the use of their gear with
photos taken in some prestigious locale—Mount Everest being a prime
example—score special commercial coups. For example:

> [From an ad accompanied with a photo of the manufacturer's
> tents on the South West Face of Everest] Karrimor, the profes-
> sional's choice. The highest campers in the world require a spe-
> cial sort of equipment. The 1975 British South West Face Expedi-
> tion selected Karrimor Box Tents, Orienteer Frames, Randonneur
> Pack Sacs, Gaiters, Overboots, and Karrimats. (Karrimor 1976,
> 55)

> [From an ad illustrated with a mountain photo.] Lt. Col. Narinder
> Kumar, conqueror of Mt. Everest and leader of the Kanchen-
> junga expedition, in a report following his triumph . . . "I have
> no hesitation in saying that the boots used by us on this expedi-
> tion were by far the best ever used by me." (Fabiano Shoe Com-
> pany 1978, 58)

In advertising, climbers' purchasing habits are more profoundly influenced by immediate associates than distant heroes. Well-known local
climbers or trip leaders hold greater sway than the "superstars," and the
former usually adopt new gear only grudgingly. From the point of view of
at least established manufacturers, this tendency is partially compensated for by the strict band and model loyalties which exist among many
climbers. "Kelty" was for a number of years synonymous with "backpack" for a great number of American mountaineers who would not
think of buying or recommending another brand. Likewise, in the 70s
climbing hardware came to be idealized, if not typified, in the minds of
many American mountaineers by Yvon Chouinard's products.

The importance of climbing gear dictates that changes be approached
with caution. The role that equipment plays in identity management
discourages obvious newness in one's kit. But neither of these features
tap the most important motive for rejecting equipment and innovations.

Ethics

Technological innovations in climbing tools are mixed blessings.
While they facilitate the accomplishment of a climb, they may inhibit the
experience of challenge in climbing for which mountains are sought in the
first place. Mountaineering, after all, is more a game to be enjoyed than a
job to be done. The satisfaction of climbing lies not in merely attaining the
mountain top but in the process of getting there. Most summits can be
more conveniently and safely reached by helicopter or other mechanical

contrivance, but such devices are purposely ruled out of the climbing game. So, too, are the technological innovations which radically decrease the uncertainty of mountaineering. Equipment used by mountaineers is circumscribed by understandings of propriety, sportsmanship, and other ethical considerations as much as by need. Making the distinction between appropriate and inappropriate gear and technique is not always easy, yet so basic is this distinction that the morality, motive, and essential definition of climbing itself rests in large part on the tools used or purposely set aside.

When is the scaling of a mountain not considered mountain climbing? When is climbing activity not within the moral or ethical spirit of acceptable behavior sanctioned by the mountaineering community? The answer to these questions is found in a simple equation. On one side are the climber's resources—the types and quantity of equipment and personnel and the ways they are employed. On the other is the challenge of the mountain itself—remoteness, altitude, objective hazard, and technical difficulty. When these two are in balance, when the tools are matched with the problem at hand, ascending the mountain is looked upon as "climbing" by mountaineers. Shifting the balance in favor of the mountain, using fewer and simpler tools, is looked upon with favor as commendable, brave, and inspiring. Giving favor to the climber by bringing to bear equipment and procedures beyond necessity is seen as immoral, inappropriate, in poor style. But what are the limits of necessity?

Perhaps one is not "climbing" when a ladder is used for upward progress instead of the naturally occurring rock or snow and ice? Not so. The Americans and British used sectioned ladders in their respective 1963 and 1975 climbs of Everest. Certainly these efforts were climbing in the classic expeditionary style. But is it climbing when people shinny up a rope dangling from a mountain above with the aid of mechanical ascending devices? This is standard procedure on big-wall climbs such as the north face of the Eiger in Switzerland or El Capitan in Yosemite. On these kinds of climbs all members in a party but the first persons up routinely follow on fixed ropes. What about turning the mountain itself into a ladder? Various pieces of metal such as expansion bolts, specialized spikes, and wedges are pinned and jammed at short intervals in a line up the mountain. Nylon or metal rungs are then attached to these devices. This is the essence of "aid" climbing and is the accepted technique for those leading long stretches of rock or ice without adequate places for hands or feet. Or what of the lesser instance where the ladder pinned to the mountain is incomplete—an occasional sling or metal spike to pull or stand on while climbing unaided in between? Finally, what about the climber who improves the friction of his or her grip by powdering the fingertips with gymnasts' chalk?

All of the procedures described above are acceptable in some circumstances; all are considered ethical transgressions in others. To be credited with "climbing" the mountain as opposed to merely getting up it, one must climb in good style by maintaining the balance between resource and challenge. Good style involves the purposeful control of the equipment and techniques used to overcome a particular mountain problem. The severity and kinds of problems dictate the appropriateness of the gear and procedures used.

Lito Tejada-Flores (1967, 23–25) puts this moral balance another way by elaborating on the gamelike quality of climbing. He has aptly noted that "climbing is not a homogeneous sport but rather a collection of differing—though related—activities, each with its own adepts, distinctive terrain, problems and satisfactions, and perhaps most important its own rules." He has identified seven basic climbing games: bouldering, the crag-climbing game, the continuous rock-climbing game, the big-wall game, the alpine-climbing game, the superalpine game, and the expedition game. These climbing games constitute a spectrum, according to the intricacy of rules associated with them. The greatest number of rules and the most complex ones are attached to bouldering—climbing of easily accessible, relatively low rock-outcroppings; the fewest are found in the expedition game, where the goal is some inaccessible and formidable mountain. These rules are applied differentially according to the objective difficulties of the climbing problem. They serve as a form of handicap to ensure a degree of uncertainty about the eventual outcome of a climb. "That is, they are designed to conserve the climber's feeling of personal (moral) accomplishment against the meaninglessness of a success which represents merely technological victory" (Tejada-Flores 1967, 23). Again, it is the problem which determines the acceptable procedure and tools. And the range of these problems is vast.

In the examples above the relative advantages of ladders versus gymnasts' chalk may at first seem ludicrously disparate. Yet the variety of climbing games is so great that these differences are sometimes overlooked. At present there is a genuine and fervent debate about the appropriateness of using gymnasts' chalk on some rock climbs. There is also little or no concern about the use of an occasional ladder on Everest. In the former instance, numerous opponents of chalk feel that its use definitely and significantly reduces the difficulty of a climb. In the latter case few would argue that a simple ladder or two would have much impact against the awesome defenses of Everest. Chalk may change the outcome of one game and ladders may have little impact on another. Good style is remaining technologically within the limits of one's chosen game.

This rejection of equipment to preserve uncertainty is, however, an uneven business. Limitations have been mainly applied to gear used in actual technical climbing—the tools by which steep rock, snow, and ice are surmounted. Less reluctance has been shown in adopting equipment which reduces the harshness of the mountain environment. More sturdy tents and comfortable boots, warm clothing and sleeping bags, drier rainwear and tastier food all find their way fairly quickly into favor in the climbing community. In spite of this partial acceptance, however, the climber's equipment remains a potential threat to the sport it makes possible. The selection and use of equipment poses important ethical issues. The spirit of climbing is in conflict with too great an assortment of gadgetry.

Ideally, the climber seeks to utilize in the most creative and skillful way possible an absolute minimum of equipment. In one sense mountaineering demonstrates a kind of stagnation, if not reversal, of societal evolution. While society at large develops toward ever more complex and differentiated role performance, a development implemented and assisted by a burgeoning array of technological devices, the climber takes another, quite opposite direction. He or she endeavors instead to broaden the range of personal skills and experience so that a few basic tools can be applied in many circumstances. This is not merely an effort to conserve weight or money; it is an integral and necessary feature of a climbing experience. By regressing to a less differentiated social order and by developing rules that limit equipment and techniques, the climber holds in abeyance the rationalization of modern industrial society. At least in the mountains the climber's world comes to be permeated with a unifying moral purpose no longer readily available in conventional society. The climber's reward is not only climbing but the willful construction of regulations governing the enterprise.

In the early 1980s Yvon Chouinard was perhaps the most well-known mountaineering equipment manufacturer in the United States, if not the world. A climber as well, he eloquently noted the ethical need to limit equipment if the experience of climbing was to retain its attraction.

We are the Homo sapiens; we are the tool users. We develop tools to increase our leverage on the world around us and with this increased technological leverage comes a growing sense of power. This position of advantage, which protects us from wild nature, we call civilization. Our security increases as we apply more leverage, but along with it we notice a growing isolation from the earth. We crowd into cities, which shut out the rhythms of the planet; daybreak, high tide, wispy cirrus clouds forecasting storms, moonrise, Orion going south for the winter. Perceptions dull and we come to accept a blunting of feeling in the shadow of security. Drunk with power, I find that I am out of my senses. I, tool man, long for immediacy of contact to brighten my senses again, to bring me nearer to the world once more; in my security I have forgotten how to dance.

So, in reaction, we set sail on the wide sea without motors in hopes of feeling the wind, we leave the Land Rover behind as we seek the desert to know the sun, searching for a remembered bright world. Paddling out, we turn to ride the shore-break landward, walking on the waves of smell of wildflowers meeting us on the offshore breeze. In the process we find not what our tools can do for us but what we are capable of feeling without them, of knowing directly. We learn how far our unaided effort can take us into the improbable world. Choosing to play this game in the vertical dimensions of what is left of wild nature makes us climbers. (Chouinard 1977, 30)

I hope this is a balanced—if brief—view of the issues surrounding equipment. For me, however, some of these arguments are less meaningful than others. While I share Chouinard's enthusiasm for the mountains, I certainly lack his talent. In spite of modern equipment, the mountain still poses an awesome challenge. There is little doubt in my mind whose resources are superior. My small bag of technological gadgetry does not abate the storm or stem the avalanche. I feel cold, hunger, exhaustion, uncertainty with little relief. My climbing tools do not render the crumbling rock more sound or the ice-plastered wall less slippery. My tent, clothing, and sleeping gear do not make me impervious to the cold. They offer no more than a fragile barrier to the hostile elements. Some argue that modern equipment may almost magically carry even the beginner to the summits of mountains. Quite the opposite. I struggle to carry my own equipment up the mountain in return for the slim margin of survival it does provide. Then again, if that margin seemed too great, would mountaineering be the same for me?

Yet this, too, is perhaps an inadequate picture. Equipment and food in the mountains are different from those products so carefully analyzed and dissected at home. To restate a basic law of sociology, the meaning of objects emerges in their use. For me there is a special moment at the end of the climbers' day when this meaning is best understood, when the part that equipment and supply play in the climbing experience becomes clear.

The sun has gone down. The day's climbing is over and we have returned to camp. This is the time when courage may be abandoned in a search for comfort and reassurance. Thin fabric walls may be all that separate us from plunging temperatures and rising winds outside, but for a while we shrink into our unnatural cocoon and rejoice in nylon and aluminum and premeasured cocoa packets, in stoves and sleeping bags and flickering candles which say in small but important ways "This is home." This time serves as a reminder that the drudgery and danger of the day are past, that given success or failure on the mountain, at least all have returned safely to share this moment together.

It is a time for communion with senses denied by the urgency of the day's deeds. When the terrible burden of a brave independence from civilization is removed, women are free to laugh and men are free to cry. It is a luxury, a moment of rest, when aching limbs need no longer be forced to action but lapse into well-earned relaxation. Toes, liberated from stiff, icy boots, wriggle deliciously in soft, dry socks. Hands that clutched only ice and rock and cold steel for hours on end now cradle the precious warmth of a cup of freshly brewed soup. Steam curls up to bathe the parched lips and face stung for so long by the freezing wind and driven snow. While armchair recollections may change one's priorities, in the mountains this is the time most looked forward to by many. The most memorable time is not the crux move on the most difficult pitch of the climb, not the spectacular panorama from the summit, or the airy rappel back down. Rather, it is the sharing of a simple beverage, safe at last in a warm tent, with the company of one's companions.

Summary

Equipment selection is a crucial phase of mountaineering preparation. The gear which is chosen must serve the many necessities of progress and survival attendant on travel in the high mountains. At the same time care must be exercised lest the equipment itself negate the climbing experience by reducing the uncertainty of mountaineering ventures, that it not become an artificial intrusion into the union between person and nature. What gear is to be used or left behind involves moral as well as practical decisions. For upward motion on the mountain to be called "climbing," the equipment must match the challenges, not overpower them. A rough equivalence between the difficulties faced and the resources employed to meet them is essential for the enjoyment of mountaineering. As we shall see, a desire to escape from an imbalance between challenges and resources in other realms of social life is a major motive for climbing mountains in the first place. Judging the balance between tools and tasks is not simple. Equipment means one thing at home, another in the mountains. Certain equipment may be seen by some people as a technological assault on the wilderness, by others as the only practical means of survival in formidable and threatening territory. Each climber, in filling his or her rucksack, must decide both the necessity and the propriety of the items taken along.

The organization of equipment is a vital phase of any climbing, but equipment is not all that needs preparing. The mountains will test gear and persons alike. The climber's body needs preparation, too. Physical conditioning is another important aspect of mountaineering.

4
Conditioning

For the mountaineer the psychological aspects of fitness are based on the confidence that he possesses the necessary skill, strength, endurance. . . . In physiological terms it means that the combined capacity of lungs, heart, and circulation must be sufficient.

R. H. T. Edwards, "Physiology of Fitness and Fatigue"

Mountain climbing places rigorous demands on the physical resources of those who participate in it. On a normal weekend climb a typical Sierra Club mountaineer will perform over one million foot-pounds of work in carrying his or her backpack to camp and climbing to the summit. This is about the same effort required to lift a one-ton compact automobile to the top of a 50-story skyscraper.[1] In addition, this work must be performed in the rarefied atmosphere of high altitude and sometimes in the face of adverse weather conditions. Then the process must be repeated in reverse from the summit to camp and on the return march to the trail head.

For the fullest enjoyment and most effective performance to be realized in mountaineering, physical conditioning is necessary. In this respect, mountain climbing is like tennis, soccer, skiing, motocross racing, basketball, football, or the myriad of other sports where performance is dependent upon physical ability as well as skill and strategy. Physical conditioning for mountaineers aims at the development of increased oxygen-carrying capacity for adaptation to high altitude and greater endurance for carrying heavy packs mile after mile over rough terrain. An efficient cardiovascular system is the most important. Strong legs are more useful than a powerful upper torso.

In any sport, conditioning may closely approximate the activity for which it prepares one, or it may be an abstract set of exercises which develop specific strengths and skills necessary in that activity. For example, Nordic ski-racers lift weights to strengthen shoulders and arms and skip rope to develop legs and lungs during the dry summer months. As the racing season approaches, they combine these abstract exercises with practice in the early winter snows. The kinds of conditioning programs followed by the mountaineer span this same range from abstract exercise to concrete climbing practice. On the more abstract side are indoor calisthenics—running in place, deep knee-bends, pushups, sit-ups, and stretching exercises which strengthen and tone appropriate muscles. At the other extreme are "conditioning climbs" encompassing all or most of the aspects of the anticipated climbing goal.

Means versus Ends

The distinction between activities viewed as conditioning exercises and those which become final objectives in their own right is relative to the perspective of the individual climber. The Southern California mountaineer climbs Mount Baldy as a day hike and perhaps Mount San Jacinto or Mount San Gorgonio on a weekend as preparation for a summer climbing season in the Sierras. The Sierra peaks are used as training grounds for bigger climbs in South America, Alaska, or the Himalaya. When the American contingent to the 1976 international climbers' meet in the Russian Pamirs arrived at base camp, they set off before breakfast the next morning on a "conditioning climb" of a 15,900-foot peak involving 4,200 feet of elevation gain (Craig 1977, 44–45, 47).

It might be said that the less abstract the conditioning activity the more likely it is to be chosen as an end in itself. Certainly this is true of mountaineers. No climber of my acquaintance looks forward to an afternoon of deep knee-bends, running in place, and pushups. Many climbers do choose, as an interim sport, day hiking in the local foothills or distance running.

Conditioning, to be effective, needs to be both a long-term and frequent activity. An exercise program needs to be almost a daily affair. As most climbers lead relatively sedentary lives in their work worlds, physical exercise for them is necessarily a conscious and purposeful undertaking. Also, it must involve relatively brief time requirements and be easy to accomplish at or near home. Running is one of the ways in which these requisites can be met. The mountain climber in Southern California can be found jogging in local parks, on the beach, and along grass median strips of wide boulevards and on numerous high school and college tracks. Local parks are the favorite haunts of cross-country joggers in the mornings and evenings. These various running activities are informal and self-initiated. However, for those who require the impetus of group pressure or the company of fellow exercisers, certain formal conditioning activities are available in which camaraderie and compunction combine.

Club-Sponsored Conditioning

Almost all of the hundreds of activities sponsored by the Southern California chapter of the Sierra Club can be used by the climber as conditioning experiences. The only limitations are available time and present level of fitness. These range from evening strolls on the beach, ending with hot chocolate or wine, to technical climbs of 14,000-plus-foot peaks in the Sierra Nevada. Other club-sponsored activities which provide conditioning opportunities are trail- and hut-maintenance parties, bicycle tours, nature and photography hikes, kyaking, and Nordic and alpine ski trips.

Two kinds of regular Sierra Club activities can be singled out as particularly suited to the conditioning needs of the Southern California mountaineer. These are the Griffith Park hikes and the program of the Hundred Peaks section. The Griffith Park Committee provides a series of conditioning hikes in Griffith Park throughout the year on weekday evenings and weekends. These hikes involve a year-round average participation of approximately 125 persons per day, ranging from perhaps 50 on a winter Wednesday night to 250 on a summer Tuesday evening. The hikes range in difficulty from a four-mile stroll gaining 1,000 feet of altitude to a nine-mile marathon walk/run with 1,300 feet of gain and descent.

Few persons attend these Griffith Park hikes exclusively as ends in themselves with the possible exception of a limited number of individuals who are seeking companionship not found in other settings. Huffing and puffing cross-country, up and down hills, through brambles and poison oak, in the dark without a flashlight, is not a very sociable evening, but it is a good way to get in shape. Socializing is reserved for before or after.

Other Sierra Club groups offer weekday and weekend hikes on the beach and in the Santa Monica and San Gabriel mountains on a less regular basis. Notable among this group is the Hundred Peaks Section (HPS). This group encourages hiking in the local mountains as a goal in itself. Frequent weekend day hikes to nearby peaks are offered. Unlike Griffith Park hikes, the HPS has a specified membership, although its activities are open to all. Currently about five hundred persons belong to HPS. These members may earn awards and emblems to be worn on clothing, for climbing a certain number of peaks. According to Jon Hardt, chairperson of HPS in 1976, about half of those who participate in section activities do so as an end in itself.

When all the day and evening hikes sponsored by the Sierra Club are taken into consideration, the opportunities for getting in shape are extensive. During one three-month winter period (November 1976–January 1977) 257 hikes were sponsored and led by twenty-one different Sierra Club groups in Southern California. A mountaineer looking for a conditioning hike could pick from an average of more than two every week-day and four every weekend day. Again, these hikes are exclusive of the many other club-sponsored activities that might also serve as condition-ing opportunities—canoeing, bicycling, trail maintenance, folk dancing, etc. The Sierra Club is an organization with a strong interest in physical exercise and fitness, in getting people ready to go to the mountains. But there are some who do not think that conditioning is necessary.

Is Conditioning Necessary?

The importance of physical conditioning as a characteristic of the well-rounded climber is debatable. For some, bulging muscles, tireless legs, bottomless lungs, and the ability to clamber inexhaustibly from summit to summit is the true measure of the accomplished mountaineer. This reflects what a friend has referred to as the "macho grunt" mentality. Such an attitude appears in many Sierra Club–sponsored climbs which feature long approach-marches, multiple peaks ascended in a limited time but with little technical rock or ice difficulty. Empirical support for this contention was furnished by a sample of Sierra Club mountaineering instructors and staff who were asked to rank their various climbing-related abilities. They judged "rock climbing" and "snow and ice climb-ing" to be among their "least developed skill(s)" while they rated "strength and endurance" as their "most developed skill."

Other climbers evaluate their mountaineering worth in terms of their ability to overcome precipitous rock. Members of the rock-climbing fraternity sometimes eschew conditioning. For certain climbers this avoidance is even an ethical issue. Among some British rock climbers, "Most things which reduce the standard of a climb are regarded as unethical. . . . Physical training, for example, is considered vaguely immoral whereas a hangover is held in high esteem, presumably because physical training decreases the difficulty of a climb while a hangover increases it" (Rouse 1975, 35). American rock climbers, while performing striking feats of midair gymnastics and rock engineering high on Yosem-ite cliffs, may subsist on potato chips, Coca Cola, cigarettes, and mari-juana. Some claim that a proper rock climb is so easy of access, requiring so little effort to reach, that the bumper of one's car can serve as the first anchor.

Even among climbers pursuing the same kinds of activities, disagree-ment about conditioning may exist. In September 1974, I spent two weeks in Zermatt, Switzerland, the well-known alpine climbing center at the foot of the Matterhorn. Staying at the Bahnhof, the traditional haunt of English-speaking climbers, were two other Americans, George and

Steve. While of roughly equivalent skill and experience in the mountains, these two had radically different views on physical fitness. For George, conditioning was a necessary part of the disciplined regimen he felt should be followed by all climbers. He ate carefully, drank little alcohol, and when he was not actually climbing, would go on a daily pilgrimage to the outdoor community gymnasium and perform a series of calisthenics on each of the pieces of apparatus there.

Around the common table at dinner, George's talk would invariably be filled with the awesome statistics of his day's exercise: "Did 500 pushups today, 150 pull-ups, and 1,000 sit-ups. Then I did . . ." followed by more details and enthusiastic proclamations about the benefits of this exercise program.

Steve was a different sort of climber. His practice, when not climbing, was to sit on the front porch, smoke his pipe, drink wine, and chat with passersby. His only regular exercise on these off days involved a trip to the grocer for more wine and the makings of some multi-calorie, cholesterol-crammed but gourmet concoction he would prepare himself each night in the basement community kitchen.

One day George's perpetual praise of the benefits of his exercise program got the best of Steve's curiosity. He decided to join George for the afternoon in his round of exercises. Those of us who remained at the hotel wondered how these two would get on. They left at 2 o'clock and about sundown came strolling back down the street. George was his usual ebullient self, filled with data about the day's achievements. Steve was pensive and a bit tattered from his experiences. I asked him what he thought of his visit to the exercise yard. "Whole thing reminds me of a trip I took to Jerusalem three years ago." "Jerusalem?" I asked, "How's that?" "Oh, you know, like the stations of the cross. Going from one to another of those damned exercise gadgets is like all the tortures Christ had to go through on his way to getting crucified" (Field notes, September 1974).[2]

In summary, conditioning varies widely in importance and purpose from one climber to another. The peak bagger pursues a kind of climbing that is little more than an extension and elaboration of a vigorous exercise program in which the number rather than the difficulty of the peaks ascended is the principal object. Peak bagging is a characteristic of many Sierra Club–sponsored trips both locally in Southern California and in the Sierras. For others, such as the rock climber, conditioning may be considered less important, even mildly repugnant. For all these differences of opinion, however, there remains the fact that mountaineering in its many forms is a vigorous and physically demanding activity. Younger climbers sometimes forego the bother of a regular exercise program, preferring to suffer along at the beginning of a climbing outing, as their bodies become accustomed to the new demands being placed on them. For older climbers, this is either too painful or impractical a procedure and they get ready for the mountains in advance, with moderate but frequent exercise. Alan Ewert supports the latter procedure.

> I'd like to emphasize the "pay now or pay later" idea when it comes to conditioning. Many of us find such exercising boring and time-consuming. "Paying later" by going on an expedition in poor physical condition is at best a hell of a way to get into shape and certainly not a safe one. (Ewert 1978, 4)[3]

With conditioning complete, the climber is ready to leave for the mountains, but before the mountain itself is met, often many miles of intervening territory must be crossed. This entails travel of several sorts, the next phase of mountaineering.

5
Travel

Climbing is widely romanticized as a way of "getting away from it all," of escaping the cloying confines of an automated, machine-dominated civilization. In contrast to urban life, mountaineering presumably offers freedom from a mechanized existence and the satisfaction of self-dependence in a wilderness world where muscle and lung matter more than horsepower and kilowatt. Yet, the facts of the climber's experience are somewhat different.

Climbers do not stroll confidently out the front doors of their homes and onto the mountain face. Mountains and mountaineers have been historically and are today generally far removed from each other. Climbers are for the most part city dwellers, and few large cities are located in truly mountainous areas. In order to approach the mountain, it is necessary for the climber to travel, using various means of transport, sometimes for great distances. Travel, then, is an integral part of the total process that is mountaineering. Understanding the opinions climbers have toward travel sheds light on the meaning of the mountains themselves. To assist this understanding it will be necessary to divide travel into two distinct categories based on the types of motive power utilized.

Power Sources

An important step in the development of the industralized Western world was the harnessing and application of the earth's latent power sources. Before this important step, humans had to depend solely upon their own efforts and those of other animals to perform essential tasks—farming, construction, and transport. Power technology made useful the kinetic energy of waterfalls, winds, tides, and steam, unleashed the energy stored in chemical sources such as oil and natural gas, and tapped the nuclear potential of atomic fission and solar radiation. The distinction between animal effort and power technology distinguishes two kinds of travel. Mechanized travel refers to the varieties of transportation which are the product of power technological development—automobiles, airplanes, and the like. Nonmechanized travel concerns the modes of transport for which human and other animal labor is the principal energy source. Both are part of a typical mountaineering venture.

The development of power technology has not proceeded at the same pace in all parts of the globe. Today's American urban dweller may depend upon mechanized power to stir the cake mix, roll up car windows, open the garage door, and score junior's arithmetic quiz at school. Some mechanical devices are even slaved to others so that owners need not bother operating the machines directly. Microwave ovens have timers attached which can be preset to cook while the chef is out of the house; television viewers can switch channels by remote control without leaving the comfort of the sofa. In contrast to this automated life style, there are other areas of the world where humans and animals are the dominant power sources. Water for washing and cooking must be carried from the stream. Grain is ground on hand-cranked mills and bread baked over hot stones in a fire. Produce is carried to and from market on horses or other beasts of burden. It is also in these remote areas that mountains are often to be found. Climbers may need to depend upon transport available in both of these settings on their way to the mountain, or provide their own.

Mechanized Travel

Today's climber is inexorably tied to mechanized transport. The days of the Schmidt brothers riding their bicycles from Germany to Zermatt, climbing the North Face of the Matterhorn, and then peddling home again before their great achievement became known, are part of mountaineering's colorful history. Today's climber counts on the machine to get him or her to, and sometimes part way up, the mountain. Nowhere is this dependence more evident than on expeditions where participants utilize a whole array of powered vehicles to move themselves and their equipment toward their objectives.

Expeditions

Expedition members and gear travel perhaps tens of thousands of miles on aircraft large and small, ship and boat, train and truck to their destinations in distant Nepal, Pakistan, Alaska, Chile, etc. Two descriptions will help highlight the role mechanized transport plays in expeditionary climbing. First, a description of the British approach to Everest in 1953:

> Arrangements were made for the party to sail for India in the S.S. Stratheden on February 12th, less two members who were to leave later by air but arrive well in advance, making preliminary arrangements for our passage through India and entry into

Nepal, and carrying out other initial tasks. With the main party safely launched, Charles Evans and Alfred Gregory (Greg for short) departed by air on February 20th as advance party; Bourdillon and I took flight eight days later, and Pugla was the last to leave, on March 1st. . . . The latter part of the journey had been more tedious than ours, for it involved long, dusty stages from Bombay in a succession of trains, degenerating into a ride on a truck, perched on top of our mountainous baggage, and finally an eighteen-mile march over the ridges which bar entry into the Valley of Nepal. . . . And in the heat and dust they had the anxiety of watching over the transference of 473 packages, weighing seven-and-a-half tons, from ship to train, from large trains to smaller trains, from the miniature Nepal railway to trucks, and finally from the roadhead in southern Nepal to the conveyor trays of an overhead ropeway on the last stage, over the high ridges to Katmandu. (Hunt 1954, 57–59).

In a second example of the role mechanized transport sometimes plays on expeditions, Kurt Diemberger comments on the Swiss first ascent of Dhaulagiri in 1950, another great mountain in the Himalayas. On that climb, a small aircraft was used to penetrate deep into the mountain's defenses. The entire party of thirteen climbers and all of their gear were flown to 16,500 feet, and some personnel and stores were lifted even higher to a glacier landing at 18,700 feet.

It was, of course, an experiment, just as everything we were doing was a unique "first-time-ever" conception: nobody had ever tried to use a "gnat" to leapfrog all the valleys in one swift bound and fly every man jack of an expedition, baggage and all, up to over 16,000 feet on a Himalayan giant and so avoid the long weeks of an approach march. (Diemberger 1971, 205)

The use of small aircraft to transport climbers and their supplies is now standard practice on expeditions to Canada and Alaska, and Katmandu today may be reached by daily scheduled jet service to a modern airport.

Weekend Climbs

Mechanized travel plays a part in the weekend climber's approach to the mountains, although the vehicles used may vary from those of the expeditioner. Where mountains and mountaineers are in closer proximity, where major population centers are near major climbing areas, then roads and automobiles, trains and aerial tramways are used to carry the climber beyond the foothills and low-lying areas into the mountains themselves.

Europe: Trains, Trams, and Huts. In the European Alps, climbers depend upon a network of cog and conventional rail lines and cable lifts to reach the mountains. Jeremy Bernstein describes one such network emanating from the French climbing center of Chamonix, up into the Mont Blanc massif:

> There are four elaborate systems of *téléphériques* that lead from the valley into the surrounding mountains, and two cog railroads, to say nothing of several lesser ski lifts. One can go from Chamonix, which is about three thousand feet above sea level, to just below the top of the Aiguille du Midi, which is over twelve thousand feet high, in less than fifteen minutes. . . . In the summit pyra-mid, a system of tunnels has been blasted out. One contains a snack bar and souvenir shop, and another leads to a *téléphérique* that conveys one in little four-man gondolas over the Vallée Blanche, a glacial valley, to the Italian frontier; there one may take another system of *télèphériques* down into Courmayeur, an Italian alpine village and climbing station. (Bernstein 1965, 20–21)

Similar rail and cable systems are installed at numerous other European climbing centers where they play an important part in bringing the climber to the start of the climb.

In Europe, mountain travelers do not regularly camp out. Rather, they spend their nights in "huts" or "refuges" which are spartan, high-altitude hotels where simple food and basic shelter may be purchased at a nominal cost. These huts serve as bases for the mountaineer and way points for the cross-country hiker. They are numerous and conveniently located, almost always on a well-tended path and sometimes at the end of an aerial tramway. Many are built of stone or other natural materials and thus blend unobtrusively into the mountain environment. Guests in the more remote huts may benefit from another form of mechanized trans-port, for it is often the case that these distant huts have their supplies replenished by helicopter. As a result of this hut system, the impact of large numbers of mountain recreationists has remained localized and manageable. The mountains themselves remain relatively inviolate. This is unfortunately not the case in the United States.

America: Roads, Cars, and Campers. At the turn of the century there were few travelers in the rugged southern Sierras. Those who did venture into the mountains from the east made their entry over any one of perhaps two dozen passes previously located and used by Indians, explorers, and shepherds. Passes were chosen primarily for their proximity to ultimate objectives. All were primitive by modern standards and involved long approach-marches up from the floor of the Owens Valley. One pass was

about as good or as bad as another. But with the coming of the automobile, this situation changed radically.

Today's typical Southern California weekend climber will spend ten
hours driving more than five hundred miles back and forth to the Sierras.[1]
From each of the four major communities along Highway 395 in the
southern part of the range—Lone Pine, Independence, Big Pine, and
Bishop, a road now stretches westward up into the mountains. These
roads terminate at Whitney Portal, Onion Valley, Glacier Lodge, and the
North Lake-Sabrina-South Lake areas, respectively. These four are by far
the most popular trail heads in this section of the range. Roads provide
quick and easy access to the high country. As a result, many persons are
now showing an interest in wilderness travel who might otherwise have
been discouraged by the arduous approaches previously required. When
in half an hour backcountry users can whisk themselves and their gear
twenty miles away and 5,000 feet up toward the passes, going to the
mountains seems like a more attractive proposition. The 8,000-, 9,000-, or
10,000-foot road-end parking lot offers a considerable head start on the
climb of a typical 12,000-, 13,000-, or 14,000-foot Sierra peak.

The convenience of the automobile is not, however, without its price.
As roads intrude into the wilderness not all mountaineers rejoice. In
some instances, roads have not only facilitated access to the high country
but affected the quality of the experience to be had there. With the aid of
the automobile and roads, many are encouraged to go where few went
before. In addition, these ever-increasing hordes are no longer spread out
over two dozen or so entry points but concentrated by their dependence
upon the automobile at the four road-ends and in the nearby surrounding
countryside.

In the United States, no hut system exists comparable to that in
Europe. Wilderness travelers carry their own food and shelter, setting up
camps along the way. Unfortunately not all of the freshly emerging
backcountry users spurred by easy auto access are knowledgeable about
or concerned with the proper hygiene and nondestructive camping techniques their growing numbers demand. Some of these visitors, a few
climbers included, call upon the outdoors to serve as more than an
inspiration and a challenge. This growing minority uses the wilderness
resource indiscriminately for fuel, garbage pit, and toilet. As a result,
living trees are mutilated and killed for firewood, animal habitats are
destroyed, and water sources are polluted.[2] In an attempt to stop or limit
these abuses, the U.S. Forest Service and the National Park Service have
found it necessary to instigate a wilderness-use permit and reservation
system. Backcountry campers in many areas are now required to obtain a
permit in advance of their trips. In the Sequoia-Kings Canyon area of the
Sierras, for example, permits are issued on a daily quota basis which

limits the number of travelers passing through any given entry point. Users are further required to abide by restrictions on wood fires, waste disposal, and selection of campsites. Obtaining permits for popular areas like Whitney Portal on such holidays as the Labor Day weekend requires application many weeks in advance.

Mixed Opinions

Mountaineers are ambivalent in their attitudes toward mechanized travel. On the one hand, they recognize that the jet plane, train, boat, etc., have been instrumental in opening up important new climbing areas in Patagonia, Nepal, Pakistan, Greenland, and British Columbia, and in speeding the trip to the local ranges. Automated transport is accepted as a natural outgrowth of these new mountaineering possibilities combined with the greater mobility and tighter schedules of the contemporary climber. Where mechanical contrivances provide quicker access to the mountains, they will be used, if not praised. Climbers have their practical side, as John Cleare's remarks about the Aiguille du Midi aerial tramway illustrate:

> Whatever criticisms climbers may level at it, the cable car is fine engineering and it does make possible, if you're a very hard Scot, the sort of day's entertainment Tom had planned for us [a climb of the Midi North Face and descent by the cable car]. (Cleare 1975, 33–34)

Other pragmatic advantages of mechanized transport are readily accepted by the climber. Aerial photography has helped expeditions to penetrate little-known mountainous terrain and serves in more well-traveled areas as the basis for one of the climber's essential pieces of equipment, the topographic map. The huts in the European system mentioned above are not only supplied but sometimes built with key materials and furnishings airlifted in by powerful helicopters. Indirectly, helicopters also provide a margin of safety for the climber. When illness or injury strike unexpectedly in some remote mountain area where ground evacuation might take critical days, helicopters rush victims to the hospital in hours, although sometimes at considerable monetary cost. This cost problem can, in fact, be monumental. In the early 1980s, high-altitude helicopter service was chargeable at a rate of $300 to $600 per hour from the minute the craft left its home pad to the minute it returned. A mountaineering fall may break the climber in more ways than one. This cost problem is not inescapable however. Throughout the Swiss Alps, travelers may purchase helicopter rescue insurance for a modest cost (about $10 per season in 1980). This policy covers the costs of any air transport necessary in case of emergency.

Limits and Restrictions

Mountaineers place definite self-imposed limits on the use of mechanical transportation and have strong feelings about those who go beyond those limits. For example, modern tramway runs from Zermatt up 3,000-plus feet to Schwartzse, the starting point from which the Matterhorn is normally climbed. Use of this tram, however, is not considered appropriate, at least on one's first climb of the mountain. Guides require that their clients walk from the city limits to the summit under their own power (although guides may pull a bit on the rope). No restrictions are placed on tramway use for the descent, but for one to be credited with a complete ascent of the Matterhorn or any other peak in that area, climbers are expected to hike directly from Zermatt. In 1974, among climbers congregating at the Bahnhof Hotel there seemed an exception to this norm that allowed climbers to "pick up where they left off." When a climb which originated in the city and progressed halfway or so was interrupted for some reason, as by a storm, that forced a return, climbers could ride the tram or train on their second upward trip and continue their climb from where they left off. This would not prejudice their claim of having done the entire climb.[3]

These restrictions on the use of aerial lifts appear similar to the norms applied to the use of fixed ropes on long technical climbs. On expeditions and sometimes in the ascent of big rock-walls, climbers may leave ropes attached to the mountain along their routes as they proceed upward so that there is a line of ropes over the difficult portions of the route from the base of the climb to the highest point reached. In case of an emergency such as bad weather or injury, this line of ropes offers a quick avenue of retreat down the mountain. When the danger is past, the ropes are used as aids in ascending to the previous high point where actual climbing is begun again. Such tactics are acceptable, if not laudable, and an ascent made in this fashion is judged complete. However, all climbing must be done without the use of such fixed ropes by at least the first member of the party ascending the route for the first time. The dangling of rope or cable down from the top of the climb and ascending this directly is strictly forbidden. Any claim to having climbed a route using such overhead ropes without first climbing in the conventional manner would be held invalid.

In the United States, climbers look with pity and disdain on those who use mechanized transport as their principal or only means of locomotion. Worse yet are those who see powered travel as an end in itself. Mountaineers see their way of life as antithetical to that of enthusiasts for recreational vehicles, four-wheel drive, and dirt motorcycles. Climbers are proud of their "freedom of the hills" (the title of a well-known mountaineering text). Conservationists' efforts which seek to limit the use of off-road vehicles usually receive enthusiastic support from mountaineers.

The Skiing Lesson

As a final note on mechanized travel, it is instructive to examine the role machines have come to play in other travel sports for a glimpse of what the future might bring to climbing. Some travel sports start out as entirely nonmechanized but, as appropriate mechanical contrivances are developed, parts of these activities, presumably the less desirable parts, are circumscribed by machines. The addition of a gas motor to the bicycle allowed fans to enjoy the fun of swooping around corners and rapid acceleration without the bother of pedaling. However, when the motor quits, today's motorcyclist is reduced from swooping and accelerating to pushing and grunting. Only a portion of the initial sport remains, and participants become wholly dependent upon mechanical devices to perform some of the tasks they formerly did themselves. Anyone noticing a motorcycle being carried on a trailer that is being pulled by another vehicle must wonder how far power technology has intruded into that sport.

The downhill skier provides an even better example. Skiing might be nominally defined as travel over snow by gliding on staves attached to the feet. That was an adequate description of the sport in this country until the early 1950s. Skiers simply went to the mountains, climbed up hills, and skied down them (see Ford 1983, 38–43). Today only a few hardy ski-mountaineers carry on this tradition, ascending to mountain snow bowls and even summits with the aid of traction devices on their skis. Formerly almost all skiers had much in common with other wilderness travelers. Their own energies and skill were all that determined the challenges skiing offered them. Then mechanical lifts were introduced. With these devices it was possible to avoid the drudgery of the uphill climb. Skiing experienced a dramatic jump in popularity. It was no longer a lowly form of wilderness travel but a popular and prestigious sport where impression-management efforts called for special clothing, yearly style changes, and being seen at fashionable places. Skiing was concentrated increasingly in areas served by lifts. Lifts, in turn, were located on or near major highways which could speed the paying customer from the city to the slopes. Expensive restaurants, bars, and other entertainments ensured that the urbanite would not feel too abrupt a separation from city amenities (or return home with unspent funds). The machine now dictated the challenge, carrying the skier to clearly marked, carefully prepared, and continuously patrolled "beginning," "intermediate," and "advanced" runs.

Equipment and technique evolved in response to the availability of these lifts. Trussed up in high foam-injected plastic boots, today's skier is crippled for any action but the downhill run, entirely dependent upon machines to provide the altitude and access which make that run possible. So incapacitated is the modern skier that he or she often dons special footwear, so-called "after-ski" boots, to get from the parking lot to the lodge or lift line. Uphill travel is limited to a few feet of gain accomplished by a painful and strenuous splayed-foot hobble or short mincing sidewise steps. In sum, skiers have come a long way since the 1950s in developing their sport, most of it downhill.

Perhaps mountaineers will not follow this same course. They seem to have accepted mechanical aid with greater reluctance than the skier. Yet, the onlooker might well wonder if the climber has not reached a point where the gear used to get up the mountain is not almost as specialized as that the skier uses to get down. So single-purpose is some of the gear that is renders the climber alien to, if not totally excluded from, other kinds of travel. It is a common practice for rock climbers to replace their painful toe-pinching special footwear with tennis shoes for the walk back down to the bottom of the cliffs. Another example is found in the modern ice-climber. Sheathed in Gore-tex to ward off wind and snow, bound up in chest, waist, and leg harnesses, wearing a crash helmet, feet encased in stiff-soled boots onto which are strapped rigid frames of metal spikes, and carrying in each hand a special steel clawing tool, the ice climber buys his freedom of the hills at the price of wearing a fairly heavy suit of armor. In fact, the rock or ice climber may secretly appreciate a ride down as much as the skier appreciates a lift up.

Nonmechanized Travel

At some point the limitations on the use of mechanical transport pass beyond the control of the climber to become technological or legal problems. Helicopters and airplanes cannot operate or land above certain altitudes, and that ceiling may be thousands of feet below the intended summit. Roads, rails, and rivers may end miles before the actual climbing begins. Laws may restrict or prohibit the use of off-road vehicles in national forests and parks. When, for whatever reason, mechanical transportation is no longer feasible or permitted and the mountain remains some distance away, climbers have recourse to a second kind of travel in which human and animal energies are the only ones used. The expedition again serves as a dramatic, if not entirely typical, example of this second sort of travel.

Expedition People-Power

Nonmechanized transport plays a vital role in modern large-scale expeditionary climbs. Powered vehicles may move the climbers' gear thousands of miles and then cease to be practicable, though the final objective remains still far out of reach. With tons of supplies and tight time-schedules, it is usually impossible for the two dozen or so climbers in even the biggest expeditions to transport their own gear to and up the mountain without considerable assistance. On climbs in the eastern Himalayas that assistance comes from two kinds of helpers.

Porters and Sherpas. It is roughly 120 miles from the terminus of road and air transport in Katmandu, Nepal, to the Mount Everest base camp at 18,000 feet. This is the first and longest stage requiring nonmechanized transportation. The route follows a path through leech-infested rain forests and over high mountain passes. Rushing rivers may have to be crossed on swinging vine-rope bridges. No pack animals in that area of Nepal are sufficiently light of weight, sure of foot, and available in adequate numbers to carry the gear for the expedition on this journey. Load carrying, therefore, falls to human beasts of burden.

Porters recruited from the local population move gear from the last point accessible to mechanical transport to the beginning of actual climbing difficulties. This contingent of laborers has little or no training for, or experience in, mountain travel, yet they represent the largest group of load carriers in any expedition. In 1953 the British hired four hundred porters to carry their gear to base camp; in 1970 the Japanese employed more than eight hundred on another Everest attempt.[4]

On the mountain itself, load-hauling assistance is still needed. A flow of supplies must be kept going upward to stock the various camps and support the lead climbers above. While this involves the transportation of less gear in absolute terms than during the first stage, load carrying is more difficult and arduous at high altitudes and in precipitous terrain. The volume of this work may still be beyond the capacity of the climbers themselves, who are often otherwise occupied in maintaining and extending the route. As a result, the job of moving supplies between one camp and another becomes the responsibility of high-altitude porters.

In the eastern Himalayas this work is the monopoly of a remarkable group of hill tribesmen, the Sherpas. Of Mongolian descent and Buddhist faith, they originally came from southern Tibet and gradually migrated to Nepal and to the vicinity of the Indian climbing center of Darjeeling (Ullman 1964a, 75). Quite distinct from lowland porters, the Sherpas are at home in the mountains. Their ability to carry heavy loads tirelessly at great height is legendary. While not generally skilled in the nuances of technical climbing, they are competent mountain travelers who follow easily in the ways prepared by the actual climbers. For the large expedition they are an indispensable and respected part of the climbing team.

Sherpas are fewer in number than low-altitude porters on an expedition. For example, the Japanese used forty-seven on their large-scale 1970 Everest attempt. They perform a vital task. In recent Everest expeditions via the normal South Col route, Sherpas have demonstrated such outstanding ability, competence, and self-sufficiency that some critics have asked who is in fact supporting whom and who are the real climbers.

Sherpa Overuse. A case in point would be the 1977 South Korean "conquest" of Everest. On that climb twenty-eight Sherpas carried loads to the South Col, 25,850 feet. Only two Koreans were able to go that high, although they were not encumbered with heavy packs and had the use of supplementary oxygen. Two teams of eight and seven Sherpas then carried to the highest camp in support of two summit attempts. With all this assistance, one Korean and the one Sherpa who accompanied him made it to the top. If nothing else, it would appear that by the late 1970s the Sherpas were perfectly capable of climbing Mount Everest by themselves (Cheney 1978, 589–90).

This application of excessive Sherpa-power, like the overuse of other kinds of mountaineering aids, is seen by some climbers as an ethical transgression. They argue that the modern day Sherpa-supported climb harkens back to the bad old days of early European mountaineering. Then, climbers, usually British, ascended to the summits of the Alps behind shepherds-turned-mountain-guides who cut snow steps, carried loads, and held the rope for their less skillful but wealthier clients. Current feeling among American and most European climbers runs strongly against the re-creation of the sharp distinctions in ability and social standing that the client-guide relationship represented, at least outside popular tourist areas such as the Alps. Most modern expeditions expect and are sometimes required to treat the climbing Sherpas as full party members, providing them with proper and complete equipment, food, and medical care on the mountain and according them full credit for their accomplishments afterwards. The Korean Everest climb is among the few recent exceptions (see also Thompson 1979).

Porter Problems. While most climbers have praise for the Sherpas, not all hired load carriers are as conscientious or cooperative. At the western end of the Himalayas, the situation is different. To reach the major peaks in this Karakoram region also requires long approach-marches from the last point accessible to mechanical transport to the base camp for the climb. Moving the expedition's gear requires considerable person-power. Misunderstandings have sometimes been generated in this region when stringent government pay structures and work agreements have been looked upon by expeditioners as binding but have been seen by the local Pakistani porters as starting points for negotiation. This conflict of perspectives has led to porter strikes, work slowdowns, and recruitment problems. On the 1975 American K2 expedition, porter recalcitrance became so acute that the expedition seemed on the brink of total collapse.

Arguments and cajoling from the climbers and even a Pakistani government representative had no effect. Only radical countermeasures could
stimulate the porters to continue their load-carrying duties. Galen Rowell
describes the final successful bit of climber histrionics:

> We told the porters that if our expedition failed at Ghoro, we
> would burn all of our equipment and money on the spot and go
> home empty-handed without paying them. To underscore the
> threat Jim pulled a ten-rupee note out of the payroll sack and
> Wick set his lighter to it. As it burned on the negotiating table in
> front of wide-eyed village headmen, the team members got up
> and walked back to their tents without a word.
>
> Later we had great news. Virtually all the porters had agreed
> to carry to Concordia. (Rowell 1977a, 174–75)

Are Expeditions Necessary?

Whether the porters be cooperative or obstructive, skilled climbers in
their own right or simply substitutes for beasts of burden, the tasks they
perform are a necessary part of the support required by all large-scale
expeditions. But climbers are beginning to ask whether large-scale expeditions are necessary. As a result of the cost and cumbersomeness of
these large parties and because of growing ethical concerns, the era of the
mammoth expedition with its vast retinue of support workers may be
coming to a close. During the late 1970s, mountaineers showed an increasing interest in small, self-sufficient climbing parties that do most of
their own hauling and dispense with fixed ropes and fixed camps, carrying all their own gear and supplies with them as they ascend. These
"alpine style" ascents are considered more sporting and are viewed as
greater achievements than climbs using the siege tactics of conventional
expeditions.

While the American K2 expedition with its more than six hundred
porters and tons of hardware and supplies was toiling up the Baltoro
glacier on the way to the climb, another, quite different mountaineering
venture was in the making. Hidden Peak, 26,470 feet, is the second
highest mountain in the entire Karakoram region (after K2, which is the
second highest in the world). The difficult northwest face on Hidden
Peak had been dismissed by experts "as too difficult for contemporary
standards" (Rowell 1977b, 254) even with the power and resources of a
full-scale expedition. In spite of this gloomy analysis, two exceptional
European mountaineers, Reinhold Messner and Peter Habler, had come
to attempt what others had deemed impossible. They would try to climb
the northwest face of Hidden Peak, as steep as the North Face of the
Matterhorn and almost as high as two Matterhorns, one on top of the
other. And they would climb it in one continuous three-day push. To

accomplish this feat they would carry only a minimum of gear in their own rucksacks. By comparison with the American undertaking, Habler and Messner brought with them from Europe only 220 pounds of gear and used just twelve porters in their approach. As the defeated Americans returned down the Baltoro, they learned that this bold plan had been entirely successful, with Messner even shooting cine footage on the summit. More such lightweight alpine-style climbs on big mountains can be expected in the future.

Whether by choice, cost prohibitions, lack of ability, or because of ethical concerns, most American climbers never go on a full-scale Himalayan expedition. Yet, wherever they do go—to the local ranges or on semi-expeditions further afield—almost all are faced with the problem of transporting their gear from the road end to the mountain base. They solve this problem in several ways.

Animals

Historically, and to a less extent today, pack animals have helped move the mountaineers and their gear toward the mountain. Clarence King and the other members of Whitney's pioneering Sierra Nevada survey and climbing party used horses whenever practicable to carry them toward and through the mountains, more than a century ago (see Farquhar 1965, 129–54; King [1872] 1970). The first ascents of Canada's Mount Logan and Alaska's Mount McKinley utilized dogsled teams to transport supplies up frozen rivers and across snowy territory in winter, in preparation for upcoming spring climbs (Sherman 1965, 1–38; Stuck 1977.) Today only a very few wilderness travelers own their own horses and those who do find trailering them a tedious and time-consuming chore. Somewhat more frequently, owners of large dogs may have their pets fitted with pack bags by which some canines can carry sizable loads.

Most of the time, beasts of burden are an impractical alternative for the contemporary mountaineer. Dogs are not allowed in the backcountry of national parks, and horses are few, expensive, and difficult to transport. Thus, the primary responsibility for moving gear and supplies in the wilderness rests with the person who will ultimately use that material. The climbers are their own most reliable and frequently called upon beasts of burden. Other backcountry visitors also carry their own loads, and an understanding of these others sheds light on the special perspective of the climber.

Mountaineering's Cousins

The mountaineer has three close cousins who seek out and enjoy self-propelled and self-contained wilderness travel: the backpacker, the trekker, and the explorer.[5] Each shares a portion of the climber's activity, technique, and territory. They are set apart from each other and from the mountaineer most clearly by the emphasis they place upon achieving certain goals, a difference of degree rather than of kind. While climbers may dislike and object to those who depend upon mechanized vehicles for wilderness travel—the four-wheel-drive and dirt-bike set, they often feel a kinship with and affinity for those who enjoy backcountry travel on their own power. Many climbers were themselves first backpackers, may occasionally be trekkers, and dream of being explorers.

Backpacking. Backpacking is the most popular form of nonmechanized wilderness travel. Its devotees enjoy the process of making their way on foot in the outdoors and supplying their needs from the few things they carry with them. They find challenge and enjoyment in facing the same requirements for self-sufficiency as the mountaineer but usually in less hostile and more easily traveled surroundings. While mountaineers' curiosity and enthusiasm for their specialized techniques and equipment may lead them toward broken and difficult terrain, backpackers more often choose to journey along established trails. Traveling a common path by day, they frequently come together at popular lake or streamside camp sites to spend the night in each other's company.

Backpackers set themselves different goals than mountaineers do. They define their accomplishments more in terms of horizontal than vertical travel. For backpackers, overcoming a short piece of precipitous terrain is a less appealing objective than going considerable distances over easier ground. Reaching mountain summits is less important to backpackers than going from point A to point B, although the high mountain places do not go unnoticed or unappreciated by them.

For backpackers the most difficult part of any trip is usually crossing passes. Hiking over passes will take backpackers to their greatest altitude, sometimes into the more demanding territory above timberline where an absence of sheltering trees may combine with the obstacle of snow on the trail. Overcoming these impediments is a significant achievement for backpackers. On arriving at the pass they may stop to eat, rest, and enjoy the view in much the same manner that climbers do on the summits of mountains. The actual trail crest may be marked with stone mounds or, on some Sierra passes, with wooden signs provided by the United States Park Service which are inscribed with the pass name and altitude. These signs may be included in photographs backpackers sometimes take of each other—photos which are similar in composition to the climber's summit snapshots. A few passes in the Sierras are even provided with registers, like those on mountain tops, which hikers may sign to provide a record of their accomplishment. But just getting to the pass is not the backpacker's goal; it is getting from one point to another.

Passes are the objective as well as subjective high points of a cross-country journey, but reaching them is not the principal motive for backpacking trips. If two routes are equally aesthetic, accessible, and appointed with catchable fish, the way selected by backpackers is likely to be the one that avoids steep high places. For this category of wilderness travel, convenience, conservation of energy, and competence considerations come first; pleasant scenery is appreciated and technical climbing generally avoided. Like climbers, backpackers may aspire to certain prestigious accomplishments. The Wonderland Trail, which encircles Mount Rainier in a hundred-mile-long continuous pathway, is one such trip. Hiking the entire two-hundred-forty plus miles of the John Muir Trail from Mount Whitney to Yosemite Valley is another. Even more ambitious is the Pacific Crest Trail, a trip which takes the hiker from the Mexican to the Canadian border, along the Sierra Nevada and Cascade ranges. The Appalachian Trail poses a similar challenge to East Coast backpackers.

It may sound as if a sizable schism exists between the backpacker and the mountaineer. For most settings and circumstances this is correct. The mountaineer, as typified by the technically skilled alpinist, and the cross-country hiker lack commonality in both goals and means. But among many outdoor enthusiasts in Southern California, this distinction is not so clear. Some backpackers accept the challenge of reaching mountain summits where technical climbing is not required. For instance, the summit of Mount Whitney is easily ascended via a broad path and is a favorite way-point of the adventurous hiker. Some climbing, likewise, is little more than high-altitude, long-distance walking with the summit thrown in for legitimacy. Those people whose goal is to hike from summit to summit by the most accessible route, amassing a long list of ascents, were referred to earlier as peak baggers. Peak bagging and backpacking are closely related. While fans of the former count summits and feet of gain per day, participants in the latter count passes and miles. Peak bagging was said to fall close to the limits of activity which could be termed mountaineering. Backpacking lies immediately beyond these limits—outside the immediate family of climbing activities but still a close relative. Unlike climbers in Europe, Southern California mountaineers are of necessity backpackers on their ways to and from trail head to mountain. Some by choice pursue a kind of climbing very close to backpacking in challenge and method.

Trekking. Some backpackers, like their mountaineering counterparts, may grow dissatisfied with the challenges of the nearby mountains and set out to find new adventures in other areas of the globe. This is trekking. While the climber seeks ever higher, more remote, and more difficult summits, the trekker goes in search of higher and more remote passes leading to seldom seen valleys far distant from conventional pathways. Treks incorporate features of extended backpacking, expeditionary mountaineering, and guided climbing.

Treks are long and strenuous cross-country journeys. They may last for two, three, or four weeks and cover hundreds of miles. With the expedition, they share a common territory—the remote mountainous areas in the Himalayas, Africa, South America, and elsewhere. They often follow the same routes major mountaineering parties take on their way to base camp, or the paths of earlier expeditionary scouting groups probing the defenses of a mountain.

Travel in this kind of terrain requires that the trekker have at least the rudiments of the mountaineer's technical skill to traverse high snow-covered passes and rocky terrain. Trekkers also need a modicum of the expeditioners' strength, endurance, and tolerance for altitude, as treks are physically demanding and often involve travel at considerable height. Like the climbers on an expedition, trekkers may have a portion of their gear and supplies carried by hired porters.

Treks resemble guide mountaineering trips in that they are often commercial ventures, organized by professionals who plan and acquire the transportation, equipment, and food, lay out itineraries, and provide trip leaders familiar with the area. In the United States, guided treks are often put together and led by the same organizations and personnel that organize guided climbing trips. A description of one trek in the Everest area illustrates these commercial adventures.

There are many ways to approach the massif of the highest mountain in the world. Perhaps the most adventurous, alpine, and least traveled access is provided by the high Himalayan valley of Rolwaling, extending from a junction in the west with the Bhote Kosi river eastward to the imposing Tesi Lapcha Pass (19,000'). The valley, some 35 miles long, runs parallel to the Tibetan region of China, from which it is separated by the towering peaks of the Rolwaling Himal.

The approach to the Rolwaling Valley from Katmandu is via landrover to Sun Kosi Bazar, then on foot across a 12,000-foot ridge into the Bhote Kosi Rober valley. The 30-day trek begins at about 4,000 feet and progresses steadily upwards through steeply terraced fields dotted with tiny, feudal villages, passing shrines built of stone along the path. Walking across delicate hanging bridges we will reach enchanting, beautiful viewpoints, and on the eighth day enter the Rolwaling Valley forest at 8,000 feet.

There are two main villages in the valley: Beding (12,000') and Nan Gaon (14,000'). Our route of ascent to Moraine Lake Camp (14,000'), Glacier Camp (16,000'), and finally Tesi Lapcha Pass, lies on the main trade artery between the Rolwaling Valley and the Everest region. Winding down past the Drolum Bau Glacier to Thami, Manche, and Thyangboche in Khumbu, we will reserve a day to either climb Kala Patar (18,192') or visit

Everest Base Camp (18,000′). After the trek out to Lukla, we will
return by charter plane to Katmandu. (Mountain Travel, Inc.
1976, 27)

Exploring. One final category of wilderness traveler is the explorer. While
even the most famous of mountaineers remain relatively obscure personages in the public view, many explorers are well-known. The names of
Columbus, Cortez, Pizarro, Livingstone, Byrd, Perry, and the like may
not be household words but they at least appear frequently in history
texts. Their deeds are celebrated or decried in biographies, novels, and
films. But these were heroes from an earlier time.

The globe on which we live is smaller now. No new continents,
mountain ranges, or river systems lie beyond the horizon, waiting to be
discovered. Even the Arctic and Antarctic are now neatly partitioned
among nations, with invisible boundaries carefully drawn between the
territories. The City of Gold was found on the Las Vegas strip, and the
Fountain of Youth is piped in at Leisure World. It is no longer possible to
annex vast new territories on the strength of an explorer's claim alone.
The time is gone when a few men and women armed with modern
weapons, religion, and courage could subjugate an entire people and
their lands, but some of the spirit of the explorer's conquests lives on in
the mountaineer.

In past centuries the explorer's task was not primarily recreational.
Rather, he was charged with the duty of enhancing the economic circumstances of his backers. This involved not only travel through un-
charted lands but an examination of the terrain and its inhabitants with an
eye for their economic potential. He looked for resources—minerals, raw
materials, arable land, animals, and markets for existing products. He
searched for means by which these sources might be exploited—cheap
power and labor, practical trade routes, feasible passes, navigable rivers.
Access to these newfound riches was assured by outright claim, conquest, or favorable trade agreement. Finally, the explorer's work concluded with maps, surveys, charts, and descriptions of the newly discovered territory. All of these efforts were done to further the interest, for the
glory, and in the name of sovereign, state, or sponsor.

Mountaineering and exploration have several common features. Explorers confronted the same essential circumstances that faced the
pioneer climber—trying to find a way through wilderness terrain about
which little was known. While climbers look for ways up and down
mountain peaks, the explorers sought routes around and through them.
Exploring was very often a patriotic, nationalistic endeavor. Explorers
were specifically charged with gathering information and making conquests on behalf of and for the benefit of those who provided them with
financial support. The spirit of this sort of explorer's nationalistic con-

quest is still to be found in major mountaineering expeditions. The desire to conquer a particular peak or difficult route for one's country has been a recurring theme in mountaineering since its inception. For example, Britisher Edward Whymper and Italian guide Jean-Antone Carrell both tried to be the first to reach the summit of the Matterhorn. They competed for more than personal glory and recognition. Of Carrel, it has been said that:

> It has been his lifelong dream that he should be the first to stand upon the summit of the peak—for the honor of Italy and his native Val Tournanche. (Ullman 1964a, 50)

During the 1930s, considerable patriotic fervor emerged around efforts to solve one of the most difficult mountaineering problems in the Alps, climbing the North Face of the Eiger, the Eigerwand, in Switzerland.

> Young Germans were encouraged to attempt the apparently impossible in a do-or-die spirit that held prudence in contempt and extolled carelessness of death as virtue. This attitude was transferred to mountaineering and resulted in many fatalities and bred a cut-throat competition between the young climbers of the countries near the Alpine frontiers. (Styles 1967, 128)

> Seldom has there been an unhappier example of how hysterical and perverted nationalism can infect even the most unpolitical of human activities. . . . Hitler himself announced that gold medals would be awarded to the first scalers of the Eigerwand in conjunction with the Berlin Olympic Games of 1936. (Ullman 1964a, 73, 74ff.)

As Ullman (1964a, 73) observed, the Alps had once been looked upon as a playground, then as a laboratory, and in the 1930s they became a symbolic battlefield.

Today's expeditionary climbing still retains considerable nationalism. Major expeditions are often carefully identified in journal reports and other media coverage on the basis of the country of origin of the participants as well as the peak attempted, year, and perhaps the route. Thus, reference is made to the *American* K2 Expedition of 1978, the *French* 1950 Annapurna Expedition, the *Swiss* 1952 Everest Expedition, etc.

Along with the possession of satellites and sophisticated military hardware, it has become a source of much pride to put a team of climbers on the summit of the world's highest mountain, Everest. Sometimes the mountaineering takes a back seat to the politics in those sorts of climbs, as

Michael Cheney observes, regarding the Korean Everest climb of 1977 mentioned above:

> Of all Everest expeditions, this was the most blatantly political and nationalistic. It was a calculated exercise in "prestige politics," financed half-and-half by the government of South Korea and South Korean business. It was sponsored by the South Korean National Assembly. (Cheney 1978, 590)

Finally, the symbolism of national conquest in mountaineering is underscored by the ritual of the summit flag-raising. Upon reaching the top of important peaks, some expeditionary climbers unfurl small flags of their nation of origin from about their ice-axe shafts. These are held proudly aloft to be photographed. This ceremony is strongly reminiscent of that practiced by explorers who planted flags of their own nation on the shores of newly discovered lands and thus symbolically took possession of that territory.

In summary, exploring is political, while mountaineering is assumed to be recreational. The two should remain distinguished from each other, yet like the relationship between climbing and backpacking or trekking, there is much overlap. Both may involve the use of technical climbing skills; both may lead to the summits of difficult mountains. The differences are sometimes more of motive than method. While explorers seek the discovery of new lands with an eye to their eventual exploitation, the climber is satisfied with the climbing. Yet, on occasion, expeditionary mountaineering serves as a symbolic form of national conquest which resembles in many ways that of the explorer.

None of the stages or modes of travel we have discussed can be said to be exclusively the province of the climber, but at the end of the road, tram, or trail is a mountain. At some point travel involves more than simple balance, becomes more vertical than horizontal, requires skill as well as endurance. This is the realm of technical climbing. The backpacker, trekker, or explorer must act the part of the mountaineer to travel through this more demanding terrain. How travel on the mountain itself is accomplished is the topic of the next chapter.

6
Technical Climbing

Technical climbing encompasses the activity which the lay public usually identifies as the sine qua non of mountaineering—the scaling of steep ice, snow, and rock. How is it possible to ascend great rock faces and ice-sheathed walls without falling off and being killed? To answer this question we need to take a closer look at the climber's equipment and the ways in which it is employed. Through the definition and explanation of some basic terms, a common vocabulary will emerge which will render future discussions of technical climbing less stilted and mysterious (see also Glossary).

Technical climbing is most clearly distinguished from other kinds of uphill travel, by use of the rope. The act of "roping up," attaching one's self and one's partner to the climbing rope, marks the dividing line between sociability and technical climbing. The rope serves to safeguard and sometimes to aid the climber's progress.

The rope is the first item of gear that many lay persons associate with mountain climbing. How that rope is used, however, is sometimes woefully misunderstood. Norm Kingsley provides an example of such confusion:

> When I first got into the game in 1953, my mother bitterly complained, "My boy's climbing mountains with a rope. Isn't that awful?" This presents a vision of a climber unfurling his rope, tootling at it as it snakes its way up the crags. Then he clips in with his ascenders and jumars [climbs up the rope] finally reaching the summit pinnacle. (Kingsley 1975, 73)

An understanding of the actual principles of rope management will help dispel such myths. My example will be limited to two climbers on a rope. This is the usual number of high-angle travel, although solo roped climbing is possible, and three or more may rope together for glacier travel or other less steep climbing.

Rope Management

As a pair of climbers move up the mountain, they proceed in the following fashion. Each is tied to an end of the rope, either directly or by use of a harness that distributes the impact of falls over the climber's body. One climber called the "belayer" or "second" anchors firmly to the mountain. This may be accomplished in several ways. The simplest is to tie a loop in the climbing rope near where it is attached to the belayer and drop this loop over a nearby projection—rock, tree stump, etc. Loops of flat nylon webbing—also called tape, sling, or runners—may be used for the same purpose if shortening the climbing rope is inadvisable or the object can be more securely or practically encircled with this material.

In the absence of a convenient projection, more subtle features of the mountain are used as anchor points. Metal spikes, called pitons, pins, or pegs, may be driven with a hammer into cracks in the rock. Pitons range in size from the postage-stamp-small, knife-thin RURP (Realization of the Ultimate Reality Piton) to the 6-inch-wide folded sheet-steel or aluminum Bongs, named for the sound created when they are pounded into the mountain. Pitons, generally provide secure anchor points, but their repeated placement and removal, also by pounding, can scar the rock and damage crack systems.

Other devices used in anchoring are referred to as chocks or nuts. These are metal wedges or cams of various shapes that can be slotted or fitted into existing cracks. They also come in a wide range of sizes. The security of chocks and nuts is variable, but they do not damage the rock and are thus preferred in areas of heavy climbing use.

When the belayer can locate no suitable rock in the immediate vicinity but solid ice of sufficient thickness is nearby, threaded hollow tubes called ice screws, or studded spikes, ice pitons, can be used as anchors. These are twisted or pounded into the ice. If rock is accessible but lacking in adequate cracks, small holes can be drilled in a blank section into which expansion bolts are fitted. This permanently alters the rock both in difficulty and appearance.

Regardless of the type of device used—rope, sling, piton, chock, ice screw, bolt—the aim is to make the anchor as secure as possible. In case of a fall this anchor must be strong enough to support the weight of both climbers and absorb the shock of one of them falling, perhaps from far above. It must be as failure-proof as circumstances allow.

When firmly attached to the mountain, the belayer takes up the rope and wraps it around his or her torso in such a way that the rope can be controlled as it is played out or taken in and can be held firmly in case of a fall. The leader is now "on belay" and begins to climb upward while the belayer manages the rope to maintain a minimum of slack between the two partners.

This is the basic belaying system. The belayer's secure position and rope-handling expertise ensure that should the leader fall, he or she will travel no greater distance than twice the height above the belay point. This may, however, be a limited consolation. The standard length of a climb rope is 150 feet. Thus, the minimal belay system would permit a leader to fall as far as 300 feet before being stopped by the rope. Modern ropes, when properly used, are capable of stopping such severe falls. By partially elongating, they absorb a portion of the shock that might otherwise be transmitted to the climber. However, in such long-distance falls the danger of hitting a ledge or other projection before being arrested is considerable. Therefore, the leader may safeguard his or her progress by placing intermediate protection points along the route. These are additional slings, chocks, pitons, etc., which are attached to the rope with metal snaplinks called carabiners. Carabiners clip around the rope but allow it to continue to slide upward as the leader progresses. In case of a fall the highest protection point acts as a fulcrum, like the belayer's position in the basic system, so that the length of a potential fall is limited to twice the distance from the climber to the last intermediate anchor point.

After climbing a pitch, the leader establishes a new belay anchor, ties in to this protection point, wraps the rope around his or her body for control, and belays the second climber up by keeping the rope between them reasonably snug. The second person climbs upward and recovers the gear left behind by the leader. Upon reaching the upper belay point, the second person may continue upward, becoming the new leader.

It is also possible for the second climber to ascend the rope itself. At the top of the pitch the leader may attach the rope directly to an anchor. The second then attaches accessory cord with prusik knots, or mechanical ascending devices—the best known being the Jumar brand—to the rope. These knots or devices slide upward when not under tension but lock on the rope when loaded with weight and may be attached to the climber's feet via slings or other cord. By alternately standing in one while sliding the other upward with the hands, the climber can ascend the rope in an exaggerated stair-step fashion.

Climbers use special maneuvers to get down as well as up steep rock or ice. To descend they may rappel, abseil, or rope down, three names for essentially the same procedure. The rope is fed through a ring or sling attached to some protection point until the middle of the rope is reached (or the rope may be looped over a convenient projection). This leaves the rope doubled, with the free ends dangling downward together. This doubled rope is wrapped around the climber's body or around a rappelling device attached to his or her harness in such a way that considerable friction is produced and the descent can easily be controlled with the hands. He or she then slides down the rope. At the bottom the rope is recovered by pulling one end downward.

Rappelling serves as an end in itself for a few enthusiasts who devote leisure time to the descent of practice cliffs, buildings, and other structures. These sport rappellers gain the start of their descent by pathway, stairs, or other less difficult means. Their goal is another slide down the rope. Experienced rock climbers and mountaineers often view rappelling as a risky and unrewarding endeavor, a necessary evil to be used judiciously and sparingly. They argue that rappelling is an entirely technical maneuver where climbing skill and ability are negated by one's complete dependence on the equipment employed. Rappelling, they say, is like trying to prepare a fine meal using packaged TV dinners. There is not much the individual can do but follow directions. Personal involvement is minimized, creativity limited, and disasters frequent enough to warrant caution. Still such climbing worthies as Yvon Chouinard started by going down the cliffs for fun, not up them. Recreational rappelling may introduce persons to rope handling and safety procedures they later go on to apply as climbers.

It is important to distinguish between free and aid climbing. In free ascents only naturally occurring features of the mountain are used for footholds and handholds. Protection points may be placed along the way, but these only serve as safeguards against a fall. Aid climbing uses the protection points themselves as holds. Pitons, chocks, etc., are placed, then metal or webbing stirrups are attached to them. The climber then stands in this stirrup, reaches up, and places another anchor which serves as the next hold. In this manner stretches of otherwise holdless and even overhanging rock and ice can be overcome.

With aid techniques and enough hardware, particularly expansion bolts, virtually any problems can be surmounted, provided there is sufficient time and patience. Thus, the use of aid, or "rock engineering," is not the most difficult sort of climbing, although it may be used to ascend the most objectively difficult terrain. The greatest challenge lies in the upper limits of free climbing where the climber dispenses with the artificial handholds and footholds and makes do with whatever meager opportunities for purchase the mountain provides. High-standard free climbing requires both greater strength and delicacy than aid ascents do.

Rock and Ice Climbing

There are two related sports in which technical climbing is looked upon as an end in itself, rock climbing and ice climbing. Rock climbing in the United States is not generally a wilderness experience. It is concentrated on accessible crags and practiced during times of fair weather. Participants are discouraged when rain or snow interrupts an outing or when the cliffs are at too great a distance from a convenient road, although they may travel some distance to popular climbing areas by auto or other transport. Because of their preference for easily reached locations and pleasant weather, rock climbers often share a common territory with day hikers, picnickers, Sunday drivers, and other members of the nonclimbing public. As a result of this mingling, rock climbing may on occasion become an impromptu spectator sport.

At Stoneypoint, a Southern California practice area in Chatsworth, weekend bicyclists, pleasure drivers, and walkers often stop in the parking area at the base of the boulders to watch the climbers and sport rappellers in action. Rappelling is particularly interesting to onlookers. Fascination with it seems to stem from the apparent precariousness of the situation. Spectators will "ooh" and "ahh" while watching rappels but will almost totally ignore an unroped climber at the top of a delicate and committing 20-foot boulder problem. A lack of awareness leads some onlookers to imagine considerable danger in the simple technical exercise of lowering oneself down a cliff on a firmly anchored 4,000-pound test rope but overlook the very real hazard faced by the boulderer performing awkward and strenuous gymnastics where a slip would produce a certain 20-foot fall onto an uncompromising parking-lot surface. In consideration of this public attention a few rappellers may even embellish their descent with unnecessary leaps and bounds for the sake of audience appreciation. In major rock-climbing areas, such as the Yosemite Valley, the climber's progress up the valley's walls may be followed by tourists with binoculars and telescopes from the comfort of their trailer-side lawn chairs. Mountaineers generally lack both the opportunity and the inclination for such public review. As Ullman comments:

> Mountaineering, by its very nature, is almost never seen by anyone but its participants. There is the climber, his companions, the mountain. And that is all. Except in the rarest cases, as on a Matterhorn or an Everest, no one is following his progress. No one is umpiring or keeping score. As near as possible in the modern world he is a man on his own, and his rewards and penalties are known to himself alone. (Ullman 1964a, 318)

Ice climbing is rock climbing's cold-weather cousin. On steep snow or ice, crampons, spiked metal frames strapped to the boots, may be used to provide the climber with surer footing. The climber will also carry an ice axe, a multipurpose tool resembling a lightweight pick adze, which is used for balance, chopping steps in steep ice and snow, or arresting slips on more moderate slopes.

Historically, the rudiments of snow and ice climbing were developed well in advance of rock craft since many of the great peaks in the Alps were most practically ascended by snow and ice routes. The Matterhorn resisted all attempts to climb it for so long in part because the climbers of the day had little familiarity with the sort of rock-climbing challenge the mountain posed. In the late 1970s, ice climbing underwent a radical resurgence of popularity as a result of subtle but important improvements in the climber's tools. It is now possible for climbers of modest ability to overcome ice problems thought formidable by experts only a few years ago.

Like rock climbers, ice climbers are interested in overcoming steep and difficult terrain, but while the former find their challenge on rock, the latter seek steep ice-filled gullies and frozen waterfalls to climb. This sort of climbing is limited to climates where temperatures and precipitation produce ice in sufficient quantity to remain for a reasonable period of time on the local crags. The Sierra Nevada, with its mild winters and warm summers, is a mecca for rock climbers but offers relatively few opportunities for the ice climber. On the other hand Scotland, with its harsh, protracted winters and tenacious climbers has been the proving ground for much of modern ice-climbing technique.

Both rock climbing and ice climbing are necessary skills for the competent mountaineer, but they are not sufficient in and of themselves to define mountaineering. Only when they combine with each other and take place in remote locales, at high altitudes, in all conditions of weather is the fullest variety of mountaineering challenge realized. Such conditions provide the ideal mountain-climbing experience, though not always the typical one.

Rock and ice climbing receive additional attention throughout the text so no more time need be devoted to them here. But our discussion of mountaineering activities is not yet complete. Climbing is a social process as well as a technical maneuver. Climbers do more than plan, drive, hike, and grapple gamely with the mountainside. They also talk to each other. Understanding some of the special qualities of this talk helps us penetrate further into the world of the mountaineer.

7
Talk

Talk is here taken to refer to all types of linguistic symbol-making, either written or verbal, from ritual rope-handling commands to fireside philosophizing. For mountaineers there are normative and environmental prescriptions for where and when talk will proceed and upon what subjects it will touch. Like all other activities, talk cannot be completely separated from the events with which it is associated. Nevertheless, it is usefully looked at as a social product in its own right.

Topic, Time, and Place

Now that the reader is familiar with the physical environments of mountaineering and related activities, it will come as no surprise that certain times and places preclude talk altogether. Struggling up a steep trail under an eighty-pound pack is conducive to deep breathing but not to fluid conversation. Two climbers on a technical portion of a climb have other restrictions. While the belayer is well-rested and secure in his or her stance and has plenty of breath and time to chat, the only person he or she can address may be a hundred feet overhead in the midst of some strenuous and desperate gymnastics. The leader's contribution to any conversation will come probably in the form of guttural utterances or colorful epithets (see Godfrey 1975, 207, for examples).

Other phases of mountaineering encourage or require talk. As we have seen, for the Southern California climber at least a portion of every climbing trip is devoted to mechanized travel. This provides an extended opportunity for conversation with one's fellows. On the trip up, climbers are in transition from workaday world to mountain setting. Early talk often centers on functional topics—mechanics of the drive, where to eat, packing of the car (or bus or boat), work matters. Later, with the city behind, conversation turns to the upcoming climb. Attempts are made to glean from fellow climbers any additional information they might have concerning the forthcoming ascent. This is a particularly noticeable tension-reducing device used by novice climbers and others faced with a challenge of unknown dimensions. More experienced climbers perhaps achieve the same end by a more subtle probing of their companions' knowledge, always bearing in mind the climber's penchant for calculated understatement.

The tendency to understate is applied in describing both one's personal accomplishments or skills and the objective difficulties of a particular undertaking. Even events of phenomenal daring, endurance, and hardship are couched in mild terms. The most arduous and hair-raising climbs, dangers, tribulations, and personal injuries are discussed in dispassionate terms. Frightful peril becomes a "very committing" situation. Tiny holds on a sheer wall thousands of feet up pose a "problem," an "awkward passage," and are "interesting." The broken finger or leg or other injury is "quite bothersome." Some understatement in English-speaking countries perhaps reflects the worldwide British influence on climbing.

The return drive is another occasion for talk. This period may be muted by fatigue after a long climb but still offers at least some opportunity for mutual congratulations or chastisement in the light of the weekend's events. The approach and return phases of travel have somewhat different points of conversational focus. Going towards the mountains, talk is characterized by information-gathering efforts, hypothesizing, anticipating, and general attempts to forecast the events of the approaching weekend. On the return the tenor changes to one of review. The events of the climb are no longer problematic but factual. Talk shifts from conjecture to analysis.

Formal Talk

In at least two situations climbers use standardized expressions to communicate with each other: when rope commands are needed and when trail greetings are called for. The expressions used in these situations typify what Lyman and Scott call frozen linguistic style. "Typically, interaction in the frozen style occurs among those between whom an irrevocable barrier exists. The barrier may be of a material or social nature, or both" (Lyman and Scott 1970, 132).

Rope Commands

In technical climbing it is important for the leader and belayer to communicate basic information about their situations: there is too much slack in the rope; the leader is anchored and ready to belay the second person up; more rope is needed by a climber to make the next move; etc. Yet climbing partners may be out of sight of each other, around corners, behind boulders, below overhangs. To convey this important information, climbers develop and employ a set of shorthand expressions to instruct their partners in rope management and advise them of other critical conditions. A climbing text provides an illustration. Note that "Belayer" here refers to whichever partner is anchored and tending the rope, while "Climber" indicates the person who is moving and being safeguarded by the belayer.

> Climber (inquiring if the belay is ready): "On belay?"
> Belayer (when ready with belay): "Belay on."
> Climber (to notify belayer he or she is beginning to ascend): "Climbing."
> Climber (when rope is too loose): "Up rope." (When more rope is needed): "Slack." (For a taut rope to hold his or her weight): "Tension."
> Climber (when safe and no longer climbing): "Off belay."
> Belayer (responding): "Belay off."
> Both (when falling rock is seen): "Rock!"
> Climber (in case of slip): "Falling!"
> (Adapted from Manning 1967, 162)

As subtlety is less important than clarity, these signals are generally forcefully bellowed back and forth between climbing partners. On a busy weekend afternoon at the local practice crags this sonorous signaling echoes almost continually. On occasion, high wind, intervening rock, or nearby waterfalls may render vocal communication nearly impossible. In such circumstances climbing signals may become so "frozen" that they pass from the realm of talk entirely, being reduced to a series of rope tugs or whistle codes.

Trail Greetings

Another sort of standardized verbal exchange occurs when strangers pass each other on the mountain path. This is the trail greeting. In the Sierras these salutations are of the same sort as would be used with strangers in more urban settings; "Hi," "How's it going?" "Howdy," etc. In the Pennine Alps, passing hikers greet each other similarly with "Grüss Gott" (Field notes, September 1974, Zermatt). In the eastern Himalayas, Sherpas carrying loads on Everest expeditions and in other areas may use a somewhat spicier salutation: "Likpadello," they say. "My sexual organ is big" (Bonnington 1976, 91).

These greetings are typical but not exhaustive. How perfunctory or expansive a particular trail encounter will be depends upon the social density, the frequency of these encounters. Close to the trail head, where many wilderness travelers are constantly coming and going, other hikers may be passed every few minutes and greetings are reduced to a smile and a nod. On the other hand, in truly remote areas, where other people have not been seen for a week or more, a chance meeting calls for not only a friendly greeting but a rest stop, a chat about origins, routes, and destinations, and perhaps even a brewed cup of tea or a shared snack.

Specialized Language

Finally, throughout the climber's talk there is a specialized language, some of which has already been indicated. Setting this prior knowledge aside for a moment, imagine how the following piece of climber conversation might be interpreted by the uninitiated. The mystery in mountaineering talk should become immediately apparent. Doug Scott is describing his preparations for departure, with Dougal Haston, from Camp 6, the highest camp on the South West Face of Mount Everest, on their summit attempt.

> I decided to travel light, and left my feathered suit behind, relying on my jumpers and ventile/nylon wind-suit. However, I packed a stove and billy for hot water, and Dougal put in his duvet boots and bivi sheet. We had two deadmen each, four pegs, and one hammer. (Bonnington 1976, 28)

Without knowledge of the context and a grasp of some basic mountaineering terminology, this might sound a bit like the effects of altitude sickness. One might ask whether this "feathered suit" is a giant bird costume with which one flies up the cliffs. Are "jumpers" alternatives to feathered suits which allow climbers to bound rather than fly toward the summits? Is "billy" simply the misspelled name of their Nepalese man-servant? Why the morbid attention to dragging four dead men to the summit, and why would one need pegs and a hammer, presumably to pound upon them, high upon a mountain face? Finally, why would Dougal want his bivi sheet when the nearest proper bed is obviously many miles away?

For clarification, a feathered suit is a down-insulated garment comprising pants and parka used in extremes of cold weather. A jumper is a hooded, noninsulated overparka. Billy refers to a billy can, an aluminum pot used for melting snow and heating water on the portable stove. The deadmen are aluminum alloy plates, roughly 8 inches square, attached to short tether lines and then to the climbing rope. These are pushed into the snow, where they act like fluke anchors, digging deeper the harder they are pulled. They are used as belay and intermediate anchors on snow slopes. The hammer is used to pound the pegs or pitons into rock cracks for anchors. A bivi sheet is a body-length light nylon sleeve into which the climber may crawl for minimal shelter if forced to bivouac or spend the night on the mountain away from camp.

It is sometimes a wonder that the neophyte mountaineer ever comes to tell a carabiner from an etrier, a piton from a piolet, a couloir from a col, a belay from a bivouac. Although a working knowledge of French and German would help unravel some of this mystery, it would not totally suffice, for the Americans have added Hexcentrics, Camlocks, alpine hammers, Friends, stoppers, Titons, Copperheads, Snargs, Hummingbirds, and cliffhangers, among other items, to the climber's bag.

Benjamin Lee Whorf (1970, 115) has pointed out that the Eskimos of North America have at least three separate words in their language for "snow." This plurality is the result of the importance this substance has in the Eskimo's life. Mountaineers are even more preoccupied with the various forms water may take below its freezing point and have developed and adopted numerous words to denote what in common parlance is simply referred to as snow or ice. Airborne frozen water is referred to variously as hail, sleet, grauppel, wet and dry snow, and diamond dust (air hoar). On the ground these are identified as firnspiegel, rime, hoarfrost, verglas, windpack, suncups, water ice, sastrugi, and neve penitente, or in larger masses as cornices, glaciers, seracs, and ice falls. Even the spaces between large ice and snow collections have names: crevasses, moats, and bergschrunds.

Talk on the hike out and the drive home begins the final phase of any climb, a phase which may continue for weeks, months, or even years after a major mountaineering effort. It involves more talk in the form of analysis, reconsideration, post-hoc strategy, and ethical review of the past climb. This is the phase of debriefing.

Debriefing

Climbers have a network of friends who share their avocation. They may be members of local clubs or organizations that have meetings and monthly programs, offer classes, and provide other social interaction opportunities for mountaineers. These meetings, along with less formal get-togethers with climbing friends, provide the stage for the final act in climbing any mountain, debriefing.

As a social phenomenon the climb is not over till the tale is told. The meaning of mountaineering events emerges in the reflective discussion and debate that follow them. Debriefing is the occasion when one's private physical accomplishments become public social topics of interest. It is here that the climbing community decides if a particular ascent is a noteworthy deed or a mediocre accomplishment. The past event is reinterpreted, clarified, and judged. The debriefing session occasions conjecture about what one could, should, or might have done in planning and executing some climb. During debriefing significant accomplishments and misdeeds become public information, and the climber accrues or loses status accordingly. This is prime time for identity negotiation.

Debriefing serves other purposes as well. It provides opportunities for the retired or inactive climber to associate with friends and to enjoy the prestige of his or her past accomplishments. It allows for the development of solidarity among climbers with regard to mutal interests, conservation issues, access to climbing areas, and government regulations. It offers a chance for the dissemination of technical information of the "how to, with what" variety as well as a sharing of approach-march and climbing-route data. The latest issues regarding ethics and style are given an airing. Finally, debriefing offers grassroots contacts for large climbing-related organizations like the American Alpine Club, Sierra Club, the Portland-based Mazamas, the Seattle Mountaineers, and others.

Untoward Events

Special efforts are made during debriefing to render untoward occurrences understandable. These events are analyzed post hoc as instances of rule violations, as examples of action contrary to what "every climber knows" is proper procedure. Appropriate action is that which is dictated by textbooks, climbing manuals, and the like. These sources are culled and cited in accounting for some debacle. Being caught out by a storm, in an avalanche, or suffering a serious fall on rock or ice illustrate the error of not heeding the telltale warning of earlier cloud formations, foolishly crossing south-facing snow slopes in the afternoon, or failing to test a foothold for soundness, tighten crampon straps adequately, place secure and adequate anchors, etc.

Climbers' talk, in the wake of some unexpected event, endeavors to reinforce the belief that mountaineering mishaps are created, not fated. Climbers remind each other that the root of most climbing accidents lies in human error, not mountain menace. Mountaineers are quick to search for plausible causes of any mishap and to reassure themselves that had the relevant rules been followed the untoward event could have been avoided.

The American Alpine Club's publication *Accidents in North American Mountaineering* provide examples of this reflexive reasoning. This annual booklet is a sampler of recent mountaineering accidents with an analysis of each which recasts the event in terms of rule violations. For example:

CLIMBING ALONE, IMPROPER EQUIPMENT—California, Mt. Shasta. Some time on the 15th of September, John Saulsberry (55) attempted a climb of Mt. Shasta from the ski bowl. On the evening of the 15th and 16th an early storm hit the area, dropping large amounts of snow down to 7000 and 8000-foot levels.
When he was reported missing by his wife, after Saulsberry

failed to return home on Saturday, Siskiyou County Sheriff
Search and Rescue began to search. The Sheriff's Department
first became aware of a missing person when a caretaker at the
bowl notified a friend, who notified the Sheriff's Department.
They sent a deputy to the ski bowl to check out the reported
incident. The deputy followed a snow plow all the way into the
ski bowl. There was some question as to what had happened
since Saulsberry had not notified local authorities about his climb
of the mountain. Because of continued extremely poor weather, a
good search was not begun until the 20th. The Sheriff's Department used helicopter and foot searches but could find no trace of
Saulsberry.

Other climbers had seen Saulsberry on the mountain and
stated he wore a green down vest and a slicker. Saulsberry had
written his wife stating that he was going to climb Mt. Hood in
Oregon but realized he did not have the proper equipment so he
returned to Mt. Shasta. Saulsberry stayed at a motel in the city of
Mt. Shasta and told the manager he was going to "climb around
the mountain." His body had not been found as of January 14,
1978. (Source: Don Bryant, Palo Alto Mountaineering School)

Analysis: Saulsberry did not adhere to four of the basic rules
of mountaineering: (1) he failed to notify local authorities of his
climb; (2) he climbed alone with little mountain experience; (3) he
was dressed improperly and carried no mountain or climbing
gear, which would include survival gear; and (4) though the
weather had been clear, there were current weather reports
which clearly indicated a fast approaching storm. (Source: Don
Bryant, and Sgt. Jourden of Siskiyou County Search and Rescue)
(American Alpine Club 1978, 24–25)

Slide Shows

One particular type of off-the-mountain social event typifies the
debriefing process. This is the slide show. Going mountaineering is a
little like having an operation—for the greatest effect it's best to pull up
your shirt and show the scar as well as tell the story. So, climbers often
augment their adventure tales with photos. Slide shows can be casual and
loosely organized events after dinner with friends or at the monthly club
meeting. At other times they are more structured and professional. There
are even a few climbers who are debriefing "specialists." For them the
slide show represents a source of income as well as an opportunty for
image enhancement. Such persons may be retired mountaineers of great
renown. Others may be well-known contemporary climbers who support
themselves in part from the slide-show circuit.

Organized climbing clubs may serve as sponsors in bringing noted
climbing personalities to their areas and may share in the profits forthcoming from admission charges and refreshment sales. At other times
these shows may be promoted by a local sport shop as a way of attracting

customers. The most common topics of the professional show are the highlights of some particularly noteworthy expeditionary climb. A rather lavish example was the 1977 Sierra Club–sponsored presentation of the 1975 American K2 expedition. This Los Angeles extravaganza featured films and slides with commentary by Galen Rowell; it was put on in a rented hall accommodating over 1,000 viewers who paid legitimate-theater prices to get in. Generally, such shows are more modest in price and attendance figures; admission costs only a few dollars and from 100 to 200 people are present.

While expedition climbing is the central theme in most of these shows, this aspect alone attracts a fairly narrow audience. In order to make the commercial debriefing as economically successful as possible, efforts are made to appeal to a broad spectrum of persons with a variety of outdoor interests and experience, from explorer to bird watcher, conservationist, and hiker. The more savvy showmen and women inform and entertain these diverse audiences with anecdotes and glimpses of flora and fauna, native custom, costume, and history in the distant lands to which their climbing trips take them.

Books

The most formal debriefing device is another sort of commercial effort, the expedition book. Leaders or prominent climbers generally are given the task of chronicling the adventures of their climb at the trip's conclusion. These books are an important source of revenue in defraying the costs of the expedition itself. Contractual arrangements with publishers are often made well in advance of an actual climb. The expedition book contains certain obligatory sections, including the prior climbing history of the proposed objective, brief biographical sketches of the participant climbers, plans and preparations, the approach journey, actual climbing, and a technical appendix. They are often augmented with maps, sketches, and photographs and also, unhappily, dedicated to those who lost their lives on the climb.

Climbers may be expected to keep regular diaries, which later serve as resource material for authors. Occasionally, heated jurisdictional disputes emerge over which climbers have the rights to publish these expedition records. While few climbers actually participate in full-scale expeditions, many purchase these books and join vicariously in the debriefing process, spending many hours discussing the strategy, tactics, and ethics of the expeditioners.

Summary

Climbers plan and condition, they select companions and equipment. They drive, fly, hike, and grapple with the mountains' technical difficulties. Then they debate and rehash their accomplishments and start the whole process all over again. This is a recurring cycle of activities. One climb often overlaps another. The climber jogs with friends, discusses the propriety of using some new gadget, selects future climbing objectives and company, and analyzes the last climb all at the same time. While a single climb may be charted through each of the stages distinguished here, the process of mountain climbing is more eclectic and protracted. It involves not just the sum of these constituent activities but a basic commitment on the part of the individual to mountaineering. For those who enjoy climbing mountains a single trip satiates only for a time. The search for mountain adventures is ongoing.

> One can't take a breath large enough to last a lifetime; one can't eat a meal big enough so that one never needs to eat again. Similarly, I don't think any climb can make you content to not climb again. . . . What I get out of climbing . . . such values as warm friendship tested and strengthened through shared danger, the excitement of obstacles overcome by one's own efforts, or the beauty of the high quiet places of the world . . . these values can't be stored like canned goods. They need to be experienced, lived—many times. (Sayre 1964, 199)

One central, recurring theme throughout this study is the climbers' search for balance. It is not just a physical balance of body on mountain that is sought but a moral balance between the challenges of the peak and the tools and techniques used to overcome them. As the difficulty of the mountain increases with remoteness, altitude, weather, lack of information, and technical difficulty, the climber brings into play airplanes and porters, specialized lightweight equipment and supplies, and sophisticated technical maneuvers. But as the problems decrease, when the mountain is not so high or formidable or distant or unknown, then the climber purposely limits the tools and techniques employed to climb it.

Mountaineers often work under numerous self-imposed handicaps. Equipment is restricted to a Spartan minimum. Mechanized transport is foregone in favor of walking. Help from others in the form of porters, Sherpas, or guides is reserved for the extremes of expeditions or for those with only limited skill, such as tourists in the Alps. Some go so far in the search for balance that they may at times even restrict the effectiveness of their own bodies by an avoidance of conditioning programs and by almost enthusiastic acceptance of heavy drinking. Those who climb less technical peaks limit the time they allow themselves to reach the summits, rushing from one top to another on a busy peak-bagging weekend. Technical hardware is employed, when necessary, with caution and restraint; fixed ropes are kept to a minimum and used only in a prescribed fashion.

Limitations, restrictions, and exclusions abound. Conscientious and continuing care is exercised to guarantee that technology and technique do not overwhelm the mountaineering problem at hand. Rules are applied at every turn to ensure that a summit reached may be counted as a moral accomplishment, not merely a technical conquest.

The climber's ongoing task is to tread the precarious ground between too much force and material, which leaves victory meaningless, and too little support and gear, which renders climbing impossible. A slip to one side may result in censure from one's climbing companions and peers, accusations of ethical transgression. A slip to the other way may leave the climber facing failure or even peril. Mountaineering is the process of overcoming physical obstacles but only when done within a carefully constructed and maintained normative framework. Mountaineering takes place on precarious ground, but it is often ground of the climbers' own choosing, rendered difficult and narrow by the rules they apply to themselves and others.

As one mountain adventure follows another, recall and anticipation of mountain experience blend together. The individual is caught up in new patterns of relationships, finds new ways of judging self and others. Through these relationships mountaineers develop images of themselves as climbers, performing a role that is special and apart from conventional ones. These emergent images are part product, part process, and part purpose for interacting with other climbers. How the climber's identity is created, maintained, and enhanced is the topic of the next part of this work.

Part Two
What Is a Mountain Climber?

8
Clubs and Organizations

Identity and Others

Identity—who we are and how we feel about ourselves—depends to a great extent on the ways other people act toward us. Given praise, we may feel pride and act proudly; being censured, we question ourselves and seek improvement. A sense of self requires more than direct perception, more than the sum of sensory stimulations, visceral churnings, and libidinal urges. It requires the perspective of others. "The individual experiences himself as such, not directly but only indirectly, from the particular standpoints of other individual members of the same social group or from the generalized standpoint of the social group as a whole to which he belongs" (Mead 1956, 202).

To understand ourselves we step outside our ideographic experience and imagine the way that others see us. We make an object of ourselves and imbue that object, that self, with meaning according to the action that others take towards us. We know ourselves through the mirrored reflections from what Cooley called the social "looking glass" of the others with whom we interact: "so in imagination we perceive in another's mind some thought of our appearance, manners, aims, deeds, character . . . and so on and are variously affected by it" (Cooley 1972, 231).

In the world of play and games, as in other contexts, it is by the opinions of others that progress is marked and accomplishment gauged. To know ourselves we seek the judgment of others. Yet, not just any others will do. Special qualities are required of those who judge. These significant others are expected to know, in general, the purposes, rules, precedents, and other subtleties of the games being played.

In the selection of evaluative others, those of like kind and mind are sought to observe and compare one's skills and talents. Caillois (1961, 37) notes that similarity of interest is a minimum prerequisite for those from whom evaluations will be accepted. "Generally, the owner of a top hardly finds pleasure in the presence of curling fans, nor does the lover of kite-flying in a group occupied with rolling hoops. Possessors of the same toys [and players of the same sports] congregate in an accustomed or convenient place where they test their skills. This is often essential to their pleasure" (Caillois 1961, 37). But common interest alone is not enough to earn others the role of evaluators of performance. More is required of them.

The results of small-group research provide empirical substance and clarification of Caillois's remarks. Camilleri, Berger, and Conner (1972) found in laboratory experiments that subjects accept others as evaluators if it is believed that they have access to objective standards by which the subjects' deeds might be measured, such as the results of nationwide testing. In another set of experiments, Webster and Sobieszek (1974) showed that persons accord credibility and import to others as evaluators if they have demonstrated the ability to perform the task being judged or if they are of high status in some task-relevant hierarchy. We value the opinion of those whose skill and knowledge we personally observe or infer from their relatively elevated organizational position. Students, in evaluating their academic progress, value both the opinions of the personable and bright fellow student of demonstrated ability and the less interesting but respected faculty member possessing institutional recognition for competence. The budding baseball player values the judgment of this year's star pitcher and the Hall of Fame member alike. Webster and Sobieszek summarize:

> . . . The effect of the evaluations from an evaluator appears to be virtually the same whether the evaluator's basis for an accurate evaluation is (1) possession of access to objective information regarding correct answers . . . (2) high task ability . . . or (3) possession of the high state of a diffuse status characteristic. (Webster and Sobieszek 1974, 86)

Those who have access to objective standards, possess task ability, and have achieved some relevant status meet the expectations for evaluators—they know, in general, the games being played.

For mountaineers, climbing clubs and organizations are one social setting in which significant others may readily be found. Climbing clubs play an important role in developing objective standards of climbing difficulty by which individual accomplishments can be evaluated. Organization members are stratified in part on the basis of skill and experience, providing status hierarchies by which task-relevant abilities can be estimated. Club-sponsored climbing activities offer occasions for direct observation of higher-status individuals where their mountaineering-related talents can be evaluated. Thus, climbing clubs and organizations offer collections of suitable evaluative others. But they do more than that.

In simple terms, the identity a climber obtains within the climbing community is achieved in two ways—through performance and negotiation. Mountaineering clubs and organizations play an important part in both processes. First, they provide occasions for evaluation, chances for the novice to display his or her mountaineering competence to more seasoned and experienced climbers. Second, beyond face-to-face encounters, organizations help develop and substantiate symbolic means by which mountaineering identities are often negotiated.

Performance

Actual performance—the skill, tenacity, courage, and wisdom demonstrated to one's peers in real climbing situations—is the first and most obvious means of achieving a reputation. The climber who leads the difficult pitch which has previously foiled others is given recognition and perhaps praise. The party member who selflessly volunteers to cross a dangerous avalanche path in late afternoon to aid an injured companion is lauded for bravery. Status may accrue to the climber as a result of personal and volitional achievement immediately perceived and recognized by others. But direct performance is not always possible. As was noted in discussing climbing activities, relatively few opportunities occur in climbing to demonstrate skills directly. These occasions are largely in the technical climbing phase which is only a small portion of the mountaineer's task and involves relatively few others. This poses a dilemma. To create, enhance, and maintain a reputation as a climber of note, one needs to be seen skillfully in action on the mountain by as many fellow climbers as possible. Yet, such opportunities are few and fleeting in practice and audiences are limited to one or a few companions.

Climbing clubs and organizations provide a partial solution. By sponsoring weekend climbs, practice days at local crags, training sessions, and similar activities, the number of occasions for direct-climbing performance before referent others is expanded. But the dilemma remains.

For some climbers, club activities provide neither adequate challenges nor appealing experiences. Club climbs usually involve objectives of no more than modest difficulty where the advanced climber finds little chance to fully demonstrate the level of his or her skills. Organization-sponsored climbs also involve large groups and necessitate greater regimentation than some mountaineers find enjoyable or even acceptable. Thus, even with the addition of club climbing activities, the occasions where direct performance can be employed in identity-enhancement efforts remains inadequate. The climber, therefore, seeks other ways of establishing and maintaining an identity.

Negotiation

An alternative to directly observed climbing performance and often a more frequent way in which climbers seek to improve their image as mountaineers is the development of symbolic representations of ability and accomplishment. Medals, awards, and signs of office may be substituted for direct performance, but these tokens require institutions and structures to produce them and imbue them with meaning. This process is aided in the mountaineer's social world by climbing clubs and organizations.

These organizations contribute to the development of classification systems of the objective difficulty of climbs. Those systems, in turn, allow for the comparison of one climb with another even if they are widely separated geographically. Clubs may keep records of climbing activity by placing summit registers, ensuring that climbing accomplishments will be remembered and properly credited. The publication of club-sponsored newsletters, magazines, and, to a greater extent, climbers' guidebooks chronicle and draw attention to recent climbing achievements and publicize those who participate in them. Finally, clubs and organizations offer a forum where the ethics and style of climbing are debated and promoted and which further qualify a mountaineer's deeds.

All of these processes reflect upon the reputation of the climber and contribute to the establishment of a hierarchy within the climber's world. Sometimes clubs and organizations do more. For some, membership in climbing clubs is a source of prestige in itself. For others, club honors and awards are tangible and meaningful aids to reputation management.

Certain climbing organizations only distinguish between members and nonmembers, with little further subdivision. Members simply enjoy whatever prestige is associated with the organization as a whole. That prestige, however, may be considerable. In fact, I would offer the tentative hypothesis that the prestige resulting from general membership in a mountaineering club or organization is in inverse proportion to the complexity of the club's stratification system. Where this intraclub system is complex, simple membership is less prestigious than in those organizations which distinguish only between members and nonmembers. For example, membership in the American Alpine Club is not granted until a climber has amassed a significant list of climbing accomplishments. Merely being a member is a powerful boost to one's reputation as a mountaineer, yet this respected organization has only a rudimentary internal stratification system by which members are classified. Other organizations such as the Sierra Club offer less prestige for membership, while they subdivide their members according to individual levels of accomplishment and skill. This prestige differential is in part a function of the diverse range of interests represented by the Sierra Club as compared to the fairly narrow focus on mountaineering activities of the American Alpine Club, but not entirely.

The Angeles Chapter of the Sierra Club in Southern California is divided into numerous activity sections, several of which are devoted to climbing. Some of these climbing-oriented sections offer various medals, emblems, and other tokens as proof of accumulated mountaineering accomplishments. Others require that participants in section activities have earned such signs of recognition as a place on the "Mountaineers List" or be in possession of a "signed-off proficiency card." These medals and lists provide for further subdivision within club climbers.

This process of producing and allocating formal signs of mountaineering achievement is illustrated by activities of the Sierra Club's Sierra Peaks Section (SPS). SPS has devised a list of some 246 peaks in the Sierras which are deemed worthy objectives for climbers. These peaks were "chosen for elevation, dominance of an area, view, and unaccessibility" (Sierra Peaks Section Peaks List, revised January 1975). This list is further divided by giving special status to fifty "Mountaineers" peaks. Even more exalted is a select group of fifteen "Emblem" peaks.

This makes possible a four-level stratification of climbers. First, one may simply become a Sierra Club member. Second, one may join the Sierra Peaks Section. This is achieved by "climbing any six peaks on the qualifying list [SPS Peak List] and submitting the list of peaks climbed to the Section Secretary (two peaks must be on a scheduled SPS trip)" (SPS, membership information, 1974), as well as by completing an application form and paying a small fee.

Third, one may aspire to "Emblem" status. This is achieved by being a section member for one year or more and "climbing 10 of the 15 emblem peaks plus an additional 15 peaks on the list" (SPS, membership information, 1974). Emblem status entitles one to purchase a small pin, signifying one's achievement, to wear on clothing. Fourth, the Sierra Peaks Section has a cadre of special climbrs who have earned a place on the "Mountaineers List." According to 1974 SPS membership information:

> Certain trips are of such a level of difficulty that it has become the policy of the SPS to require participants to be on the SPS "Mountaineers List." Those SPS members wishing to be placed on the list must have been observed for their competence and attitudes by people authorized to sign the Mountaineers List Application Form which is available by sending a stamped, self-addressed envelope to the Mountaineering Safety Chairman. Activities to be "signed off" include ice axe and snow travel skills, rock climbing skills, endurance, and general mountaineering attitudes. A completed form should be sent to the Mountaineering Safety Chairman, who submits it with his recommendations to the SPS Management Committee for approval or disapproval.

Other Sierra Club sections make distinctions among their members similar to those within the SPS. The Desert Peaks Section and the Hundred Peaks Section also award emblems to those who successfully reach a specified number of summits on approved peak lists prepared by these sections. More difficult to obtain than these pins is the "sign-off proficiency card" issued by the Rock Climbing Section. To obtain such a card, applicants must demonstrate their command of a series of climbing skills at a field testing session. Possession of this card is a requirement for participants in Rock Climbing Section activities.

Some persons are highly motivated to obtain formal recognitions of climbing achievement. On a spring climb of the normal route (read very easy) on Florence Peak in the Sierras, sponsored by the Sierra Peaks Section, I encountered a participant who illustrated, if not typified, this desire. This was a middle-aged woman who was concerned about almost nothing else in her mountaineering experience than climbing enough peaks "on the list" to qualify for an SPS emblem. She had already earned such an emblem in the Hundred Peaks Section, which she wore with apparent pride on her cap. Her jacket was festooned with sewn-on patches commemorating other areas she had climbed, including "Mt. Whitney" and "The John Muir Trail." As her performance demonstrated and as she revealed in conversation, she had little interest in and virtually no talent for climbing. Even the simplest obstacle required considerable boosting, coaxing, and tugging from other group members for her to overcome it. Other climbers informed me that this was the accepted procedure for helping her along and had been followed in previous section-sponsored trips.

This is an extreme example. It is an exceptional person who ascends mountains solely for the status granted to those who succeed, without obtaining any intrinsic satisfaction. Perhaps only in the confines of club activity and structure is this sort of motivation possible. Certainly the mountaineering organization is the only place where tangible signs and categories of past performance are so readily available. Nonetheless, formal emblems and predetermined stratification systems hold a considerable appeal for some persons who are unwilling to or incapable of making more complex informal identity-management efforts.[1]

The existence, if not the extent, of this appeal is recognized by the Sierra Peaks Section. The application for inclusion on the SPS Mountaineers List contains this note.

> Some concern is now being expressed that designation as Mountaineer [inclusion of one's name on the Mountaineers List] is being considered a status symbol. While hardly the purpose of this list, this cannot be entirely avoided since such a designation is in fact an acknowledgement of some demonstrated capability on the part of the SPS member. (SPS, member information, 1974)

Clubs simplify the effort required to gain a reputation as a climber. Procedures for obtaining given levels of recognition are often clearly set forth in leaders' handbooks or other literature. Likewise, the status enjoyed by those who earn these various levels of achievement is relatively unambiguous and similar for all. The aspiring climber, in search of formal recognition of his or her accomplishments, knows what must be done to achieve the club-sponsored tokens and classifications and what impact these will have on his or her reputation as a mountaineer.

It might appear at first glance that with the provision of these formalized procedures and awards, the mountaineer's problems of status attainment and verification would be neatly solved. Novices, in taking up the sport, would immediately join their local climbing clubs and work their way up in the hierarchy, collecting signs of their growing assortment of climbing deeds as they progressed. If such a system prevailed, one could imagine the most seasoned and respected mountaineer as the individual who is finally distinguished above all the other members by election to some club office. In this exalted position, he or she would preside over club banquets and other functions in some ceremonial outfit (knickers of the purest tweed?), carrying signs of the importance and heavy responsibilities of that office (club bolt kit?), and bedecked with symbols of past conquests like generals' campaign ribbons or boy scouts' emblem bandolier. But, this is far from what actually occurs.

It is my impression that in America, at least, existing clubs can neither accommodate nor interest the majority of climbers on a full-time basis. Above all, the American climber sees himself or herself as an individualist and thus does not often totally embrace climbing organizations, although many are members at one time or another. Because of their origins within these clubs, formal signs of recognition such as emblems, medals, and lists are eschewed by many. Even for those few who do most of their climbing in formal groups, there is a dearth of tokens to denote their accomplishments, a paucity of categories to classify their climbs.

Mountains offer greater diversity of challenge than a three-category scheme of SPS List Peak, Mountaineers Peak, and Emblem Peak. Mountaineers are more varied in experience and skill than a four-stage hierarchy of Sierra Club Member, SPS Member, Emblem Holder, and Mountaineer would suggest. These classifications of mountain difficulty and climber ability are severely limited in scope and applicability. What more does the "Mountaineer" aspire to do? How are mountains beyond those covered in the peak list of a club's home range to be classified? Would Mount Everest, K2, Nanda Devi, Mont Blanc, or the Matterhorn qualify as Emblem peaks?

If all that organizations did to distinguish between peaks and climbers was a simplistic sort of categorizing, their contribution would not seem very great. So far, it may appear that climbing clubs are for the most part interested in making distinctions on a local, intraclub basis. To a limited extent this is true. Some organizations mainly sponsor less demanding activities and are made up of members of only modest skill. For these groups, simple classification schemes suffice. More typically, however, the climbing club serves two different sorts of climbers.

First, such clubs are the training grounds where the beginning mountaineer receives initial instruction. After this early socialization, only a relative few continue their mountaineering experience exclusively in club-sponsored activities. They divide their mountaineering time between club and individually arranged trips with the number of the latter increasing in proportion as skill and experience expand. Later, the more advanced individuals may return to club activities but in new roles—as trip leaders or instructors. Such a pattern is fairly typical of Southern California Sierra Club climbers.

Novices get their introduction to the sport in the Basic Mountaineering Training Course (BMTC). Progressing through the club's Leadership Training Courses, they may achieve leadership status themselves or earn a place on the Mountaineers List and subsequently contribute their own efforts to teaching BMTC or leading trips. Independent climbs will still be more common for advanced climbers than for beginners. The simple, truncated, and somewhat arbitrary classification schemes are adequate and appropriate for learners and serve that purpose well.

Clubs continue to exert influence on the reputation-building efforts of even those who only infrequently participate in club-sponsored activities, but this influence is less direct. For the advanced climber, clubs are looked to more for standards of comparison and sources of information than for definitive evaluation of personal ability. One of these standards is the classification of peak difficulty.

Rating the Climb

Climbers have found it desirable to be able to express the difficulty of a particular climb by referring to standard rating systems. At the time of this writing at least eight such systems are in widespread use, none of which have received universal acceptance. In America, the most popular are the Yosemite Decimal and the National Climbing Classification System (NCCS) schemes, both evolved from the Sierra Club system illustrated below. In addition, there are also English/Welsh, Australian, Extended Saxon, Scottish, and Union Internationale des Alpinisme (UIAA) Alpine schemes. The Yosemite, NCCS, Australian, and Extended Saxon are solely alphanumerical; the English/Welsh and the UIAA Alpine rankings are adjectival and numeric; and the Scottish scheme is exclusively adjectival. For comparison, the same pitch of technical climbing might be rated and referred to variously as "5.9" (Yosemite). "F9" (NCCS), VIIc (Extended Saxon), "Extremely Severe 5b" (English/Welsh), "18–19"

(Australian, "Very Severe" (Scottish), and "6 Superior" (UIAA Alpine) (*Mountain 28*, 1973, 14; Mendenhall, personal communication, 1979; Prochazka 1981, 16–19).

Classes and Grades

How do ratings correspond to the actual challenges encountered by the climber? A look at one popular variant of the America system will illustrate. The Mountaineers, a Seattle-based climbing organization, use a modification of the Sierra Club system in which all climbing difficulty is divided into six classes (adapted from Manning 1967, 109–10, 144).

Class 1 Cross-country hiking. Hands not needed.
Class 2 Scrambling, using hands for balance. Rope not usually necessary or desired.
Class 3 Easy climbing. Elementary climbing technique useful. Rope may be desired and important for safety of less experienced climbers. "The exposure or drop is often such that a beginner feels a bit queasy about being where he or she is. Handholds and footholds are necessary; these will be quite large and easy to locate. Imagine climbing a steep, narrow staircase which has been placed on the outside of a tall building without benefit of a railing: scary but easy" (Roper, 1976, 20).
Class 4 Roped climbing with belaying. Ropes will be used by almost all party members. It "usually involves steep rock, much smaller holds and great exposure . . . an unroped fall on Class 4 could be your last" (Roper 1976, 20). Belays should be anchored. Some moves may be so difficult they would be considered Class 5 except for short pitches and abundant protection.
Class 5 Roped climbing with protection. The leader's progress is safeguarded by the placement of intermediate points of anchorage to the mountain between the belayer and the next belay point, as described in Chapter 6. Class 5 is further subdivided by decimals, from 5.0 to 5.12 and, more recently, 5.13, the latter representing the current limits of human capability to adhere to and progress up the mountain without artificial aids. Climbs of 5.10 to 5.12 difficulty are further subdivided into four subclasses each; 5.10 a, b, c, d, and 5.11 a, b, c, d etc. It should be noted that upper limits are continually expanding—the 5.13 category was nonexistent in 1981 and some day there may be a 5.14. The Australian system, in recognition of the ever-increasing difficulties of climbs being done by today's cragsmen and women use an open-ended numeric system. When a climb is done which is qualitatively more difficult than any which has preceded

it, it receives one higher number. The Australians were
doing 28s in 1982.

Class 6 Direct aid. Upward progress is made by using chocks,
pitons, slings, and other devices directly as handholds
and footholds. Aid climbing is subdivided into five levels
from A1, very easy, to A5, requiring difficult and insecure placements.

The rating assigned a given route is not based on an average but on
the most difficult move encountered in the entire climb. Thus, ratings
represent the maximum difficulty likely to be encountered. If both free
and aid climbing are part of a single route, the maximum difficulty of each
will be stated separately in rating that route. If the hardest move done free
is a 5.6 and the most demanding aid move is A2, then the climb would be
rated "5.6–A2." The maximum-difficulty principle is important, for two
climbs of the same rating may not represent the same degree of challenge.
To illustrate this variability, consider that the northwest face of Mount
Humphreys in the Sierra Nevada is rated class 4. This difficulty is justified
by no more than 50 feet of moderately difficult climbing while the rest of
the roughly 2,800 feet of ascent from the west is class 2 or 3. On the other
hand, when George Willig ascended one of the World Trade Center
towers in New York using mechanical devices attached to a cable permanently fixed to the building, all 1,350 feet of his climb were of equal
difficulty—a very easy A1.

Mountain climbs are divided into grades which indicate the time,
commitment, strenuousness, and general seriousness of a climb. Six
grades are delineated by the Mountaineers (Ferber 1974, 110). Grades are
applicable only to roped technical climbing, not to scrambling or
approach marches, however arduous or easy these might be.

Roman numerals from I to VI represent the grade of the climb. Grades
I and II climbs are relatively easy and can be completed in a few hours.
Grades III and IV indicate a serious climb which will take most of a long
day (Roper 1976, 21). Grades V and VI are multiday endeavors involving
considerable difficulties. George Willig's ascent and the Mount Humphreys route would both be grade I. By comparison, most Himalayan
climbs of high peaks are multiday, sustained technical undertakings
rated at grade VI.

The existence of rating systems affects identity-management efforts
in two ways. First, these systems provide a common yardstick by which
the skill of two climbers may be measured. A climber who has led one or
more established routes rated 5.11 is accorded more prestige than another
climber who has only followed 5.2 routes. It will be recalled that to lead a
pitch is in general a greater challenge than to follow. This is a result of
modern rope-management techniques which render the follower's posi-

tion considerably safer and less complicated than the leader's. Likewise, climbers with a successful history of successful grade V or VI climbs enjoy more respect than those capable of no more than short grade Is. Second, rating systems affect the climber's identity management because classes and grades are sometimes manipulated by climbers to reflect more favorably on their own achievements. This generally occurs when a route is first rated but is also possible when the initial ratings are reconsidered by climbers who are out to make names for themselves.

> Finally, there is always the question of who numbered the route. Perhaps it was a young hero seeking to impress the readers of an alpine journal with his derring-do. However, since assigning a high number leaves the hero open to the scorn of competitors, who in a later copy of the journal will demonstrate their superiority by giving a lower rating, some expert practitioners of climbsmanship deliberately underrate the peak to protect their reputations. (Manning 1967, 143)

While some climbers reject as unimportant the simpler formal rewards for mountaineering achievement such as emblems or a place on the Mountaineers List, they are unlikely to reject all forms of formal recognition. Those who scoff at club membership and tokens may be quick to correct what they feel are errors in the rating scheme applied to routes they have climbed, forgetting perhaps that those classification schemes are also, often, the products of formal climbing organizations.

Ratings in Context

Ratings are idealizations, not precise assessments of existing conditions. They are based on a hypothetical set of seldom obtained conditions—warm dry rock, stable snow, settled weather, and climbers of "average" ability (Manning 1967, 43). They purport to evaluate the difficulty of moves likely to be encountered, without regard for the natural environment in which they occur. They do not take into consideration objective hazards such as rock-fall or avalanche danger or the subjective trauma of the gaping abyss below. Alan Rouse notes in his discussion of grading systems that "the danger involved in some particular series of moves may reduce to wobbling jelly a climber who would otherwise be perfectly capable of making them" (Rouse 1975, 35).

Without consideration of the subjective experience a climber may have on a given route, the variation between individuals in courage and concentration is ignored. This necessary oversight renders ratings considerably more tenuous as guidelines than they might seem. To illustrate, in the beginning of my own climbing career a companion and I once set off to climb two adjacent peaks in the Palisades area of the Sierras. Both were rated class 3 so we anticipated no undue difficulty. Mount Galey lived up to our expectations. It was a stimulating but simple scramble up a wide, moderately angled ramp which required no more than basic balance and a little extra leg and lung power to reach the summit. With the experience of Galey behind us, we thought that Temple Crag would be as easily surmounted. We were very wrong.

The class 3 section of Temple Crag is short—about sixty feet long—and involves only one serious move. Objectively that move involves only a short hop from the top of one large boulder to another, across a space of perhaps five feet. The rock on which one must land is rounded and without obvious holds but is at least two feet wide at the top. The reader can mentally rehearse this simple act from experience and conclude that it might be easily accomplished without the need for ropes or other mountaineering gadgetry. In the children's game of hopscotch, youthful players frequently must make greater leaps to bypass squares occupied by their own and competitors' markers. Nor was the landing place smaller than the hopscotch square. The experienced climber would see no more than a simple challenge, be over the gap in a twinkling, and be on his or her way to the summit. But we were not experienced climbers. We lacked their selective perception. We saw more.

The two key boulders are not chalked-in squares on a sidewalk. They are prominent points high on a mountain peak. They are the keenest part of a serrated knife-edge ridge. The gap between them is only five feet, but to us the points seemed to stick out from the rest of the mountain into an eternity of empty air. The blade of the ridge is so thin here that although only five horizontal feet separate these boulders, they hang a fearsome 1,000 vertical feet above the upper talus slopes on the right and a less dramatic but still awesome 400 feet from the ridge base on the left.

The thought of what we were required to do to pass this obstacle was so terrifying to us as novices that we retreated. Even with a rope, the prospect of a fall into that awful empty space was more than we could face. In fact, such a fall would probably be safer than a typical tumbling third-class fall, as there were no projections to strike against. But it did not seem that way at the time. We finally reached the summit by another route, one more difficult but less harrowing.

Objective rating systems are sometimes poorly articulated with subjective experience. They tell us about the mountain but not the mountaineering. They summarize the ease with which holds may be found but say nothing about the boredom, exhilaration, or terror that grasping or moving over those holds may entail. They require other information to be understood.

Ratings assigned to climbing difficulty are a fine example of what philosophers and ethnomethodologists refer to as indexical expressions (Mehan and Wood 1975, 93). Indexical expressions are communications which require contextual information to be understood fully. When Blumer (1969, 2) notes that "the meaning of . . . things is derived from, or arises out of, the social interaction that one has with his fellows," we are reminded that all symbolic interaction is context-dependent to a certain extent. Climb ratings are no exception.

Referring to a climb as class 3 or 5.6–A2 is less a precise and exhaustive description than a starting point for interpretive action. The point will not be elaborated further, but it is well to bear in mind that even in formal settings for which club or organization ratings and stratification systems are available, identity rests in large part with the volitional actor. The labels attached to climbing deeds are less predetermined and arbitrarily assigned than they are negotiated and emergent.

Ratings Rejected

Rating schemes are not for everyone. While many climbers debate the merits and weaknesses of one system or another and carefully correct any misuse of their own pet schemes, a few reject ratings altogether. This minority contends that the only important feature of any climb is the subjective experience of the climber. The reward for climbing, they argue, is in the doing of it, not in gaining glory points on some arbitrary and dispassionate rating schedule. These climbers are strong supporters of those who find the motive for mountaineering solely in the intrinsic satisfaction it provides. The more verbal proponents of nonrating are occasionally heard poking fun at traditional classification schemes.

On one trip with the Sierra Peaks Section (SPS), I was told of the "other" SPS, the mythical "Sierra Ponds Section." This latter group is devoted to seeking out naturally occurring bodies of water to bathe, splash, skinny-dip, and otherwise play in. As it is important to classify these various watery objectives, a scale of difficulty of water entry has been developed similar to the scheme applied to mountains. The veteran climbers who were my informants described the system with feigned seriousness as follows (Field notes, June 1975):

The Sierra Ponds Section recognizes six classes of water that range from very easy to quite difficult to enter and remain in.

Class 1 Very easy. A hot spring or spa.
Class 2 Easy. A sun-warmed pond or tarn.
Class 3 Moderate. A mountain lake.
Class 4 Difficult. A mountain lake fed by snow runoff or glacial melt.
Class 5 Very difficult. A mountain lake with pieces of ice still floating in it.
Class 6 Extremely difficult. A frozen mountain lake. Mechanical aid required to enter the water.

Another tongue-in-cheek rating scheme has been suggested by Bert Brown (1978, 20). He describes with tedium and exactitude the mathematics required to develop probability statements about the likelihood of a fatality on a given route due to objective dangers such as rock or ice fall or avalanche. He then facetiously proposes that with such a system climbers could brag about how close they came to getting killed. We might hear boasts like: "I did a 0.4 on the Willis Wall" or "Did you hear about Harry? He survived three 0.5's!"

Peggy Berglund has offered yet another rating-scheme spoof. Her system is based upon one of the most reliable and valued behavioral indicators of the climber's subjective experience—a cursing scale. The system works this way.

> You can grunt and cuss varying amounts depending upon difficulty. There are levels of cussing, like a two-shit-one-damn-three-grunt climb. Or maybe a five-mother climb. Wow. You get the idea. "That was a hard one," means the air was blue and there might be other words to use but I don't know them. (Berglund 1978, 18)

Such a system, Berglund points out, has two advantages. First, it takes into consideration all pertinent variables, "the rock, the weather, the condition of the climber, the amount of protection and the quantity of blood shed." Second, "the beauty of this system is that it can be applied to any area and is already universally used in all languages, whether consciously or not" (Berglund 1978, 18). Finally, Brink and Kelman (1981, 41) propose a rating scale for the "epic" quality of mountaineering adventure stories told by climbers. These range from "E1.Underestimation of or delay in completion of a route resulting in being late to dinner with your significant other" to "E10.Getting lost or hung up on an isolated route where rescue of injured climbers and recovery of bodies require an elaborate and dangerous effort" and so forth.

Record Keeping

Registers

There are 246 peaks on the Sierra Peaks Section's approved list of mountains in the Sierra Nevada (1983). On or near the summit of each of these lies a special weathertight aluminum or brass box or tube. The outside of the container bears the citation "SC" or "Sierra Club" and, after additional information, the elevation and peak name in raised numbers and letters cast in the metal of the lid. Inside, one finds a small spiral notebook or writing pad and perhaps an old ballpoint pen or pencil stub.

This is a summit register, another formal aid to the mountaineer's identity-enhancement efforts. In these registers successful summiteers may
enter their names and other self-descriptions and comment briefly on
their ascent. Summit registers offer a relatively permanent and at least
semi-official record of one's climbing deeds.

Summit registers are one specific case of a more general class of
identity-enhancement devices referred to here as *signatures*. Understanding the role of signatures in fostering and furthering reputations helps
clarify the meaning of summit registers.

There are numerous social situations in which persons desire to make
some brief indication of their presence or are called upon to do so. They
may be required to answer roll calls or sign in for security purposes at
buildings, or they may wish to certify bank drafts. Adventurous sorts
such as mountain climbers might wish to mark the extent of some wilderness exploration while other adventure seekers such as juvenile gang
members might want to signify their presence on a rival gang's turf.
People may accomplish these goals by making their marks, signing their
names, inscribing brass placques, carving initials on trees or in stone, or
writing on walls with spray paint. Whenever an indication of one's
presence takes some tangible and relatively permanent form, I refer to it
as a signature.

The act of signing may impart status to the place at which it occurs or
to the person doing the signing. When some important person visits a
little-known place and leaves some record of his or her visit, that place
may gain in status. On the east coast of the United States, a number of
inns, restaurants, churches, and other establishments claim to have
served George Washington ("George Washington slept here"). Those
places which substantiate their claims with the first president's name
written in his own hand in an old guest-book do enjoy a certain distinction. The San Gorgonio Inn in Banning, California, a favorite haunt of
rock climbers returning from Tahquitz Rock and Joshua Tree National
Monument, proudly displays in its foyer an old register containing
Grover Cleveland's signature, presumably to the same effect.

In certain circumstances, it is not the place but the person who gains
status by signing. Ed Hillary, son of a New Zealand beekeeper, and John
Hunt, a retired British army colonel, would have remained obscure
personages had they not been, respectively, one of the first two men to
stand on the summit of Mount Everest and the leader of the expedition
that put him there. It is doubtful that such individuals would have been
recognized for their beekeeping and military exploits, but it is now *Sir*
Edmund Hillary and *Sir* John Hunt to whom we refer, both knighted by
Queen Elizabeth for their mountaineering achievements.

Even the statuses of persons of high standing may be enhanced by
visits to important places. Pope Pius the XI became all the more impres-

sive a personage for his ascent of the Monte Rosa, the second highest peak in the Alps, but that peak gained little prestige from the pope having ventured there.

Often the procedures for noting one's presence are structured and norm-governed. Guest books, attendance sheets, bank checks, and mountaineering summit-registers all provide for the ordered recording of signatures and related information. There are, however, times when people desire to note their presence in some place but can find no formal provisions there for doing so. When people mark their presence in urban areas by impromptu and relatively unstructured means, their efforts may be referred to as graffiti.

When a mountain is climbed for the first time, no ready-made register will be found. On this special occasion it is traditional to construct a cairn, a pile of stones arranged on or near the highest point. Spaces between the stones of the cairn provide a repository for subsequent registers. Cairns may be inconsequential or monumental according to the time, energy, and architectural talents of the climbers. A solo climber on a first ascent whose safe return is threatened by rapidly increasing avalanche danger may construct little more than a hurried grouping of a dozen nearby rocks stacked a few inches high. In contrast, the cairn atop Olancha Peak in the Sierras is almost six feet high, composed of several tons of stone hauled and piled, so I was told, by a large group of Boy Scouts who ascended the peak together and devoted several hours to the effort.

In the absence of registers provided by climbing clubs, temporary ones may be created by climbers writing their names on odd bits of paper and putting these in film cans, plastic baggies, or other available weather-resistant containers. More durable receptacles such as surplus ammunition cans, mason jars, and tin cans have also served this purpose.

> We climbed for about two hours and ended up about 200 yards south of Mt. Mendal [sic]. We decided it was closer so we climbed to the summit. We were very mad not to find any register on the top. So we wrote our names on a piece of paper and put it under a pile of rocks in a plastic bag. We ate our lunch, what a view. (From Mount Darwin summit register describing an ascent of adjacent Mount Mendel, Sierra Nevada, July 16, 1970)[2]
> A tough climb for us since we had no rope or anything. Brought a little pitch wood and cooked coffee and soup at the top. Thrilling view—hope we got good pictures—saw five mountain sheep on ridge one-half mile south. Found no register so we are leaving paper and pencil in soup can. (Dragon Peak summit register, Sierra Nevada, August 17, 1946)

As the popularity of a peak grows and it is climbed more often, makeshift registers will usually be replaced by more enduring climbing-club registers.

Certain regularities in the entries of summit registers may be observed. These records usually convey two kinds of information. First, they identify the signer in name and often in broader social contexts. Second, they chronicle the kind of achievement that obtaining the summit represents.

Despite the undoubted importance names and naming play in one's identity (see Gross and Stone 1970, 178), persons often seek to communicate more about themselves. This additional information takes the form of brief catalogs of the consensual social groupings with which they identify. The summit register, then, is sometimes an impromptu "Twenty Statements Test" (Kuhn and McPartland, 1954: 68–76). In addition to their names, climbers may note their places of residence and employment, club affiliations, school or religious affiliations.

Norman Clyde   March 20–'27   Independence
(University Peak, Sierra Nevada, March 20, 1927)

Marek Glogoczowski–Klub Wysokogorski
Polaska—Poland
(Mount Ritter, Sierra Nevada, June 18, 1970)

F. Jerry Mattsa, D.D.S.
Highland General Hospital
Oakland, California
(Mount Ritter, Sierra Nevada, July 4, 1970)

8-3-61   Father Leo Hoeffer S.C.—L.P.C.
Sierra High Physics Department—San Mateo
(Mount Ritter, Sierra Nevada, August 3, 1961)

Wayne Bourquardez
USFS Mammoth Lakes, California
Also Pasadena, Texas, University of Houston
(Mount Ritter, Sierra Nevada, September 16, 1962)

The importance that people give to the reaching of some goal such as a mountain summit is in rough proportion to the difficulties overcome in achieving it. The more demanding a climb, the greater is the credit for its achievement. Not all persons climbing a peak experience the same degree of objective difficulty. Some may be harried by storms and darkness, inching their way up near vertical rock faces, while others, approaching from another direction, arrive at the sunny peak after little more than a stiff uphill walk. Both reach and sign the same summit register but the achievement which that signing represents varies widely.

Persons who have climbed peaks by easier routes compose register entries which attend less to the actual climbing than to the context in which it occurs. If a climb is a mundane achievement, its recording may be embellished by listing other accomplishments in that region. This may involve noting the direction of the approach march, hiking speed, or the listing of climbing and travel itineraries.

> July 12. The two old goats mentioned above also made it. We came in over Bishop pass and then Muir pass to Wanda Lake. Tomorrow we will get Mt. Huxley on our way to Mt. Darwin, where we expect to meet Flemming and Curran for the ascent of Mt. Darwin. Then out to Florence Lake. (Mount Goddard, July 12, 1966)
>
> 9/1/63. On a 16-day knapsack route, from Lake Edison (2nd recess) up Cabbot pass to Dussy Basin (details in other book) attempt on N. Palisade tomorrow. Have climbed Gabb, Abbott and Darwin. (Mount Sill, September 1, 1963).
>
> Climbed from below lake in Glacier Creek leaving at 9:00 a.m. and arriving at 11:30 a.m. Unbelievable view but rather windy. (Mount Sill, July 14, 1964).

When persons reach a peak by some difficult route, they may briefly outline their efforts and the problems they met. A truly outstanding achievement, the completion of some heretofore unclimbed route, allows the participants to *name* their route and comment upon it in some detail.

> 25 June 1968. Traverse from Starlight which was climbed for the first time by its north buttress which we named "The Piper at the Gates of Dawn Buttress" after Kenneth Graham's *The Wind in the Willows* (III, 5.7). Begins on right side of large flat-iron slab west of Clyde Couloir, working out onto the slab over two ceilings, then runs alongside a long right-leaning snow patch and onto a rib which comes out just east of the summit. (Doug Robinson, Vulgarian Youth Section, Carl Dreisbach, North Palisade, Sierra Nevada, June 25, 1968).

Signing registers identifies a climber with those who have preceded him or her to that peak, including perhaps even the early pioneer ascents and those made by other well-known mountaineers. This is particularly true if the peak is seldom ascended, so that many years of climbing history are compressed into a few pages of the register.

Registers are used to promote more than just the accomplishments of individual climbers. Climbing clubs and organizations have certain territories which they regard as their own home ranges. In these limited areas they claim responsibiity for record keeping, trip organization and leadership, and sometimes for rescue operations. The summit register serves to advertise the power and purview of these clubs and delineate their territorial boundaries. When different organizations claim jurisdiction over the same territory, a mild form of competition may ensue. Each club vies for the climber's attention by placing its own register on a peak, sometimes even if one has already been provided by another organization.

For the most part, this sort of summit register duplication is limited to the nearby and readily accessible peaks, more easily and frequently reached by the Boy Scouts, youth groups, and religious organizations who are the principal augmenters of existing records. The Hundred Peaks Section of the Sierra Club has placed 268 registers on peaks in the Southern California area. In addition to these, the climber may find other registers of mixed ancestry—painted tin cans, ammunition boxes, and the like, festooning the more popular peaks. Not all register overlap, however, is local and low-level.

Two California chapters of the Sierra Club, one in Los Angeles and the other in San Francisco, claim as a common concern the entire Sierra Nevada within the state. The Angeles chapter's Sierra Peaks Section provides registers in the southern portion of the range, while the Loma Priata chapter attends to the northern peaks. Their relative monopoly is marred from time to time by registers formerly provided by the California Alpine Club, the "Sun and Sea" religious activity group, and, occasionally, a Boy Scout contribution. The summit of Mount Shasta in northern California is an interesting transition point. Near its summit are two almost identical registers lying side by side. One was placed in 1931 by the Mazamas, a Portland-based climbing club that claims the Cascade mountains as home range. (Mount Shasta is the southern-most of the major Cascade peaks and the equivalent of an "emblem" peak for the Mazamas). The other register was provided by the Sierra Club in 1955. The Sierra Club maintains the climbers' refuge at the foot of the mountain and, evidently as a result of that commitment, considers Mount Shasta a part of its territory.

Summit register boxes sometimes contain more than register notebooks. Religious tracts occur frequently in the more popular areas. Occasionally the notebook itself is missing or full or in use, at the time, by another summiteer making an extended entry. In these instances, pieces of maps, candy wrappers, paper bags, and the like will be pressed into service as materials on which to sign. Some persons wishing to make a more personalized contribution to the register leave business cards in lieu of signatures.

Not all registers are found on or near mountain summits. In the European Alps and in parts of Canada it is more common for the record of climbs in a particular group of peaks to be entered together in a substantial hardbound ledger. This valuable book is left in the care of the custodian of the hut or hotel where climbers may stay on the way to and from the mountains. These ledgers become an important reservoir of information for both historical archives and contemporary news of recent climbing activities.

While most signers may not be aware of it, signing some summit registers provides considerable longevity for the climbers' deeds. In policy, if not in practice, Sierra Club summit records are eventually recovered from the peaks and forwarded to the club's national headquarters. From there they are sent to the University of California at Berkeley, where they become part of a permanent collection in the historical archives of the Bancroft Library. The records atop Mount Rainier in the state of Washington are placed, recovered, and permanently stored by National Park Service personnel, and it is claimed that those who sign the National Park Service register maintained atop Mount Whitney will eventually find their names on microfilm in the Library of Congress.

Summit registers provide a widely distributed, readily available, and relatively permanent way of recording one's climbing deeds. But this is not enough. A climber in search of an improved reputation needs more than just these features. Even though climbers who follow will duly note one's name and accomplishments, how many will follow and how soon? Others may not come that way for some time. If they do, their own success, perhaps on a more difficult route, may eclipse prior climbs. Nor are the occasional descriptions of new routes found in registers of much use to those who wish to repeat a climb but are in need of guidance from those who have made the climb before.

Registers do advertise one's deeds and they do provide information, but that advertising is limited, access to that information is poor. Wider audiences need to be reached more rapidly with a wider range of data. This is the function served best by journals and guidebooks.

Journals

Mountaineering journals provide a forum in which the values of the climbing community are developed and reinforced. Journals are important in helping define the social meaning of climbing for its participants. As Dennis Ford points out,

> If mountaineers could derive the "meaning" of their climbing apart from the similar experience and accounts of others, then how account for the parallel development of climbing and climbing journals? For the mountaineer, the "meaning" of a climb often lies in the constellation of accounts and experiences [of other climbers] which provide a context for his own experiences on the mountain. (Ford, 1978:13)

Climbing journals serve as a medium through which the experiences and opinions of other climbers can be shared. They provide a means of evaluating one's own standards and accomplishments against those of other climbers, and, for some mountaineers whose exploits are published, they provide an important means of reputation enhancement.

Most climbing clubs and related groups publish summaries of the recent accomplishments of their membership and sometimes of nonmembers in periodic magazines, newsletters, and journals. Taken together, these constitute an extensive body of literature. For example, at the level of national organizations, the American Alpine Club publishes the *American Alpine Journal*, while the Alpine Club of Canada puts out the *Canadian Alpine Journal*. Similarly, Scotland, New Zealand, Japan, England, France, Germany, Austria, Poland, and other countries have their own national and regional publications. Swiss climbing deeds are disguised as the activities of the Swiss Foundation for Alpine Research reported in *Mountain World*. On a more local basis, the Cambridge and Harvard mountaineering clubs publish *Cambridge Mountaineering* and *The Harvard Mountaineer*. The Seattle Mountaineers put out the *Mountaineer*, and *The Climber's Club Journal* has obvious journals. These organization-sponsored publications range in quality from slick and sophisticated annuals of over 300 pages with textbook price tags to the irregular and sometimes irreverent coverage of local club "freebie" flyers.

Fewer in number but no less important than club publications are the commercial American climbing periodicals: *Summit*, *Climbing*, *Mountain Gazette*, *Off Belay* (no longer published), and the best-known English-language climbing magazine, *Mountain*, published in Great Britain, as well as others not published in English. All are common in mountaineering shops and on mountaineers' shelves. While these are profit-oriented publications, they are similar in many respects to the club-sponsored products. They are directly dependent upon reader contributions for much of their material, and that readership often has climbing-club ties and reads club publications.

The range of potential subject matter in climbing publications is wide. Mountain wildlife, glaciological studies, high-altitude physiology, equipment testing, climbing technique, obituaries, book reviews, and editorial statements about conservation issues all may be included.

Whatever else mountaineering journals and magazines cover, they devote a portion of their pages to significant climbs and expeditions. These articles describe both the objective and subjective characteristics of the climb and climbing setting. This sharing of the climber's subjective experiences is what sets journal reportage apart from information sources such as registers and guidebooks. Journals report the climber's perspective and interpretation of the obdurate circumstances of the mountain world. They share with the reader glimpses of fierce or friendly fauna, photogenic or edible flora. They tell us of the climber's hopes and feelings, trepidation and despair; of cold feet, skinned knuckles, clenched teeth, hemorrhoids, and the view at sunset.

Subjective Glimpses. Below are two examples of the climber's subjective experiences as reported in the *American Alpine Journal*. They are at once typical and unusual. They are typical in the way they reflect a style of reporting used in some journals which seek to highlight the human experience over the technical description. Yet they are unusual, too, for they touch upon the ends of an emotional continuum seldom approached in common understanding. Rarely does climbing engender supreme elation or acute despair. Usually mountaineers vacillate through the middle ground of emotional experience from drudgery and concern to amusement and relief.

First is Peter Metcalf's moment of appreciation on Mount McKinley in Alaska:

> The air was crisp, cold, calm, and clear, making the climbing in the twilight of the Alaskan night almost magical. At about 9,600 feet, I turned around to see the moon rising above Mount Huntington while the first orange rays of morning began striking its upper half. At the same time, I could watch the last subdued pastel colors of sunset disappear off the west side of Mount Hunter. This scene alone would have made the climb worthwhile, but it was only a preview of greater glories to come. (Metcalf 1976, 315)

Next, a different kind of moment, a moment of sorrow. Willi Unsold tells of the death of his twenty-four-year-old daughter, Nanda Devi, as they climbed on the mountain for which she was named.

> Because of the high winds and continuing snow, we decided to head down. . . . Pete, Andy, and Devi had now been at 24,000 feet for nearly five days. We were packed for departure when at 11:45 Devi was suddenly stricken. She had time only to say with great calm, "I am going to die," when she lapsed into unconsciousness. We tried mouth-to-mouth resuscitation and CPR, but with no sign of success. Within 15 minutes, I felt her lips growing cold against mine and I knew that we had lost her. . . . As the enormity of our loss slowly sank in, the three of us could only cling to one another for comfort while tears coursed down our beards. . . . We agreed that it would be most fitting for Devi's body to be committed to the snows of the mountain for which she had come to feel such a deep attachment. Andy, Peter, and I knelt in a circle in the snow and grasped hands while each chanted a broken farewell to the comrade who had so recently filled such a vivid place in our lives. My final prayer was one of thanksgiving for a world filled with the sheer beauty of the mountains and for the surpassing miracle that we should be so formed as to respond

with ecstasy to such beauty, and for the constant element of danger without which the mountain experience would not exercise such a grip on our sensibilities. We then laid the body to rest in its icy tomb, at rest on the breast of the Bliss-Giving Goddess Nanda.

And so the three of us climbed down—in the mist of tears and anguish. Our bodies performed automatically those actions necessary for survival—with little assistance from our numbed minds. The blizzard continued unabated. (Unsold 1977, 21–22)[3]

Objective Data. Of the objective data reported in journals, there is less to say. When space or information is limited, journal accounts shift their contents from people to places. They tell of approach marches and directions, of times and distances, of routes and ratings and particular difficulties along the way.

In each issue of the *American Alpine Journal,* roughly one-third of the pages are devoted to a section entitled "Climbs and Expeditions." The articles reported in this part of the journal are abbreviated accounts of climbing activity throughout the world. Each report is a brief summary of the "facts" surrounding a given climb, with less attention paid to the involvement of the climbers. An example is provided in Rowell's (1977b) account of the Hot Tuna Tower in the Sierra Nevada:

> *Hot Tuna Tower, Open Book Route.* This tower is located on the east side of Wheeler Crest and is visible from U.S. 395 at the beginning of Sherwin Grade, north of Bishop, California. It is the largest tower in a pink band of granite that intrudes the otherwise grayish granite rock. An open-book splits the east side of the tower, but ends in a ceiling two pitches from the summit. In February, David Belden and I made the laborious 3,000 foot approach to the tower and were surprised to find a F10 section in the easier-appearing lower section of the open-book. Higher, we came across a section neither of us could lead. After many tries, I threw a nut over a flake and made a five-foot tension traverse out of the difficulties. When the ceiling itself loomed directly overhead, it was David's lead. He found the rock coated with orange plates and knobs, climbed the pitch quickly, yelled for joy, and rated it F6. The next pitches to the summit were equally enjoyable. The 1,000-foot face took six hours and is rated NCCS IV, F10, A2.

The "First" Ascent. Journals bring to the climbing public news of mountaineering accomplishments at both the personal and the pragmatic levels. While their styles and contents may vary, one characteristic is shared by almost all journal accounts, an emphasis on newness and discovery. In general, the interest shown a climb is in inverse relation to the frequency with which it has been repeated. The fewer times a climb has been done, the greater is the mountaineer's interest. Routes move from "new" to "classic" (or into obscurity) on their third or fourth repeat. The greatest attention is focused on the first successful ascent. Journals reflect this interest. The event most often reported, given the most space, and most eagerly sought by the climber is the first ascent. Journal coverage of a first ascent can provide a powerful boost to a climber's reputation by bringing this most important of mountaineering achievements before extensive and attentive audiences.

The first ascent is the plum, the prize, the most prestigious accomplishment in the mountaineering world. The first ascent is the pioneer adventure into the vertical unknown. Basically three sorts of "firsts" are recognized. Most obvious is the climbing of some peak never before successfully scaled. The zenith of all summits to be reached in the Alps was the Matterhorn, first climbed in 1865 after years of repeated attempts. A second kind of "first" is the scaling of some peak by a new route. When all the significant summits in an area have been climbed, interest shifts to climbing them by more difficult routes, first the harder ridges and then the faces. Mount Everest was climbed for the first time by the British in 1953. They also achieved another "first" when they successfully surmounted the difficult South West Face in 1975.

The third type of "first" ascent is made by repeating older climbs in better "style." Often improvements in style are in terms of eliminating the need for mechanical contrivances, large parties, or both. Reinhold Messner and Peter Habler undoubtedly scored a "first" when in 1978 they reached the summit of Everest on their own lung power without the use of auxiliary oxygen apparatus. Other stylistic firsts include solo climbs, unroped climbs, or ascents done entirely by free climbing that had previously required aid techniques.

Why are first ascents so valued? First ascents offer the highest level of uncertainty concerning outcomes. They may pass over unknown ground if they are new routes, reach untrodden summits if the peak has never been climbed before. Yet in retrospect, these climbs may prove to be of only modest difficulty which dozens or more subsequent climbers will trundle up with relative ease. This subsequent ease does not reduce the prestige value of the uncertain first success. The Hörnli Arete on the Matterhorn, the route by which the mountain was first climbed, is a case in point.

Before its first ascent, the Matterhorn had been attempted fifteen times over a span of many years by various combinations of British, Italian, and Swiss climbers. When it was finally conquered, four of the summiteers perished on the descent. The climbing of the Matterhorn focused world-wide attention on mountaineering (Queen Victoria tried to have the sport declared illegal) and brought both fame and infamy to Edward Whymper and the guides who accompanied him to the summit. This was undoubtedly one of the great first ascents in the history of mountain climbing. Consider the situation on the same route on that mountain today. In a publication of the Mountain Guides Office in Zermatt, at the foot of that great peak, we learn:

> Today, climbing the Matterhorn of Switzerland, once a feat which took years to accomplish, can be done with good conditioning and a skillful guide. It is interesting that on a pleasant day, the climber might encounter some mild congestion on the Matterhorn. It has happened that as many as 60 people accompanied by their guides were on their way to the top [120 people per day not counting those climbing without guides; including the latter brings the total to roughly 180 climbers]. (Mountain Guides tourist brochure, Zermatt 1974, 1)

Annually the Matterhorn is climbed by thousands of tourists who, for a rather sizable fee, can have themselves almost literally hauled to the summit by stout, sure-footed local guides. In 1865, the combined energies, years of experience, and expert mountaineering of some of the world's best climbers were required to discover the key to the mountain and overcome this obstacle. Today little more than adequate physical condition and plenty of vacation spending money are the basic requirements for reaching the summit.

This does not mean that the Matterhorn is any less a mountain now than when it was first climbed. It is still steep, unstable, storm-prone, and high. These objective qualities are in no way diminished because of the frequent visits it receives. What has changed is the knowledge climbers have about the mountain.

The first ascent team is faced with a challenge greater than the one met by those who follow. Those who go first are not sure their enterprise will succeed at all, although they may know of prior failures. They can never be certain until they have finished the route, reached the summit, and safely returned, if the climb is at all possible. Therein lies the appeal of the first ascent. Climbers are motivated most highly when the outcome of the climb remains unknown. That is precisely the situation with first ascents. Impossible barriers, easy terrain, or intermediate difficulties may lie ahead. Each pitch is new territory presenting new problems that must be solved in turn. Will skill and strength be adequate for some difficult and committing move above? Is there enough equipment to get past the overhang, can it be done without aid, or can a way be found around it? Will the problems be solved in time to escape the ridge before it is threatened by lightning from the impending storm, before the gullies are swept by avalanches in the afternoon? The answers to these questions unfold as the first ascent party works its way upward.

Those who follow a route after a first ascent have a different sort of experience. Much of the exploration and uncertainty is absent. They *know* the mountain can be climbed, for it already has been. Often they know much more. Mystery is replaced by certainty, in particular because of the publicity that first ascents receive and the detailed descriptions that journal accounts provide. It is difficult to ignore this wealth of information if one is researching the climbing possibilities of a particular region or peak. Few indeed are the climbers who set a journal aside after reading only of the driving directions and approach march, overlooking the report of the technical climb.

In order to reintroduce the element of uncertainty, the spirit of mystery or exploration, the mountain may be approached from another direction or restrictions may be placed on equipment, technique, or personnel used in repeating a climb. This substitution of new routes and improved style for simple peak bagging serves a necessary and important purpose in the social world of the climber.

Each new year brings a steady increase in the number of climbers taking to the mountains in search of fame and recognition for their deeds. Also with each passing year a rapidly diminishing, finite number of unclimbed summits remains to be claimed. Already mountaineers must travel considerable distances, often to other continents, to find unclimbed peaks of significance. If these reciprocal trends of more climbers and fewer summits were to continue unaltered, the mountaineering community would soon suffer from acute ritual poverty. Reputations could only be improved upon by those few with the time and money to visit the world's most obscure high places.

The shift to improvements in style as "firsts" in their own right offers at least a partial solution to this problem. With this new interest later ascents do not go altogether unnoticed. They are granted credence and reputational worth of their own in proportion to the extent that they improve on the style of preceding climbs. And stylistic improvement is ready at hand. The core of these improvements is the placing of increasingly demanding self-imposed restrictions on the climbing to be done. These include limits on the time that will be taken, the amount and type of gear to be used, and the people who will participate on a given climb. While peaks themselves may be finite in number, the stylistic strictures that may be imposed by those who climb them create a virtually limitless range of new challenges. By placing more and more stringent limits on what is deemed to be proper style, older routes are continually rejuvenated as desirable climbing objectives. Opportunities for reputation improvement are thus provided for succeeding generations of climbers.[4]

In fits and starts and with some disagreement, the movement toward upgrading the status of stylistic improvements and downplaying simple summiteering has permeated the climbing community. But the first ascent is not forgotten. It is the basic standard by which later climbs are judged.

> The "ultimate experience," if there is such a thing, is to make the first ascent of a major natural line. . . . Since first ascents are becoming less frequent, repeat climbs should be in at least as good a style as the first ascent and, in view of the continuing improvements to equipment and technique, in better style whenever possible. (Ferber 1974, 223)

The first ascent is not free from stylistic judgment. In the wisdom of hindsight and comfort of the local pub or club meeting-room the new climb will be thoroughly dissected, evaluated, and judged. Each crucial move, decision point, and application of hardware will be considered and debated as to its necessity and appropriateness. If perhaps a few of the devices and procedures employed are not up to the currently held stylistic standards, the climb will still be allowed to stand as a legitimate accomplishment. Minor faults are more permissible in first ascents than in later ones. With this tentative acceptance of their deeds, first ascenders may bask for a time in the glory that their achievements bring them. But, if subsequent investigation or later ascents reveal omissions in the first party's reporting, their reputations may be jeopardized. Cleare and Smythe explain the normative requirements for full disclosure of one's methods in British rock climbing. They note that:

> The leader of a genuine first ascent may use as many pegs, slings, chockstones, lassos . . . and so on as he likes. . . . However, it is his bound duty to declare each and every one of the above bits and pieces. If he forgets even one little sling, and it later comes to light—and it's astonishing the way these things are found out—then Public Opinion might well come down on him as vindictively as a tired customs officer at Dover. (Cleare and Smythe 1966, 99)

Cleare and Smythe perhaps oversimplify things. Their remarks leave the impression that the first-ascent party has carte blanche in the techniques and equipment that its members may employ as long as they are forthright in their subsequent reporting. This is incorrect. If too much aid, fixed rope, porter power, or other mechanical or human assistance is used in achieving the climb, the entire effort may be dismissed as an ethical transgression. For example, among many American and British rock climbers the use of expansion bolts is expected to be judicious and limited. Royal Robbins discusses these expectations in the making of first ascents.

>   OUTRAGES— There is . . . an area . . . which concerns first
> ascents done in a style which lies significantly outside the mores
> of a climbing center. . . . It is not too much to expect a due regard
> for the values generally held in a climbing center. Thus, for an
> American to visit Britain and put a new route on Dinas Crombeck
> by placing bolts would be boorish. It would reveal a gross insensi-
> tivity toward the values of the locals where sense of style kept
> them from climbing the route in such a manner. One would not
> be surprised if they exercised their right to remove the offending
> bolts. . . . Similarly, if someone put up a bolt route next to Horse-
> man in Shawangunks, he would be ill-advised to expect his
> ascent to be honored, or even find its way into the guidebook.
> A local consensus would probably decree that it go. (Robbins
> 1973, 81)

These discussions of style may seem tangential to the major concern—the ways in which reputations are gained and maintained in the
climbing world; yet by placing ever more stringent restrictions in the
name of style, existing peaks and crags continue to offer new challenges
to up-and-coming climbers.

How do these stylistic requirements affect the climber's own experience of the mountains? Do some climbers find new intrinsic motivation in
these additional difficulties? Do others conform only out of a desire for
recognition and fame? Probably a little of both motivations enter in, but
with an important difference. Self-satisfaction is often based on a personal sort of covenant. One may be quite pleased with oneself over a
climbing accomplishment judged quite unstylish by others. Ask yourself
how you would feel about having climbed the Matterhorn, even with a
guide. But, reputations within the climbing community are made only
after approval of style and action. Climbs accomplished without adher-
ence to contemporary stylistic norms are likely to be discredited or demeaned by other mountaineers. Even a climb of the second-highest
summit on earth, the 28,250-foot Himalayan giant K2 is not free from such
censure as Galen Rowell illustrates in describing his meeting with the
leader of a Japanese expedition to that mountain.

>   We thought a lot of him as a person but we didn't have too
> much respect for his expedition because he had 61 climbers and
> over 1,000 porters on K2 to attempt just a repeat of the normal
> route and we didn't think that was really what mountaineering
> was all about. (Field notes, 1979)

Considerations of style are necessary in any discussion of identity management among mountaineers.

Guidebooks

One product of clubs and organizations that poses a formal aid to establishing the reputations of mountain climbers, remains to be discussed—the guidebook. The guidebook represents a synthesis of objective rating systems, technical descriptions, and historical records of first or early ascents. Guidebooks are by far the most potent sort of record keeping which may contribute to a reputation in the climber's world. Royal Robbins's veiled threat above that a climb done in poor style might not "find its way into the guidebook" suggests the importance of this sort of recognition.

Guidebooks do two things that journals and magazines do not do so well: they provide a permanent record of first ascents and they ensure that this knowledge of first ascents continually comes to other climbers' attention. As was noted before, a climber's reputation depends upon three things: an objective rating system by which climbs can be compared; a permanent record of one's deeds; and a means of disseminating that record throughout the climbing community.

Clubs and organizations have developed effective rating systems, although these schemes are often too sophisticated for club-sponsored activities. Summit registers help provide a relatively permanent record of successful climbs, but they have the disadvantage of reaching only limited audiences. Journals and magazine articles communicate climbers' accomplishments to broad audiences but that communication is a one-shot affair. Journals and magazines are not repeatedly reread and reviewed, although they may be kept for later reference. More typically, readers anxiously pore over the latest edition's new climbing discoveries while last issue's triumphs fade in both memory and stature. A reputation built on a single climb reported once in a journal or magazine will provide a fleeting moment of glory at best. Guidebooks fill this void by permanently and clearly identifying a given climb with the persons who first successfully completed it. For example:

Mt. Olympus—West Peak.
First recognized ascent 1907 by L. A. Nelson and ten members of The Mountaineers. There is serious doubt of the first-ascent claims of Col. B. F. Shaw and H. D. Clock (1854), Col. M. Simmons (1854), and B. J. Bretherton (1890). (The Mountaineers 1979, 141)

Mt. Hood—Eliot Glacier Headwall.
First ascent 1935 by Russ McJury.
(Dodge 1975, 53)

Mt. Rainier—Mowich Face, Edmunds Headwall.
This was the original route on the Mowich Face. . . . The face was
pioneered by John Rupley, Don (Claunch) Gordon, Fred Beckey,
Tom Hornbein, and Herb Stealey on June 23, 1957. (Beckey 1973)

Mt. Assiniboine—North Face.
July 1967, Y. Chouinard, J. Faint, C. Jones.
(Putnam and Boles 1973, 100)

Guidebooks ensure that climbers' accomplishments will continually
come to people's attention. Journals are neither a compact nor a convenient source of information on climbs in a given area. Journal articles are
often arranged by first ascent chronologically, not by geographic position. To locate the record of a first ascent in a journal, a researcher usually
must begin by knowing when it occurred. As a result, researching a
climbing area through journal and magazine articles can prove tedious or
even fruitless, for regional information is just the sort some climbers seek.

The newcomer and the novice who wish quickly to learn about local
climbing possibilities and who wish to compare their cragsmanship with
prevailing standards turn to the guidebook for information, thus generating an ongoing and expanding audience. Guidebooks do not fade into
obscurity with time. While journals are set aside or sometimes discarded
when new ones arrive, guidebooks are clung to with tenacity, becoming
dog-eared but cherished companions. As the years pass, revised editions
of the guide to some area may be enthusiastically acquired but the older
versions are retained and referred to frequently.

Guidebooks and to a lesser extent, journal reports can change and
even create climbs. Climbing is the serial connection of one physical effort
with another in order to achieve upward spatial mobility; a "climb" is a
more abstract construct. It is more than the sum of the actions used in
climbing. Climbs become entities in their own right when they are published in guidebooks. They are given names, a history, geographic location, and a rating relative to other climbs. This in turn leads to a response
from the climbing community. Reified in this way, climbs acquire a
prestige value which reflects on those who subsequently ascend them.

If a label has been attached to a climb, if something has been
published about it, it becomes a much more attractive proposition for most people. It has a price on it, and a climber can buy it
with his own effort and skill, and sell it in the bar to his friends
afterwards, to whom it also has a definite value. Since a climb
may acquire this value, the climber himself inherits associated
prestige, which can be potted and weighed, climb by climb.
(Cleare and Smythe 1966, 30)

Not all of the effects of guidebooks are positive. A published route description may inadvertently "undo" a climb as easily as it creates one. In their searches for objectivity and thoroughness, guide authors may describe a route in such exhaustive detail that nothing remains to be discovered on the actual climb. With each technical problem and often its solution meticulously detailed in advance, the only unknown remains the limits of one's physical resources and perhaps the weather. In that case, one might as well test those resources directly by taking up gymnastics or cross-country running and dispense altogether with the unnecessary formality of climbing. Lito Tejada-Flores puts it this way:

> What happens when your local climbing area is no longer an exciting place, when a whole range loses its aura of mystery and attraction, when a climbing area feels "used-up". . . ? We might call this the *no more adventure/no more wilderness* syndrome.
>
> Guidebooks can contribute to the above syndrome in several ways: by over-describing an actual route so that it no longer contains any puzzles or enigmas and route-finding becomes a lost art. Or by over-describing a whole area, so that it's no longer possible to find your own short cut on the approach, no longer tempting to look for alternate lines of attack. (Tejada-Flores 1974, 81)

Guidebooks can contribute to a more than just the psychological devaluation of certain routes. A flattering published description of a climb can lead directly to the demise of that route as a desirable climbing objective. Climbs which are praised in guidebooks quickly draw the attention of climbers seeking the prestige associated with them. This sudden popularity can have a devastating environmental impact. Nearby streams polluted, fragile meadows overrun, parties queued up at the base of a route and knocking rocks down on one another as they climb, cracks and vital handholds destroyed by frequent and indiscriminate piton placement, trash and excrement strewn about, trees girdled and killed from their frequent use as rappel anchors are just some of the negative effects that guidebook citations can have on some climbs and their surroundings. Tejada-Flores shares a similar view.

> One of the most obvious impacts of a guidebook is the way it influences one's choice of climbs and the resulting frequency of use of certain climbs. If a climb is described by a guide as ugly, grungy, or a real drag, it is thereby saved—at least from a rash of further ascents; while the guidebook author who has been too lavish in praising a certain route can often reproach himself for having destroyed it, or at least for having turned it into an ugly thoroughfare. (Tejada-Flores 1974, 81)

As an example, the Yosemite Valley rock-climbing routes, exemplified by those on Half Dome, are documented, described, mapped, discussed, and itemized in minute and excruciating detail in dozens of climbing guidebooks published in many languages around the world. Here, Bart O'Brien describes climbing the great northwest face of Half Dome, twenty years after its first ascent:

> But since the passage of these pioneers, Half Dome has been assaulted by hundreds of unthinking mountaineers. The closer we got to the actual base of the climb, the more garbage we saw. Knic and I were dumbfounded. Here we were, standing at the base of one of the world's truly beautiful mountains and one of North America's greatest rock climbs. . . . Knic and I rifled through the garbage. Every conceivable type of can was present. There was even a broken Gatorade bottle. . . . We found two fine water bottles . . . and our friends carried out a plastic tube tent, several yards of nylon cord, a couple of water bottles, and a knife. Perhaps the final irony was that under a rock, along with several cans and broken bottles, we found a somewhat mildewed but serviceable pair of climbing shoes. . . . The way was marked with fixed pitons and bolts, and the rock bears the scars of the passage of hundreds of climbers. . . . Cans and useless old slings littered every ledge. . . . At the far end of a ledge was a stained paper bag. . . . Inside we found a broken bottle of benzoin. We could hardly believe it. . . . Here, six hundred feet off the ground, some climber had broken and abandoned his bottle of chemical courage.[5] (O'Brien 1978, 466–70)

Records and ratings are the major formal tools by which reputations are created and improved in the climber's world. But sometimes these devices become more than impartial information sources or aids to impression management. The presence of ratings and records lends not just assistance but a certain urgency to the search for an improved reputation. Standards of style, once established, must be lived up to. If a route is described as "classic" in the guidebook, some climbers do not judge themselves fully experienced until they have climbed it. But the impact is more profound than just encouraging a particular style or the climbing of certain routes.

Records and ratings bring about a basic change in the challenge that is mountaineering. They shift the focus of interest away from the difficulties of the mountain to the problems of gaining a reputation as a mountaineer. As the mysteries of the mountains diminish following the publication of journal articles and, especially, guidebook descriptions, there is a corresponding increase in attention to the actions of other climbers. A climber no longer asks "How can it be climbed?" but rather "Has it been climbed by so-and-so?" or "How many people have climbed it before me?"

Competition

Mountaineering for the most part is a cooperative enterprise. Ropemates must safeguard each other as they proceed upward. Expeditions require the cooperation of fairly large numbers of persons. Yet different rope teams and expeditionary groups may be in keen competition with each other. The publicity and prestige brought on by the possibility of appearing in print in journal articles or guidebook descriptions accentuate this competitive urge.

This represents a fundamental change in the meaning and purpose of mountaineering—from sport that is the intrinsically rewarding search for a sense of controlled elation, to an activity based on competition with other people where reward lies in defeat of others. This introduction of competition as a recognized element in the motives for climbing is denied and rejected by some groups and joyfully embraced and encouraged by others.

Peak Bagging

Climbing competition usually takes two major forms, peak bagging and speed contests. Earlier we mentioned that peak bagging was a form of mountaineering where the quantity of the climbing is emphasized over quality. Peak bagging may be likened to other sorts of avocational collecting. Persons who collect coins, stamps, cameras, bottles, etc., often work to complete some assemblage of these objects with defined limits. They seek at least one representative of all of the types included in a set—a U.S. penny from each year they were minted, one each of all the Leica camera models manufactured, a sample of each style of Coca-Cola bottle made, campaign buttons from all twentieth-century presidential elections.

While the individual items in any collection may be valuable in their own right because of their rarity or other intrinsic qualities, the ultimate goal of collectors is to complete the set. For peak baggers, these sets may be summits of a given altitude, within a given geographic region, or peak groupings otherwise identified and formally recognized by clubs and organizations.

An early peak bagger was Hugh T. Munro of the Scottish Mountaineering Club, who researched and listed all the peaks in Scotland over 3,000 feet in height. He then made it his lifelong goal to climb all 538 of these summits. He was only two peaks short of finishing the set at the time of his death. A typical goal for peak baggers in the United States is the set of 52 peaks over 14,000 feet high in the state of Colorado.

Climbing a large number of peaks on the Hundred Peaks Section (HPS) approved list is an objective of peak baggers in Southern California. Most HPS list peaks offer little or no technical difficulty. The majority have trails or fire roads leading to the summit. This ease of access may diminish the challenge of a single peak but is compensated by the large number of climbs necessary to establish an enviable record. Peaks considered suitable for HPS climbs generally must be in the Southern California area, be not less than 5,000 feet high, involve at least 1,000 feet of gain, and be at least a half-mile from any other qualified peak. While these requirements do not seem particularly impressive, climbing 100 such peaks is a considerable accomplishment. As of May 1983, 633 HPS members had reached 100 or more of the summits during their hiking careers, and 117 had climbed 200 or more and 82 had completed the entire list (Field notes, May 1983).

Peak bagging is a venerable institution among climbers. Geoffrey Winthrop Young recounts the historic drama of Alpine mountaineers anxious to complete a summit set.

> At Courmayer we ran into an electrically charged atmosphere. Our arrival was enveloped, almost literally, by the agitation of a notable Austrian mountaineer, Dr. Carl Blodig. . . . He was one of a few great mountaineers who had made it their interesting ambition to ascend all the peaks in the Alps of more than 4,000 meters in height. Now, some years before, the doctor had finished them off, all sixty-five of them. Then, most inconsiderately, two new points were climbed and entered on the maps. . . . Thus, the doctor found himself well over fifty years of age, and faced with these two formidable additions. Moreover, during the intervening years his competitors were overhauling him. Another Austrian, Dr. Puhn, had even equaled his record. Well, to put the matter shortly, H. O. had promised to help the doctor [Blodig] to his final victory if this season should prove kind.
>
> We arrived to find it almost too late. . . . Dr. Puhn had used the fine weather well and had actually gone ahead in the race. . . . It could hardly increase the commotion in the region that another famous competitor, Ing. Pfann was said to be already bivouacing out for the same ascent. (Young 1926, 301–2)

"H. O." provided the needed help. A few pages later we learn of Dr. Blodig's eventual success.

> The gray-bearded Doctor took off his hat, and gave three cheers for the Climbers Club. For him it must have been a very inspiring moment. He was on the last and the latest of the four-thousanders. He was the first man to complete the list. (Young 1926, 310)

Peak bagging is not truly a zero-sum game (agôn in Caillois's classification) where one can win only by defeating others. Obviously more than one person can complete a set of peaks and be recognized for this achievement. But, in practice, not all climbers are oriented strictly to their own roster of peaks climbed. Some also keep an eye on others trying to complete a set. As in the example of Dr. Blodig and his competitors, climbers are sometimes interested in being first to complete their collection of summits. The speed of climbing as well as the number of summits reached becomes a concern of the competitive mountaineer.

Speed Climbing

Speed climbing is the second major form of competition. The object of this sort of contest is to climb an established route or set of summits in the quickest possible time. One kind of speed climbing not involving technical terrain is a sort of timed peak bagging called "fell running" in Great Britain. The Welsh "Fourteen Peaks" is a classic of this form of competition. This is a long distance cross-country run that connects the summits of fourteen hills or peaks in a 22-mile course involving 11,000 feet of ascent and slightly more descent. An early record for this course was established in 1919 by Eustace Thomas and members of his Rucksack Club who completed the distance in 20 hours. By way of comparison, in June of 1973, Joss Naylor, a Cumbria sheepherder, finished the entire route in the incredible time of 4 hours and 46 minutes. Another impressive time and distance challenge is the climb from summit to summit of Africa's two loftiest peaks, Mount Kilimanjaro and Mount Kenya. Rusty Baillie and Barry Cliffs descended 14,000 feet, drove 400 miles over bush country roads, and then climbed some 12,000 feet—all in 23 consecutive hours (Cleare 1975, 145).

Speed contests are not reversed for climbing simple terrain. They may take place on major technical climbs as well. Competition may not be as formally organized in the high mountains as in the local hills, but an impressive time which is recorded on an established technical route is not likely to go unreported by the speedy summiteers. In the following example, the French mountaineer Lionel Terray boasts not only of his significant repeat climb of the north face of the Piz Badille but also of the time that climb took.

> Casin and four companions made the first ascent in three terrible days of climbing in a storm, and two of the party had died of exhaustion on the descent. Rebuffat and Bernard Pierre had taken almost as long over the second ascent. Since then the face had been done four or five times, but never without a bivouac; the fastest ascent having taken nineteen hours of actual climbing. . . . Finally, there remained nothing above us but sky: it had taken us seven and a half hours for the two and a half thousand feet of face. . . . We had thus accomplished a feat that was considered stupefying at the time, yet without my mistake in route-finding, and if we had forced the pace from the very beginning, we could have knocked over an hour off this "record." Terray 1963, 213, 216)

Perhaps the most controversial kind of competition is speed rock climbing. In this sport, climbers take turns ascending the same rock pitch while protected with a rope from above. The object is to try to beat the climbing times of others on that route. Speed climbing originated in the Soviet Union. The first formal climbing contest took place in the Crimea just after the Second World War, and for many years this was exclusively a Soviet sport. Beginning in the 1970s, the Russians repeatedly sought to have this kind of contest adopted as a world championship sport with the eventual aim of establishing it as an Olympic sport. The British have been strongly opposed to such a move. Denis Grey, the General Secretary of the British Mountaineering Council (BMC), wrote in a letter to *Mountain* magazine: "Once the Soviets get their World Championship, an Olympic event could easily follow. I think that the B.M.C. would consider resigning from the U.I.A.A. [the official world mountaineering body] if these proposals were adopted" (Grey 1976, 42).

In addition to the British, the American, Swiss, and Yugoslavs are opposed to this kind of speed climbing competition, but the Poles, Czechs, Hungarians, East Germans, and Japanese have adopted the sport and support the Russians. Other nations have not taken public stands so the issue remains unresolved. (See also Brniak 1980, 36–38.) Since a sport needs to be practiced on three continents by about sixteen countries before it is eligible for Olympic standing, it may be a number of years before enough worldwide interest is generated in this relatively narrow sort of climbing activity to gain official recognition. On the other hand, public interest in such contests may be aroused by the increasing media coverage of rock climbing. In the summer of 1978, ABC's "Wide World of Sports" covered almost in its entirety George Willig's (of World Trade Center Tower fame) two-day big-wall climb in Zion National Park, and a few weeks later viewers watched Henry Barber soloing traditional hard-rock routes in England. Willig has returned to the TV screen in other "Wide World of Sports" specials—climbing Devil's Tower in Wyoming, in May 1979, and Castle Rock in Utah, in June 1980. Media coverage of rock climbing and mountaineering events is much more common in Europe than in the United States.

Not all climbing is clearly competitive,[6] not all comparisons of climbs are based on fixed and firm standards of personal performance and peak difficulty. Some mountaineers deny or downplay the need for interpersonal comparisons and decry the impact of rating scales and guidebooks. At least a portion of all climbers' efforts to advance their reputations lies outside the regularized schemes of identity development made possible by clubs and organizations, in a subtle but important area of informal impression-management techniques. In the next chapter, one of the most intriguing of these techniques, the collection and employment of souvenirs, is discussed.

9
Souvenirs

Goffman (1959, 22–30) identifies that part of a person's performance which serves to define the situation for observers as "front." Front is the expressive equipment by which an actor's identity is supported and confirmed. This includes manner and deportment, one's physical appearance, and the setting in which the performance takes place.[1]

Settings involve the physical layouts, characteristics, and background items which supply the scenery and props for action played out in a given locale. Settings serve to underscore identity claims made by actors. Teachers support their roles by blackboards, desks, and seating arrangements. Palmists and spiritualists communicate their seeing powers through shaded rooms, gypsy clothing, and crystal balls. In thinking about the scenic aspects of front, we most typically imagine the living room in a particular home (Goffman 1959, 22). Here, furniture and decor give substance to the claims of persons identified with that setting (see Csikszentmihalyi and Rochberg-Halton 1981). People wishing to be seen as well-read, for instance, might display appropriate magazines on coffee tables and important literary works on bookshelves. In the mountain climbing community such works might include Whymper's *Scrambles Amongst the Alps*, Geoffrey Winthrop Young's *On High Hills*, Rebuffat's *Starlight and Storm*, and Kurt Diemberger's *Summits and Secrets*. Mountaineering club periodicals and commercial climbing journals also attest to knowledge of and interest in mountain sport. In these settings, actors may employ a special sort of prop, the souvenir.

Souvenirs provide evidence of visits to or experiences in places ordinarily considered strange, foreign, or forbidden. They serve as reminders of the physical locales and conditions from which they came and lend credibility and substance to verbal accounts of events and circumstances in estimable but distant places.[2] Souvenirs allow actors symbolically to bring the action home, to capture and transport the novel excitement and prestige of interaction with exotic peoples and places to everyday surroundings.

Souvenirs may be defined as representations of the sign-equipment employed in some exalted primary place that are transported to another, less notable secondary locale and used in action there. Those tokens take three forms. First, they may be simple reminders of the sign-equipment available in some important locale. Painted serving trays from Hawaii feature scenes of volcanos, beaches, and palm trees—the props available for performance in situ. Photos are a special case of such reminders and will be discussed separately below. Second, souvenirs may be replicas of sign-equipment normally utilized in the prime setting. From Hawaii, again, come manufactured grass skirts and leis. These replicas allow actors to recreate portions of the action associated with the prime locale. In this way it is possible for visitors to Hawaii later to demonstrate their hula skills to friends at a February Minnesota luau. To avoid excessive cost, fragility, or cumbersomeness, replicas of sign-equipment may not always be exact copies. Size and material may vary from the original. Thus, visitors to Paris purchase miniature tin Eiffel Towers; "flower" leis are constructed of nonperishable plastic. Children's toys could be viewed in the same light—as replicas of adult sign-equipment scaled down to fit youthful bodies and to be less expensive and perhaps less harmful than the adult counterpart. Third, souvenirs may be actual sign-equipment that no longer serves its manifest function, removed from some setting for use in another. War mementos such as helmets, flags, swords, and firearms typify this sort of token. These are not only useful in dramatic reenactments but lend authenticity to performances since at least a part of the play, the props employed, are genuine.

Some souvenirs may be found as naturally occurring objects or artifacts in a prestigious setting. These are most effective as tokens if they mark the time and place of one's visit. Theater programs, party or wedding invitations, and airplane ticket stubs serve this purpose well. Other artifacts are designed for some utilitarian function and secondarily as souvenirs, reminders of some locale and the typical action which takes place there. Restaurant menus, cocktail napkins, swizzle sticks, and matchbooks emblazoned with the name of the establishment from which they come are examples. Finally, there are mementos, bric-a-brac, jewelry, ash trays, embroidered pillows, and other paraphernalia manufactured specifically as souvenirs.

Often souvenirs are designed to remind audiences why places are important, memorable, or noteworthy. Ash trays from Southern California may have drawings of Disneyland, Santa Monica beaches, or scenes from Hollywood. Satin pillows from Washington, D.C., are printed with scenes of the Capitol, the Washington Monument, or the Lincoln Memorial. Other souvenirs are exaggerations or abstractions of native dress styles or activities. Thus, tourists to Mexico often return with huge sombreros and bulls' horns, and visitors to Germany collect lederhosen and beer steins. All these trappings attest to one's access to and performance in settings other than the locale in which they are displayed. An actor surrounded by these props reminds his audience that he has been to important places and has seen and done important things. The claim that these places and events are important is reflexively underlined by the fact that someone felt them worthy enough to commemorate by making souvenirs featuring them.

For the mountain climber, souvenirs are not as easily available as to the lowland tourist. Nonetheless, some are found. Perhaps the most popular souvenir other than photographs is the only permanent commodity readily available to the mountaineer—rocks. This is not because of any widespread geological interest on the part of climbers. Rather, common rocks become special when they are found near the summits of mountains. Many climbers have rock collections, one or more stones from each of the various peaks they have climbed. This is not an affectation of novice climbers alone. When two members of the heavily-financed 1953 British expedition became the first in history to reach the summit of Mount Everest, they too had an interest in souvenirs.

> I took up my ice axe, glanced at Tenzing to see if he was ready, and then looked at my watch—it was eleven forty-five, and we'd only been on top fifteen minutes. I had one job left to do. Walking easily down the steps I'd made in the ridge, I descended forty feet from the summit to the first visible rocks and taking a handful of small stones thrust them into my pocket—it seemed a bit silly at the time, but I knew they would be rather nice to have when we got down. (Hillary 1955, 235)

Rock collecting is not a newfound habit among climbers. When the Matterhorn was climbed for the first time in 1865, "Whymper . . . went to the highest point on the ridge and broke off the real physical summit of the Matterhorn, a small pyramid of mica schist as big as a cricket ball which repeats in micro-scale many features of the mountain itself. He put the rock in his rucksack and joined the others" (Clark 1965, 130). This was an act typical of Whymper's other climbs: On the Pointe des Ecrins in 1864, "according to my custom, I bagged a piece of the highest rock" (Whymper [1891], 88).

Sometimes rocks are augmented or supplanted by other naturally occurring mementos: small pieces of animal bone, bird feathers, or unusual pieces of wood found along the trail or on the mountain. However, the similarity between one rock and another, between one piece of wood and another, reduces the symbolic value of these items unless they can be clearly identified with the place where they originated. To this end, the rocks and other items in the mountaineer's collection may be individually identified by tags, or even more elaborately by labels like those painted on museum exhibits, telling the peak name, the date it was climbed, and the altitude.

Not all souvenirs are found ready-made or naturally at hand. Some are created by the purposeful or inadvertent efforts of souvenir hunters themselves. Certain settings are so important, possessed of such ritual potency, that they imbue ordinary physical objects with extraordinary character. In the first manned Apollo moon launches, a considerable problem was created by launch personnel secreting coins, religious objects, and other trinkets aboard the space craft. The collection of such items was said to exceed 100 pounds and forced officials to monitor strictly the activities of workers on subsequent flights. Apparently a penny is worth one cent until it has been to the moon and back. It is then worth a great deal more. Similarly, stamp collectors seek envelopes postmarked in unusual places and value such mail roughly in accordance with the inaccessibility of the locale from which it comes.

Interest in unusual postmarks sometimes plays a role in mountaineering finance.

> Gordon Palmer, a stamp collector, suggested that the Vagmarken expedition might add an interesting side effect by carrying illustrated cover envelopes to Mt. McKinley. From the public sale of these envelopes, the Sir Edmund Hillary Nepal school building fund would receive all proceeds. Each team member signed his name (before departure) to 500 envelopes which had a picture of the objective peak printed thereon . . . and these envelopes were apportioned: 100 each to be carried to the summit and notarized as to this claim ($5 each), 400 to be brought to base camp ($1 each). (Camphausen 1973, 38)

The 1975 American K2 Expedition also created souvenirs to generate funding for their endeavor. "However the expedition still needs contributions. For any donation of $10 or more, the K2 team will send an autographed postcard of K2 from Base Camp" (Recreational Equipment 1975, 45).

From an earlier attempt on Mount McKinley comes another example of souvenirs in the making. Until 1932 Mount McKinley had been climbed only once. In that year an attempt was again made to ascend this highest point on the North American continent. Park ranger Grant Pearson was part of the summit team. He describes this exchange between himself and a fellow ranger who was to remain below with the support team.

> Before John Rumohr took the dogs down, next day, he ambled over to me and fished a gold-nugget watch chain out of his

pocket. "Here, Grant. I want you to take this to the top for me."
"What for? Is it good luck?" "Sure." Then he broke into a broad
grin. "But what I really want is to be able to say I've got something that's been to the top of McKinley." Alaskans are as crazy
as Americans about souvenirs. I've often thought that right there
I missed a wonderful opportunity to get rich. At the top of that
mountain I should have filled my pockets with pebbles, which I
could later sell for handsome sums as souvenirs from the continent's highest peak. (Pearson 1962, 145)

Items of clothing or equipment which have accompanied one to some
special place may take on this souvenirlike quality. One mountaineer
remarked in showing off his collection of climbing paraphernalia, "See
this hat? I sewed it out of a piece of old blanket in the Theodole hut before
we did the Breithorn. It even has built-in ear patches. It's quite a
souvenir. . . . This is the sweater I wore on the Rimpfischorn bivouac.
I've had it thirteen years and take it everywhere" (Field notes, Switzerland, September 1974).

Most, but not all, souvenirs are limited to inanimate objects. Under
certain bizarre circumstances, actors at some primary locale may themselves become souvenirs in another. Warriors defeated in battle have
been enslaved and used to enhance the prestige of their captors. Less
lucky perhaps are the conquered people who appear (in part) as souvenirs in the form of shrunken heads or scalps. Lest these practices be
dismissed as those of people long ago or far away, remember that meetings between a big-game hunter and his quarry in the wilds sometimes
still result in the latter's stuffed head being displayed on a den wall back
in "civilization."

All souvenirs, especially ones created by actors themselves, increase
their sign potency according to the clarity and duration with which they
are associated with the important locales they signify as well as according
to their physical proximity to these places. Envelopes taken to the actual
summit of McKinley were more valuable than those taken only to base
camp. Mountain summit registers similarly have considerable impact as
sign-equipment. Their easy identification with a given summit and their
extended tenure in these exalted places render them highly prized, albeit
illegitimate, souvenirs. Within the mountaineering community, summit
registers are looked upon as public property not to be appropriated by
individuals. The theft of such a register is viewed in much the same light
as horse thievery was in the Old West, a heinous crime indeed. Still, it
goes on. As a deterrent, the Sierra Club in placing some of its registers has
bolted the containers directly onto the rock. Registers themselves,
however, remain portable.

Another class of valued and valuable sign-equipment is created not so much by proximity to some important locale as by longevity in mundane surroundings. Objects remaining in ordinary settings for extended periods of time also acquire special meaning. This is particularly true of common artifacts which may have been used by more than one generation of persons. This special class of souvenirs is referred to as antiques, and if they are associated with a single family line, heirlooms.

Climbers' Equipment as Souvenirs

The equipment used by mountain climbers is simple and limited yet much value comes to be attached to it over time. It was just suggested that proximity to and duration at some primary locale were important features of effective souvenirs. In practice, mere age and signs of wear often are taken in the climber's world as indications that some article has been frequently and for extended periods of time in prestigious places. Old equipment, therefore, is not necessarily discarded but may come to serve in the role of souvenir. This retention of older gear is sometimes erroneously interpreted as a sign of the climber's frugality. Instead it illustrates the creation and maintenance of powerful sign-equipment. The same mountaineer who faithfully trades in the family station wagon every three years, regardless of its condition, will with equal faith and diligence spend hours sewing patches on the seat of a pair of threadbare surplus army pants that he has climbed in for fifteen years. Battered and shapeless hats are still worn and cherished; sweaters and wool shirts are given new leases on life with reinforced elbows and collars. The same ice axe may be used for a lifetime.

Equipment showing signs of wear is of increased sign-potency. The possessor of such gear is presumed to have had experiences roughly equivalent to the wear shown on the article. Thus, new, commercially produced equipment is anathema to the climber concerned with appearances. Learning the symbolic value of new and used equipment is part of the socialization process of the budding climber. Novice enrollees in the Sierra Club's Basic Mountaineering Training Course proudly display their store-fresh jackets, packs, tents, etc., to their fellow students on course-sponsored field trips. After a few of these encounters, however, they recognize that the equipment used by their leaders is quite different from their own—threadbare, patched, faded, and subtly changed in many ways to mark it as different from the new products that might be purchased at a store. This realization leads some students to begin modifying their own equipment by shopping at thrift stores and generally emulating the leader cadre.

Ruth Mendenhall, a well-known Southern California climber with almost forty years of experience explains this penchant for one type of worn gear.

R. G. M. Do you have an explanation for the clothing they wear in the mountains? Why is it that people who are reasonably well-to-do will wear tattered clothing to climb in?

R. D. M. Well, if there is nothing wrong with it, it's all right. Why not keep on using it? And anyway, don't you look a little suspiciously at people who are dressed too well and everything they have is new? You feel these people have not been around much. . . . The dirtier and raggedier they are, the better climbers they are. (Field notes, March 1977)

Climbers sometimes take steps to increase the apparent "experience" of their gear and, thus, its symbolic value. New clothing and equipment are more misused than openly abused in this process. This must be done with subtlety, of course, or the symbolic value of the article would be discredited. New hats are handled with inordinate clumsiness so that they fall occasionally to the dusty ground. Brush is allowed to scrape gently past new packs and jackets along the trail. Streams are forded though log bridges are nearby, and dirty hands are wiped on pants and shirts. These and other acts lend "character" to one's equipment and in general dull the painful glare of newness. Nor are these items quickly cleaned and renewed upon return from the mountains. Spots on clothing remain. Packs go unwashed. While actual damage to gear will be repaired soon enough, the repair itself occasions further opportunity for distinguishing one's equipment from its store-bought counterpart.

Some climbers not only restore their gear to its original condition but "improve" upon it with various additions and modifications. Ice-axe carrying loops are sewn on older model packframe bags. Formerly, drawstrings were installed in the cuffs of climbing breeches, and leather "rappel" patches were sewn on pant bottoms. Overpants and sometimes knickers are appointed with a "glissade" patch on the seat. Additions and repairs are often of contrasting color and pattern with those of the articles they augment. Black buttons are sewn on a black wool shirt with red thread by a college professor (Field notes, January 1976). One architect-climber sewed bright blue seat patches on his beige overpants and dyed his boxer shorts brown (Field notes, March 1976). Red shoelaces outsell the brown-boot-colored variety 20 to 1. Zippers, tie strings, and webbing straps are appended to packs, tents, and clothing to serve a myriad of functions both practical and decorative. Some persons may even alter their gear before it is used. Manufacturers of clothing and other mountaineering gear available in kit form also do a considerable business in materials to modify the final appearance of those kits.

> Examples pictured on this page show some of the things that can be done by you, while you are making a FROSTLINE kit. These are not stock kits, but rather have been customized by people to "add an extra personal touch. . . ." In this way you can create "one of a kind garments" that will be as unique as you are! (Frostline Catalogue, Fall/Winter 1976, 33)

Beyond the purposeful modification of conventional equipment, "experience" may be provided to equipment by selective acquisition of previously used items. Such equipment usually has been identified with or served in some other capacity prior to its use for mountaineering. The time of transition of such gear from other purposes to climbing equipment may be difficult to judge. Thus, signs of wear accreted over time, from whatever cause, are credited to experience in the mountains. Examples are to be found among some of the climbers who buy their shirts and pants at military surplus outlets, thrift shops, and rummage sales. These purchase proclivities lead to some highly individuated outfits. One fairly well-known Southern California Sierra Club leader and climber with a Ph.D. and an important administrative position in a research firm accents her diminutive stature by wearing green wool marching-band pants with a broad yellow stripe down each leg. Another Sierra Club trip leader leader, a retired Navy man, insists his thrift-shop tuxedo pants are the best climbing attire.

A mountaineer reading these lines may wish to set forth alternative interpretations for the acquisitions of signs of experience in his or her personal equipment. These might take the form of appeals to the "good old days": "You just can't buy them like that anymore"; "They only have wool like that in surplus stores"; "The new ones are too tight in the legs"; "The old style were more roomy; I get mine at Goodwill." Or there are appeals to practicality—some cost/benefit formula is implicit: "There are probably three more years left in that jacket"; "The new ones cost too much"; "Why get a new one when you can fix this one up?" And relative to cleaning: "Why wash it everytime?"; "It will just get dirty again after a little while." And on contrasting repairs: "I didn't have any black thread handy and the red is just as strong."

In spite of the possible motivations of practicality, poverty, energy conservation, or unavailability of materials, Ruth Mendenhall reminds us that the way American climbers dress and appoint themselves "also has something to do with style. European climbers dress much better" (Field notes, March 1977). Climbers in this country dress better as well when engaged in nonmountaineering activities—cleaning house, washing the car, working in the garden. Whether or not the signs of wear on climbers' equipment is an intended or latent function of gear selection and maintenance practices, the fact remains that the degree of climbers' experience communicated through the appearances of their equipment is an important adjunct to identity development.

It has been tacitly assumed to this point that souvenirs are useful in impression management only when employed while one is safely ensconced at home, far from the trials and uncertainty of the outside world. In part this is true. The home provides an excellent place to store and employ these items in their best light. Consider the ways these items are displayed.

The majority of climbers, in Southern California at least, are professional persons or students aspiring to professional status. As such, their homes, if sufficiently large, reflect little of their personal interests in the most public of front regions—the living room and dining room. These remain carefully neutral, symbolically bare stages which can be appointed with props stored backstage according to expected audience and type of performance.

This studied neutrality protects against the eventuality of a particular front being presented for some unanticipated audience for whom it is not intended. Like the welfare recipient who hides what few possessions of worth he or she has when the social worker visits, so, too, the mountain climber conceals the souvenirs of his avocation from potentially unsympathetic audiences (see Goffman 1959, 40).

Mountaineering as yet does not enjoy the popular acceptance of skiing, scuba diving, sports-car racing, and other recreations involving some objective risk. Many a climber has heard derisive remarks behind his back, following the public sharing of some climbing experience. When Rick Ridgeway and Chris Chandler, members of the 1976 American Bicentennial Expedition to Mount Everest, presented a slide show and discussion of their successful climb, they completed their program with a call for questions from the audience. From the ensuing hubbub and rumble of audience members talking softly among themselves came a clearly voiced opinion: "They must be crazy to do that!" (Field notes, March 23, 1977).

To avoid such perjorative judgments mountaineers may reserve the most valued and potent souvenirs of their climbing adventures for permanent display in the more intimate surroundings of the den, family, work, or recreation room.[3] These areas are shared more often with companions and compatriots than curiosity seekers or casual company. Here the climber is asked not "Why do you climb?" but more often "What have you climbed?" "By which route?" "In what season?" "With what technique and gear?" It is in answer to these latter questions that souvenirs are most useful.

In semisecluded areas of climbers' homes, one may find a rock collection, perhaps on the shelf with the mountaineering books. The odd bits of wood and other naturally occurring souvenirs are here as well—a selected item serves as a paperweight on the desk; a decoration on the magazine table, perhaps along with the climbing periodicals. It is the "created" souvenir, however, which is most likely to attract attention and to be used in support of identity claims. For a climber this is most often an item of equipment. It, too, shares the same physical location as the natural artifact—table, desk, shelf, wall, mantel, unused corner. A few of these items may be labeled; all are supported with verbal accounts of their genesis and meaning and, in turn, lend credence to these stories of mountain adventure.

Outside of the home there are other souvenirs which serve to bolster identity even while one is engaged in further adventure. The world traveler formerly emblazoned luggage with stickers noting past ports of call. Owners of trailers and camper-vans festoon the windows of their vehicles with decals marking the parks, cities, monuments, states, etc., which they have visited. The mountaineer, also, carries with him a certain amount of portable sign-equipment—the gear he wears and packs. Thus, the trail, the campsite, and the route to the summit become places and occasions for the use of souvenirs in identity embellishment.

A qualification should be introduced here. Goffman (1959, 23–24) suggests that the concept of "front" be divided into two parts: settings that represent the scenic aspects (e.g., furniture, decor) and personal front, or items more intimately identified with the performer, such as clothing and personal decoration, marks of rank, and such relatively immutable attributes as sex, age, and racial characteristics. In the mountain world this useful distinction requires one modification. When only clothing, decoration, and other easily altered articles are taken into account, personal front and setting blend together. Although all the climber's gear, including what he or she wears, carries, or packs, are "items that we most intimately identify with the performer himself and that we naturally expect will follow the performer wherever he goes" (Goffman 1959, 24), they are also the "furniture, decor . . . and other background items which supply the scenery and stage props" for performance (Goffman 1959, 22). Personal front and setting depend upon a single set of objects and these may be few in number. Goffman (1959, 22) recognizes that this synthesis between personal front and setting may occur, albeit infrequently: "It is only in exceptional circumstances that the setting follows along with the performers; we see this in the funeral cortege, the civic parade, and the dreamlike processions that kings and queens are made of."

In the mountaineer's arena of action a more useful distinction than that between personal and scenic aspects of front might be between portable human artifacts such as packs, clothing, and gear identified with the individual, and fixed natural features such as boulders, trees, meadows, streams, and mountain backdrops identified with a particular locale. Even in the fanciest (or messiest) of camps, this collection of equipment extends only a short way beyond the individual's immediate grasp. (The expedition base camp is a possible exception.) Often a climber's kit contains little more than one or two items of extra clothing, a small amount of food, minimal climbing gear, and a rucksack to carry these things in. Yet, with this paucity of sign-equipment, identities are fostered and upheld. Although the absolute number of props is limited, they are selected with care and their use is purposeful and practiced. Thus, with this additional clarification over the earlier usage, I shall refer to the mountaineer's equipment as "setting."

Traveling souvenirs of past experience are employed by climbers while in the mountains in much the same fashion and to the same effect as they would be used at home. Even while among other climbers and in mountain surroundings, tokens (generally items of equipment) used as props in the here-and-now serve to remind one's fellows of accomplishments there-and-then, on other peaks with other companions. As items of equipment, these vary from conventional souvenirs only in the requirement that they retain functional utility as well as sign potency.

In the field, equipment-souvenirs also serve as an account against inadequate performance. When one's identity is supported by appropriately experienced gear, one can have a bad climb without being adjudged a bad climber. Without the support offered by these trappings, claims of ability and past accomplishments may rest heavily on present and observable performance. The veteran has no advantage over the novice in his image-making efforts, save skill alone, if he is unknown to his companions.

The transition in use of equipment from utilitarian to symbolic purposes, or the creation of souvenirs through retirement of equipment, bears brief mention. The retirement of equipment may come about for three reasons: an article is no longer capable of fulfilling the purpose for which it was intended; the climber is no longer interested in or capable of using the gear for its intended purpose; or the article has been supplanted by gear more advanced in design, strength, versatility, or efficiency. Each reason for retirement bespeaks a different kind of past experience. Gear which is unfit for further use often indexes some dramatic event which rendered it thus and as such becomes a powerful prop. The broken piece of climbing hardware is a good example.

Recall from the discussion of technical climbing that various mechanical devices are used to assist in and safeguard the passage of difficult portions of a mountain. Climbers may employ as anchor points various steel spikes or aluminum wedges driven or fitted into rock cracks. These pitons and chocks are connected to the rope by metal snaplinks or carabiners, and this system is used to protect and aid the climber's progress. Pitons, chocks, and carabiners are made of metal alloys and are exceptionally strong. In a severe fall, however, these pieces of equipment may be subjected to such tremendous forces that they are deformed or broken, with dramatic, if not fatal, consequences. Therefore, the mountaineer who uses a bent and twisted chromemolybdenum steel piton as desk decoration, or the crushed chock or broken high tensile-strength aircraft aluminum carabiner as a paperweight, has dramatic proof indeed of his or her (mis)adventures. These souvenirs place the climber symbolically at the very center of action and are strong evidence of the danger, if not the difficulty, overcome.

A climber who boasts a broken rope in his souvenir collection has a truly phenomenal prop. As the key element in the climber's safety system, the (extremely rare) rope that fails brings, in most cases, traumatic injury or death to its unlucky user. Thus, the climber who punctuates his mountaineering adventure tales with the frayed remnant of a rope to which he was previously attached is guaranteed the undivided, awe-filled attention of his audience.[4]

Gear which outlasts the individual's desire or ability to use it and is relegated to souvenir status is less dramatic than bent pitons and the like but more common. Ice axes, with their hardened steel alloy heads and aluminum, fiberglass, or hardwood shafts are tremendously durable in normal snow-climbing use.[5] They may serve and be identified with a climber for a lifetime—and more.

> CLYDE ICE AXE ON DISPLAY—The mountaineering ice axe used by Norman Clyde, renowned for climbing exploits, has been given to the Inyo County museum by Frances Kilpatrick of Independence. The axe bears Clyde's name. . . . The museum owns a number of Clyde's possessions which are destined for a mountaineering exhibit at the museum. (Inyo Museum's News Bulletin, December 1976, reprinted in Mugelnoos, no. 530, February 16, 1977)

As climbers grow older, they are no longer as capable of the severe gymnastic contortions needed for the highest-standard rock climbing (although a gain in endurance may be some compensation). Special rock climbing shoes and bags of gymnasts' chalk used to make fingers stick to slippery polished stone are hung up for the last time. When persons retire from climbing altogether, they find crampons, axes, snowshoes, etc., useful as decoration and conversational stimulus.

> We were talking in the judge's den when he learned about my interest in mountaineering. He told me to pick up an unusually shaped piece of wood propped against one wall, otherwise covered with books. The stick was T-shaped and roughly the size

and shape of a gardening pick, crudely carved but smoothed, apparently from considerable handling and use. As I held this item, he explained its source and uses and launched into the story of his adventures. "I got it from a native for twenty-five cents. . . . The porters rest their loads on them at brief trailside stops. . . . I used it as a kind of one-legged stool. . . . It was handy for balance in many places." The stick seemed a sort of legitimating device to open up the story of his travel in Nepal. (Field notes, October 1976)

The judge's return to his judicial duties in Southern California altered this useful aid for walking to a helpful prop in talking. George Herbert Mead could not have hoped for a finer illustration of the basic interactionist proposition that the meaning of objects resides in the way in which persons act toward them (see Blumer 1969, 2). Nor could I ask for a better example of the creation of a souvenir.

The utility of souvenirs rests on their authenticity and prior association with prestigious places. With some of the examples discussed these may be uncertain qualities. Souvenirs range from obvious fakes to presumably real artifacts. Distinguishing one from the other is especially difficult when sign-equipment claimed as original may, in fact, be a replica. Pieces of the "true" Cross sold to Middle Eastern travelers and of "ancient" Aztec art treasures offered to tourists in Mexico illustrate the problem. While souvenirs increase in importance according to their physical and temporal association with some important place, that association is not always certain. Sombreros are manufactured and sold in Texas as well as Mexico; rocks are found in valleys as well as on mountain tops; embroidered pillows commemorating the American bicentennial may come from Taiwan or Korea.

As a result of the uncertainty of origin of many souvenirs, their utility as sign-equipment depends more upon appearances than their actual genesis or history. They are intended to impress at first glance, not on close and studious inspection. To this end they are sometimes carefully displayed in complementary contexts, identified with labels, certified with notarized stamps, and substantiated with verbal accounts.

However, not all souvenirs are of doubtful authenticity or in need of artful display. One class of souvenirs is routinely believable and convincing—photographs.

Photographs

Photographs are the most potent of props. They offer both the ultimate proof and the basis for final rejection of identity claims. They can simultaneously convey information about important settings, the actors found there, and the action they pursue. They are parsimonious ("worth a thousand words") and credible ("pictures don't lie"). With these features they are a grave threat to misrepresented identities and a potential boon to legitimate ones.

Climbers use photos in several ways—to illustrate the precipitousness, difficulty, or hazard of some climb, to record experiences with prestigious or fond companions, and to act as direction-finding aids when distant views or aerial pictures are available in advance of the ascent. Most commonly, photos are used by climbers to commemorate and certify the reaching of mountain summits.

Mountain summits are small places with large symbolic potential. If that potential is to be exploited photographically, the panorama below the peak along with the summit itself must be captured simultaneously on film. The reader can well imagine the compositional difficulties this may pose if the mountain top is at all spirelike. Photographers cannot pose their subjects on the summit and then conveniently back up until background features are all included. They shortly run out of mountain top to stand on. The solution to this problem is often found in substituting two types of photos for one. The first of these clearly identifies the subject with the locale, associating the climber with other objects presumably found on or near the mountain top. The second substantiates the claim that the summit has in fact been achieved with panoramic views of the scenes below.

On some mountain summits props are at hand which are useful in identifying climbers with the locale. For example, the summit of Everest is but a simple snow ridge not noticeably different from thousands of similar summits around the world. However, since the 1974 Chinese ascent, the difficult-to-distinguish place has been marked by a singular tripod flag pole erected by that party. Subsequent climbers have posed themselves beside this recognizable structure and in so doing have certified their visits.

Such props are surprisingly abundant. The distribution and frequency of cairns and summit registers was suggested earlier. In addition, the urge to proclaim particular political or religious perspectives has led, at times, to sizable artifacts being lugged to some unlikely mountain peaks. Doug Scott comments on this practice.

> We were quite pleased to leave that place and the next morning get to the summit of Mt. McKinley. I must confess that being the highest point in the U.S.A. we half expected to find a mini-statue of liberty on the top here at least. It was quite nice just to find this one little pole which marked the top. (Field notes, March 1978)

Scott's expectations are realistic. The second highest point in the USSR, 23,406-foot Pik Lenin in the Pamir Mountains, is adorned with a large bust of Lenin. The spectacular Drus in the Mont Blanc massif in France is topped with a three-foot-high Madonna. The Matterhorn sports a yet larger cross. On Argentina's Aconcagua, at 22,834 feet the highest point in the western hemisphere, still another cross resides. This latter cross serves as more than a marker for the summit. It is also the only memorial to a Japanese climber who died atop the peak in 1973 and whose exposed and frozen body continued for years to lie unburied a mere twenty feet away. (Brush 1976, 37)

On occasion, preparation for summit photos are made in advance of reaching the mountain top. Ice axes may be wrapped on the day of the final assault with small flags and pennants commonly representing one's country or climbing-club affiliation and sometimes a major funding source. Some climbers carry or wear special items of clothing for summit photo sessions.[6] Others may leave tokens buried beneath rock or snow as religious offerings or simple proofs of visitation to be found by subsequent climbers. Edmund Hillary describes the mountain-top activities when Everest's summit was first reached.

> Tenzing had made a little hole in the snow and in it he placed various small articles of food—a bar of chocalate, a packet of biscuits and a handful of lollies. Small offerings, indeed, but at least a token gift to the Gods that all devout Buddhists believe have their home on this lofty summit. . . . Hunt had given me a small crucifix which he had asked me to take to top. I, too, made a hole in the snow and placed the crucifix beside Tenzing's gifts. (Hillary, quoted in Hunt 1954, 206)

These busts, religious mementos, flags, and the like undergo the first half of the souvenir creation cycle. They are ordinary objects transported to extraordinary locales. Then, rather than being returned to their more mundane places of origin, they remain at the prime locale but are often recorded on film. The pictures rather than the objects themselves are used in later front work. Whatever inherent political or religious value these props may have lends further credence, reverence, or patriotism to the scene.

A second frequently employed credentialing device is the summit photo panorama. This is a series of photos showing the view of surrounding terrain in all quadrants from the summit. Panoramic shots are of critical importance in documenting bold and distant exploratory mountaineering. When climbs are reported that border on the limits of what is currently deemed feasible in the mountaineering community, they will be examined with particular scrutiny. Lacking proof of the sort provided by photo panoramas, spectacular achievements may be cast in doubt. It was this sort of difficulty the Chinese faced in 1960. At that time they claimed to have ascended Everest for the first time via the North Col under adverse conditions. The summit was supposedly reached at midnight by a single climber, thus ruling out documentary photographs (see Dyhrenfurth 1980, 42).

Panoramic summit photos, when available, are powerful legitimating devices. They are virtually impossible to fabricate, as Dr. Frederick Cook found out when he claimed to have climbed Mount McKinley for the first time and offered as proof a bogus picture of his companion, Ed Burrill, standing on what he claimed was the summit. The ruse was discovered and revealed by another party of climbers who attempted the peak six years later.

> Our mountain detective work was based on the fact that no man can lie topographically. In all the mountain ranges of the world there are no two hillocks exactly alike. We knew that if we could find one of the peaks shown in his [Cook's] photographs we could trace him peak by peak and snow-field by snow-field to within a foot of the spot where he exposed his negatives. And now, without going out of our way, we had not only found the peaks he had photographed, but we had found as well . . . he was not going towards Mount McKinley but he was high up among the peaks of the head of glacier No. 2—at *least a day's travel out of his course*! (Brown, quoted in Jones 1976, 61)

In summary, photographs are a powerful and effective class of souvenirs, offering substantial proof of mountaineering experience and successes.

Conclusion

Taken together, souvenirs are potent and pervasive supports to identity claims. Their utility can be highlighted by imagining performance without them. When identity must be wrought from a single performance, unsupported by history, reputation, or past accomplishment, that action becomes proportionately more cathected and difficult. Ordinarily, to prove who we are now, we use tokens of what we have done in the past to bolster our accounts. In the imagery of the theater, on an empty stage, where no program announces one's past performances, where no props lend support or remind of distant adventure, identity claims are difficult to substantiate. The prototype for dehumanizing experience, for denial and rejection of identity claims is found in the total institution. There all souvenirs of past performance, all props denoting achievements in other times and places are literally and systematically stripped away and replaced with uniform settings—with neutral, bare stages.

While no collection of props can ever constitute a performance, while settings do not make the play, they do potentiate it. In recent years, much attention has been given to analyzing the verbal gambits actors employ in substantiating their identities (Sykes and Matza 1957; Lyman and Scott 1970). I suggest that the props they employ in performance might also be appropriate and fruitful topics of study. The souvenir is one special class of such props of considerable use to the mountaineer in his or her impression-management efforts.

Summary

Part II has focused on the development of the climber's identity. The role played by formal climbing clubs and organizations in this process is varied and pervasive. Clubs provide instruction, set standards of performance, and develop lists of objectives for beginning climbers. By providing standardized ratings of technical difficulty, clubs make comparison of one climb with another possible. Clubs offer rewards and signs of recognition for specified achievements. Through the placement and maintenance of summit registers, climbing organizations offer a way in which mountaineering successes may be preserved and documented. Journals bring news of specific mountain adventures to broad audiences and thus offer a potent aid to reputation enhancement. Mention in guidebooks gives even more permanent and powerful support to a climber's image.

Ratings and registers, journals and guidebooks serve to speed the flow of information within the climbing community. Desirable peaks are identified and located, feasible approaches and routes are outlined, potential difficulties are described in advance of actual encounters with the mountains.

The existence of standards and records, especially as set forth in guidebooks, influences both the social and physical qualities of the climbing environment. With the sharpening of distinctions between climbing difficulty and climb achievement has come a subtle shift from intrapersonal to interpersonal competition. For some mountaineers the intrinsic satisfaction of climbing is replaced by the glory of journal article bylines and guidebook citations. As accomplishment takes ascendance over process, the mountains themselves may be treated with neglect or even disrespect, resulting in damage to ecosystems and even the rocks themselves.

Souvenirs also assist in the management of mountaineering representations. They serve as props in support of tales of mountaineering deeds, as graphic aids to accompany stories of difficulty encountered and daring required. Mountaineering clothing, equipment items, other objects found in or carried to prestigious locales, and especially photographs are useful in this capacity.

Souvenirs are of interest beyond their utility in climbers' impression-management efforts. They offer a clear illustration of the more general phenomenon of the social construction of reality. By negotiation and agreement common rocks are transformed into cherished mementos, broken tools become treasured keepsakes, and we are reminded again of the power of society's members to create and define the world around them.

In the final part of this book attention shifts to perhaps the most pressing of questions regarding mountaineering and its participants. Why do they do it? What calls men and women to this demanding and sometimes dangerous work? What special sight allows climbers to see beauty and purpose in bare, windswept rock, ice, and snow? Or are climbers perhaps driven upward by less tolerable conditions elsewhere in their lives?

Part Three
Why Do People Climb Mountains?

10
Accounts

"Why do people climb mountains?"[1] That is perhaps the most often repeated inquiry in the annals of mountaineering literature. Not that mountain climbers show much interest in the question. They do not. Those who write about climbing, on the other hand, feel an almost universal need to justify or excuse the activity which is their subject matter.[2] They seek to make sense out of mountain climbing to a presumably skeptical readership. Before I review some of the traditional responses to the basic question of why people climb, I want to discuss the general process of responding to socially problematic behavior. Lyman and Scott (1970, 111–43) refer to this process of explaining behavior that is inappropriate or untoward as offering "accounts."

Accounts are the linguistic devices called into play when taken-for-granted expectations about the ways people will act in a given situation are violated. Accounts are not necessary when behavior follows common sense, when it consists of routine patterns in an appropriate cultural context. Conversely, they are often required to restore normal social interaction when a person is accused of having acted in some immoral, erroneous, perverse, unruly, or unseemly way. To some persons the climbing of mountains has appeared as just this latter sort of untoward behavior. As a result it has become the mountaineer's ongoing task, in the management of his image before conventional society, to account for his actions. Two categories of accounts—excuses and justifications—have been delineated, along with a complementary form, explanations.

The distinction between excuses and justifications is twofold. First is the issue of whether or not the act in question in fact possesses some unacceptable quality. Second is the question of the actor's responsibility for his or her behavior. To justify an act is to reject the notion that the behavior in question is untoward but to accept responsibility for that behavior. Conversely, to excuse an act is to accept its untoward character but reject full responsibility for performing it. For example, the climber may justify his acts: "Climbing is *not* a sign of mental illness! It is the highest form of creative self-expression." Or he might excuse his behavior: "Personally, I think it's crazy to climb mountains but I go along because my wife likes it so much."

While both types of accounts involve imputations concerning the act and the actor, their emphases are different. To justify is to assert the positive value of an act in the face of a claim to the contrary. It is the quality of the act which is seen as problematic. To excuse is to mitigate or relieve one of personal responsibility for questionable behavior. Here it is the role of the actor which is negotiable.

Justification: I did it, but *it* (the act) was right, a proper thing to do.

Excuse: I did it, but *I* (the actor) was acting rightly, behaving properly.

Common to justifications and excuses is a claim of access to realities overlooked by others: in justifications to a perception of the objective act; in excuses to an understanding of the actor's subjective experience.

An alternative to the account is the explanation. According to Lyman and Scott (1970, 113), explanations refer "to statements about events where untoward action is not an issue and does not have critical implications for a relationship." This suggests that there is some category of inquiry which calls only for an exchange of commonsensical information without additional interpretation of motive. "Why did you get here at 7:30?" is perhaps a call for an account. "What time is it, 7:30?" calls for an explanation.

Although not an account per se, the explanation will be utilized in discussions below. Whether an account or an explanation is called for is not always clear, in part due to the variability of who can be held accountable and by whom. "The vulnerability of actors to questions concerning their conduct varies with the situation and the status of the actors" (Lyman and Scott 1970, 133). The mountain-climbing community, particularly in its beginnings, was and is made up of a high proportion of professional persons. Many climbers historically and at the present time are well educated; middle- and upper-class; scientists, technicians, engineers, and the like. These higher-status persons are able to resist calls for accounts more effectively than, say aficionados of cockfighting, dog racing, bowling, wrestling, professional boxing, or other sports whose participants and fans have frequently been lower-class individuals.

With this introduction to accounts in mind, let us return to the question of why people climb. The traditional answers offered to this question have been of four major types. Climbing has been accounted for variously as a ridiculous, sublime,[3] purposeful, or natural activity. "Ridiculous" here denotes the basic assumption of some that climbing mountains is essentially a foolish enterprise and that its particants must be emotionally ill, morally corrupt, or both. "Sublime" calls attention to those who focus upon the artistic, poetic, spiritually uplifting, or even transcendental qualities of mountaineering while ignoring the more prosaic character of the climbing enterprise as cold, hard, and sometimes dangerous work. The third type includes explanations of climbing as a practical, purposeful, and even necessary job to be done, usually in the name of scientific inquiry. Finally, there are accounts of the modern-day mountaineer with the central theme that climbing is natural and requires no explanation.

Ridiculous

To the sober person adventurous conduct often seems insanity.
Georg Simmel, *On Individuality and Social Forms*

Dragons and Monsters
"Climbing mountains is ridiculous!" This is a widely held traditional as well as contemporary opinion. Historically, mountains, far from being sources of recreation and reverence, were viewed with fear and loathing. Ullman (1964a, 17–18) reminds us that when we ask "Why do men climb mountains?" the simplest answer, even if an evasive one, is that most men and women do not.

Among ancient peoples throughout the world and among primitive peoples today, mountains are looked upon less as part of the actual earth than as a separate supernatural realm between the mundane world of living people and the heavens. This realm was the dwelling place of spirits: in the tradition of the East, of gods and ghosts; in the tradition of the West, of monsters, wraiths, and demons. For example, the city council of Lucerne, Switzerland, is known to have forbidden access to a small lake on the side of a peak in that district where the spirit of Pontius Pilate was said to dwell, lest he be disturbed and cause much damage. Peter III of Aragon was among the many "honorable and trustworthy" men to report the sighting of "a horrible dragon of enormous size" during mountain travels (Styles 1967, xiv). Indeed, as late as 1723, Johann Jacob Scheuchzer, scientist and fellow of the Royal Society of London, was to publish "a reasoned catalogue of Swiss dragons arranged according to cantons" (Beer 1967, 89). This in the age of Sir Isaac Newton, another Royal Society fellow.

Fosca Mariani reviews some classical perspectives on mountains:

> *Horridae frigoribus Alpes*, says Tacitus while Polybius describes at length the "harsh and sterile" alpine region and Silius Italicus recounts their squalor: "The shadow of towering peaks hides the sky from our sight. There is no spring up there, no trace of summer's splendour. Hideous winter reigns supreme."
> (Mariani, in Styles 1967, xiii)

The same attitude persists in more recent times. Voltaire is said to have cursed the Alps because they interfered with nations mingling naturally with one another.

Those who were forced to travel in the mountains did so with disgust and trepidation. Mountain travelers of the early 1700s "would solemnly commend their souls to their maker before risking the crossing of what today are considered the most prosaic Alpine passes, and to the occasional unhappy wanderer on the higher slopes it was merely a question of whether a bandit, a three-headed dragon or the ghost of Pontius Pilate would waylay him first" (Ullman 1964a, 19). Under such circumstances it is little wonder that the climbing of mountains for the enjoyment therein would be considered ridiculous.

Then, in the latter half of the 1700s, the Enlightenment produced a widespread and conspicuous change. Europe was astir with seminal ideas and events. The American and French revolutions were in foment. Science was on the ascendant, sweeping before it centuries of superstition. The beginnings of industrial civilization were on the horizon. The high places which had been heretofore ignored and avoided became objects of interest and even cherished goals. People began to visit remote alpine areas for the enjoyment of viewing the "immense icicles"—glaciers. Travelers on the famous grand tour "no longer gazed up from their valley inns with horror but with admiring awe" (Ullman 1964a, 33). The horizons of the world were changing. Mountaineering was about to come of age. "Monsters and dragons disappeared. Points of view were turned upside down, nomenclature inside out. What before had been inhospitable, savage, repellent, terrifying became splendid, august, majestic, sublime" (Mariani, in Styles 1967, xiv).

This shift from the ridiculous to the sublime was not universal. While the next century and a half brought with it a meteoric rise in mountain sport and the Alps became the "playground of Europe," not everyone embraced the mountains with equal fervor. A new kind of science was to emerge in the latter part of the nineteenth century which once again found reason to disavow mountaineering. Dragons were gone from the mountain passes and peaks but not entirely forgotten. There were some who found demons lurking in yet another hiding place—the minds of men who climbed mountains for the joy of it. The evil without was transformed into an illness within.

The Evil Within

It seems that the psychoanalyst finds the motivation for mountaineering in a kind of internal possession model (Glaser 1972, 485) where climbing is the "disguised manifestation of a conflict between basic instinctual needs and social restraints" (Csikszentmihalyi 1975, 8). In this perspective, mountaineering is reduced to a sublimated penis worship—the expression of latent homosexual desire. Alternatively, the climber may be manifesting veiled death wishes engendered by unresolved guilt concerning these sexual proclivities.[4] In general, activities which involve risk, such as mountain climbing, are "enjoyed because of a masochistic release from guilt about sexuality and aggression" (Bergler, quoted in Csikszentmihalyi 1975, 7)

Lacking the central sexual theme and broader in scope are psychiatric explanations of climbing. These again emphasize the non-normative qualities of the mountain climber's personality. One study serves to illustrate the presumed psychoneuroses possessed by the mountaineer. Z. Ryn (1971, 453–67) of the Psychiatrical Clinic of the Medical Academy in Cracow, Poland, studied a group of thirty active and experienced mountain climbers. The twenty men and ten women subjects were evaluated through the use of numerous methods.[5] These included

> psychiatric and psychological examinations (Cattels's personality questionnaire, Bender, Benton, and Graham-Kendall tests), and auxiliary methods such as electroencephalography, radiology, etc. In the psychiatric examinations . . . special attention was given to childhood diseases and trauma in the past, and illnesses connected with mountain climbing. For purposes of personality evaluation, information was collected about emotional states during climbing. Mental and psychopathological experience at high altitude were specially analyzed. (Ryn 1971, 456).

Ryn's study was a fairly comprehensive look at the psychological qualities of mountaineers. If some abnormality were present, one might expect such a thorough investigation to unearth it. What did this research find that typified the personality of the climber?

> On the basis of the psychiatric and auxiliary examination, the following clinical disorders were established in the studied group of alpinists: personality disorders in 7 persons (5 men—25 percent, and 2 women—20 percent), neurosis in 4 and psycho-organic syndromes in 10 persons. . . . Neurological symptoms of focal central nervous system damage were noted in 4 persons. . . . Pathologic electroencephalograms were found in 11 persons (6 men—30 percent, and 5 women—50 percent). (Ryn 1971, 461).
>
> In summary, two main personality types were distinguished: schizoidal-psychasthenic and asthenic-neurotic. The first, more frequent type, was characterized by such traits as secretiveness, reserve, emotional sensitivity, and avoiding contents [sic] with people; in spite of lack of self-reliance and feeling of inferiority, and high aspirations. As a rule these persons were hyperactive, independent, unconventional, and eccentric. They were emotionally labile, oversensitive, obstinate, excitable, and aggressive and submitted to social and collective discipline with difficulty. (Ryn 1971, 458).

Others have studied the effects of mountaineering itself on the individual and concluded that the stress of climbing, hypoxia, and the mountainous environment combine to impair mental functioning and otherwise alter behavior.

> Numerous changes were noted at 5,000 meters. There were large increases in the areas of paranoia, obsessive-compulsiveness, and depression, as well as smaller increases in anxiety and hostility.
>
> There was also a significant increase in the Bender-Gestalt score at 5,000 meters. When data on the 10 most frequent mistakes made in drawing the designs are compared with data on a normal group of adults and a group of psychotic patients, there is a surprising similarity between the changes seen moving from 3,810 meters to 5,000 meters and those between normals and psychotics. (Nelson 1981, 23)

Two professionals in the mental health field who reviewed this manuscript suggested that the meanings of these descriptions are not as obvious as they might seem.[6] One reader argued that expressions like "penis worship" and "latent homosexual desire" are not used by psychoanalysts with pejorative intent, to indicate pathological conditions; they simply are part of the theoretical language of psychoanalysis and are used to characterize people's psychological state, not to criticize it. The other asserted that any category of persons, carefully studied, will be found to have its share of nervous disorders and borderline states. With this caveat, interpretation of these data is left to the reader.

However, the nonclimbing layman might find in such research an easily grasped answer to the question of why people climb mountains: "Because they are crazy." To impute this conclusion to a psychoanalyst or psychiatrist may be incorrect. That it represents an opinion held by persons outside the field of psychology is less debatable. For some of the detractors of mountaineering, the activity is ridiculous, its participants are a few eccentric, inadequately socialized, or downright sick individuals, and it certainly is nothing to be taken seriously. But there are others who find in mountain climbing the glorious, uplifting, quintessential statement of human accomplishment. For them climbing is quite the opposite of ridiculous. Climbing mountains is sublime.

Sublime

But how splendid is this intimate dialogue between man and the forces of nature!
                              Rebuffat and Tairraz, *Between Heaven and Earth*

Beauty and Religion

The sublimity of mountain climbing manifests itself in two ways: as an environment to be experienced and as a medium for creative self-expression. Some say that they go to the mountains to appreciate their beauties and to receive their blessings as the passive recipients of an all-encompassing beneficence. Woodrow Wilson Sayre, who, with only three other novice companions, attempted to climb the North Face of Everest in the early 1960s, typifies this view in his listing of the personal values for his involvement in climbing:

> First on my list I would mention beauty. There are the colors: black rock and ultramarine shadows, pure white swell of snow, turquoise and amethyst crevasses, and the diamond glitter of sun on ice. In the afterglow of sunset the air itself becomes pink and gold. And there are the infinite clean shapes: wind-carved snow, fluted ice, weathered stone, and cloud-brushed sky. (Sayre 1964, 212)

Maurice Herzog, upon his return from Annapurna, the first of the great 8,000-meter Himalayan peaks ever to be climbed, was similarly affected: "The mountains had bestowed upon us their beauties, and we adored them with a child's simplicity and revered them with a monk's veneration of the divine" [7] (Herzog 1953, 311).

The religious character of the mountaineering experience, suggested by Herzog, is a recurring theme. Sayre enumerates values he feels are common to most climbers. He cites one: "This is the sense of communion with God. Those who experience it quite often feel it is the most important value of all" (Sayre 1964, 218). Lunn recounts how the early mountaineering literature saw the climber's activity as "a form of worship as well as sport." He quotes Geoffrey Winthrop Young on "the mystical attractions of mountaineering," its "religious fervor," and the fact that its early history had "the character and many of the phases of a religious movement" (Lunn 1957, 46). Tyndall, the scientist and skeptic, is likewise quoted: "Some people . . . give me little credit for religious feeling. I assure you that when I walk here and gaze at these mountains, I am filled with adoration" (Tyndall, quoted in Lunn 1957, 46).

Still others find the mountaineering setting the manifestation of divine handiwork. Caught at night on the Dufourspitze at over 15,000 feet in the Swiss Alps, one nineteenth-century climber reflected:

> We felt ourselves to be in the presence of a novel and most inspiring revelation of the omnipotence and majesty of God. How could we even think of the fatigue we had endured, much less complain of it? . . . If you believe mountains to be the direct work of the Omnipotent Creator, you will welcome the indescrib-

able beauty of the surroundings, and the assured possibility of priceless experiences, which can only be enjoyed during a some- what lengthy sojourn on the highest peaks, and then only at hours when one is least wont to be there. (Ratti, quoted in Noyce 1950, 143).

Creative Self-Expression

The business of spending the night out with minimal protection in the mountains is referred to as bivouacing. A bivouac, in American terminology, is a camp made only with a few items of equipment carried incidentally in the climber's rucksack. Such an evening out, without warmth of sleeping bag or shelter of tent, perhaps pinned to some precipitous face, is a memorable event. A few may be planned; most are the result of emergency delays—none are soon forgotten. All seem to focus on the second form of the sublime experience in mountaineering— creative self-expression.

Essential to such creativity is the ability to reinterpret, reform, and recreate the painful, the frightening, the problematic objective experi- ence—first as a subjectively manageable challenge and finally as an accomplished deed. During the climber's day, creativity comes with physical action, with the use of body in synthesis with the mountain, is grasp and plod, in stretch and balance, in sweat and skin on stone. At night only action of the mind remains. Limbs which were celebrated in their rhythms by day become angular lumps, drawn tightly together for warmth, serving no useful purpose.

Thus, the bivouac becomes the prototypical medium for the creative act in the mountains. Motion is replaced by contemplation. These sleep- less hours of shivering in enforced idleness make the climber a stranger to his deeds. These are hours set aside from the engrossing moment-to- moment struggles of the day. They demand that the climber attend to the radical schism between everyday experience and the mountaineering world. In bivouac, reality is no longer merely experienced but is under- stood. And if the understanding that the mind constructs is not found horrible, it is often found sublime. These are the moments often acutely miserable in their objective character yet so pregnant with self-con- sciousness that they may evoke the most vigorous accolades for the mountaineering experience. We can observe this process clearly in the writings of Gaston Rebuffat, especially by comparing his descriptions of the generic bivouac in his introduction to *Starlight and Storm* with his later discussions of his own experience.

His introduction tells us that "this book is the autobiographical record of a young man's life devoted entirely to high mountains" (Rebuffat 1957, 19). It is also a clear outline of the joys that mountaineering should bring to other young men and women who might follow in his steps. He tells pointedly how one ought to go about the business of appreciating the mountains and the climbing of them. But, introductions are, in some books, the last sections written. They distill, foretell, and set the tone of the events which are to follow for the reader—but which preceded for the writer. The author's reflections thus guide the reader's anticipations.

Rebuffat looks back upon is own experience and, in an act of creative synthesis, tells us how the bivouac should be subjectively perceived. Only later do we learn how these thoughts were born from quite adverse objective circumstances. A bivouac ought to be seen like this:

> At the end of the day, the mountaineer looks for a ledge, lays down his sack, hammers in a piton and attaches himself to it. After the hard, acrobatic effort of the climb he is lost—like the poet—in contemplation; but to a greater degree than the poet he can be a part of the hills around him. The man who bivouacs becomes one with the mountain. On his bed of stone, leaning against the great wall, facing empty space which has become his friend, he watches the sun fade over the horizon on his left, while on his right the sky spreads its mantle of stars. At first he is wakeful, then, if he can, he sleeps; then wakes again, watches the stars, and sleeps again; then at last he stays awake and watches. On his right the sun will return, having made its great yellow voyage below this shield of scattered diamonds. (Rebuffat 1957, 22)

Eighty pages later, we learn of Rebuffat's own, quite different experiences in bivouac.

> It was still only eight o'clock and a long night of sleepless inactivity lay ahead. Tensed with cold, hooked into the [Mt.] Badile by a piton like pictures hanging on a wall, we endured only for the sunshine to come. (Rebuffat 1957, 104)

And again, on the Aiguille du Roc:

> It was six o'clock, at the end of September, and we had to bivouac at the gap. All night it had snowed; we were soaked and frozen, for the light snow penetrated everywhere. Above all we had to be careful not to fall asleep. From time to time I would pull out my hand to sweep away the snow that was cloaking us. By early morning a foot and half of fresh snow covered everything. I withdrew my hand, slightly frostbitten, into a damp pocket with melting snow, and hesitated to take it out again. (Rebuffat 1957, 109)

My point is not to argue that all climbers are possessed of a need to misrepresent their actions or are oblivious of their surroundings to the extent that they cannot recall from one moment to the next how cold, hard, and tiresome their experience was. Far from it, both the acute bodily discomfort and the emergent subjective satisfaction of beauty created in retrospect from these experiences are remembered with equal clarity.[8] The real need illustrated here is to create some meaningful reality from which the physical challenges of the mountain world can be evaluated and met. When physical action is limited, that challenge often becomes one of appreciating some presumably inherent beauty in the setting at hand. But when action is possible, when daylight returns, then motion becomes an important component of these creative acts. New and expanded possibilities arise. It is in the blend of action and appreciation that this creativity finds its fullest expression.

I will return to this form in the next chapter when an examination of the psychology of climbing brings us to a discussion of the flow experience. For now, note the descriptions of some rock-climbing enthusiasts concerning their sport. When asked to characterize their actions, they responded: "It's a physical poem," "It's almost like an art, putting different combinations of moves together in order to get to the top," "It's an aesthetic dance" (MacAloon and Csikszentmihalyi 1974, 132–33).

At least one author, Harold Drasdo, in *Ascent*, has specifically argued for the "extensive and important" likeness of climbing to art and, therefore, for the climber as an artist (Drasdo 1974, 78–79). Such allusions to art, dance, and poetry clearly indicate the bond between action and awareness for those who define climbing as sublime. Diemberger provides another example:

> Then followed the dream of a rock-climb, vertical, overhanging, pitonless, with innumerable small holes and wrinkles—perfect free-climbing on a sheer wall, with an infinity of air around us. At such moments you are gloriously conscious of your fingers, your muscles; of the toes of your boots winning a hold on the rough Brenta rock; of the wall, close to your face, shining black, brown, and bright ochre amid the grey—like flower patterns in a carpet— and all of it high above the comb down there at the foot of the climb. You are enmeshed in a bright web of thoughts, on which you climb ever higher, pulling yourself upwards from hand-hold to hand-hold, foot-hold to foot-hold, towards an ever-increasing freedom, while everything below you falls away as you exalt yourself all the time.
>
> Down there at the bottom, you see the shadows of the towers lengthen, and feel that you belong to your mountain with every fibre of your being and yet, at the same time, here, high above the abyss, utterly free of mind and spirit, you are acutely aware that you have arms and legs—and a body to waft you upwards, because you have learned to overcome fear. (Diemberger 1971, 67)

In climbing, this cycle endlessly repeats itself. Toe and hand tentatively touch the rock in search of holds, then, with muscles tensed, a delicate push and pull through boot soles and fingers moves one upward to new possibilities for purchase, a new search for vertical motion.

Thus, for some, the experience of the mountains is sublime. This experience may be found in the passive appreciation of natural beauty or in the active merging with the mountain through the dynamics of climbing. Though the passive condition is the prototypical setting for the creative enjoyment of mountaineering, it is not common, usually being the by-product of uncontrolled circumstances in which enforced idleness and self-consciousness combine. It is the active state which predominates, and it is the action of climbing per se which is sought by the mountaineer as an end in itself. The essential element of these experiences is that they offer a potential for creative action. The climber's ongoing task is the construction of subjectively manageable challenges from the obdurate mountain environs and then the attempt to meet those challenges.

Not everyone, however, is satisfied to have climbing bring joy to its participants alone. Some have asked that the mountaineer seek more than simply a pleasurable experience. These persons call upon the climber to pursue his sport with attention to the ways in which it might benefit others. Some climbers have taken up this challenge, approaching mountaineering not merely as a joyful self-aggrandizement but as a meaningful and important duty. For these mountaineers, climbing is not necessarily sublime but has a practical purpose.

Purposeful

It is above all through the study of mountains that the progress of a theory of the Earth can be accelerated.
Horace Bénédict de Saussure, *Scholar Mountaineers*

Climbing mountains is said by some to be a necessary antecedent to the intellectual pursuit of basic scientific research. This justification is of importance, for it helps legitimate the participation of one group of persons likely (for other reasons to be discussed later) to involve themselves in climbing activities—professional persons in applied science. In the early period of mountaineering development in Europe and later in the United States, climbing mountains was often justified in the name of science.

Horace Bénédict de Saussure was an eighteenth-century Swiss philosopher and natural scientist noted both for his scholarly research and his pioneering climb of Mont Blanc. He illustrates the preoccupation of climbers of his time with science as an account: "My object was not only to reach the highest point, I was bound to make the scientific observations and experiments which alone gave value to my venture" (de Saussure, quoted in Noyce 1950, 58). This was no idle claim. When de Saussure and his party at last succeeded in reaching the summit of Mont Blanc, he spent four and a half hours "in activity with hygrometer, electrometer and thermometer, hours limited by the difficulty in . . . breathing" (de Saussure, quoted in Noyce 1950, 58). By comparison, today's climber, while vastly better equipped, would probably tarry no longer than the time required for a brief rest, a small snack, and few photos.

Thirty years after de Saussure's ascent science was still linked with mountaineering, though climbing as sport was on the horizon. In the early years of the nineteenth century most of those who climbed mountains still utilized, or at least invented, scientific reasons to justify their climbing, particularly on an undertaking as serious as an ascent of Mont Blanc. John Cleare illustrates:

> In fact when the first Americans, Doctors William Howard and Jeremiah van Rensselear climbed the mountain [Mont Blanc] in 1820, they borrowed scientific instruments from the generous Dr. Paccard, who had made the first ascent and still lived in Chamonix.
>
> Seven years later when two Englishmen unsuccessfully attempted the Jungfrau "for the fun of the thing" continental critics expressed shock at the complete lack of any scientific justification for their attempt. (Cleare 1975, 16)

John Tyndall was "one of the outstanding mountaineers of the Golden Age" (Lunn 1957, 44), as well as a professional scientist. He was an early member and president of the British Alpine Club. He resigned his membership in that organization, however, as a protest over remarks made at a club dinner. In his opinion the remarks invidiously "reflected upon the value of science in mountaineering"[9] (Tyndall, quoted in Lunn 1957, 45). Such was the strength of the bond between science and climbing.

Today there is considerably less concern for scientific motivation in climbing. Local and small-scale climbing activities are seldom associated with scientific enterprise. In some circles, mild ridicule may be directed at those who continue to mix research and the mountains. I have been chided from time to time for carrying a field notebook into the mountains and conducting interviews with climbers found there. "Who do you think you are, the Roper Poll?" echo the detractors (also see Snyder 1973, 16).[10]

Certainly science plays nowhere near the importance it did in the past. The concern for scientific underpinning, however, is not entirely an historical artifact. Most of the major Himalayan expeditions in the 1950s and 1960s included among their members professional scientists who were responsible for collecting data for various high-altitude research projects. For example, the American Everest Expedition of 1963 had two glaciologists, two cinematographers, a research physiologist, the clinical psychologist James Lester, and the sociologist Richard Emerson. All these were in addition to the expedition's regular staff of specialists, including three physicians and a radio operator. Nor was the inclusion of these persons mere scientific window dressing. The social scientists Lester and Emerson were as active in conducting field research as their physical-science counterparts. Both systematically studied members of the climbing team high on the mountain, in addition to participating in the mountaineering effort. Their roles as scientists were recognized as of considerable importance.

The extent to which this scientific interest is motivated by the requirements of funding sources is yet to be determined. Large expeditions cost a great deal of money. In addition to soliciting free equipment and supplies from manufacturers, it is necessary to locate additional funding sources. These sources have sometimes been foundations and groups that may require a part of the expedition's efforts to be directed toward conducting certain scientific research as a condition of their support.

As a climber and a sociologist, I suspect that if the exigencies of a climb were to preclude either research or a successful summit bid, especially in some remote area such as the Himalayas, the research would be the first to go.[11] Ullman seconds this guess. He argues that those who climb mountains, "who aspire, struggle, and suffer . . . are driven by far deeper and more human forces than a scholarly interest in rock strata, oxygen consumption, or trigonometrical surveying" (Ullman 1964a, 22). These conjectures aside, the time devoted to scientific observation in large-scale expeditions during the first three quarters of this century has been considerable. This is attested to by the often voluminous appendices to official reports of expeditions, appearing frequently in the book form mentioned in Chapter 7. These appendices chronicle the research conducted and provide brief summaries of their findings in layman's language. The tone of the reports clearly indicates that it is meaningful and important work being reviewed, in no way tangential to other expedition goals.

Many of the recent investigations conducted by expedition personnel have, in turn, benefited the climbing community itself. Basic research into physiological reactions to high-altitude stress has aided in the understanding of the acclimatization process, nutritional requirements, and especially, the etiology and treatment of altitude and cold-related disease and injury—notably, cerebral and pulmonary edemas, frostbite, and hypothermia. Equipment has been continually refined as well. For a time one of the most signficant developments was reasonably lightweight and reliable high-altitude oxygen apparatus. Such apparatus allowed mountaineers to live, work, and climb, sometimes for weeks, without serious impairment of health at altitudes formerly thought bearable only for a few days. With continued research and repeated ascents of major peaks with the aid of supplementary oxygen, the physiological and psychological borders of the possible have been pushed back. Now even the highest of the world's mountains are being tried without oxygen-dispensing devices. Our knowledge of social and psychological processes in mountaineering has, as yet, benefited less from the limited work so far conducted in these areas.

As important as science motivation has been however, it is still not the definitive explanation of the mountaineer's activity. It has, in Ullman's words, "helped pay the way and presented a cloak of respectability for the eyes of 'practical' onlookers" (1964a, 22). One type of account remains to be considered—or perhaps it should be considered an anti-account. There are some who feel that the climbing of mountains requires no explanation, that it is a natural activity.

Natural

"Why do people climb mountains?" Rebuffat muses that had he ever been asked that question he would have responded, "That's what we are made for" (Rebuffat 1957, 119). There are those in the climbing community who find the search for a motive, this continual asking "Why?" an unnecessary endeavor. For them, climbing is natural. One of the best American mountaineering instruction manuals, *Freedom of the Hills*, comments on this "naturalness":

> Climbing is a joyous, instinctive activity; unless restrained, most children will scurry up trees, garden walls, building facades, and anything else steep and enticing. While society, in the form of parents, teachers and the law, discourages these activities, some determined individuals persist and eventually find their way back to the peaks. [They follow] the suggestion of one climber "to remember our arboreal ancestors, retreat intellectually a couple of million years and make like monkeys, defying gravity with our own impetus." (Ferber 1974, 181)

Thus, climbing is alleged by some to be an instinctual pattern which manifests itself freely in childhood and is dampened only by the socialization process.

Others contend that climbing is the expression of some cultural trend toward exploration and discovery peculiar to the Western world.

> The spirit of exploration and adventure is so ingrained a part of our modern civilization that we are apt to take it for granted. Is there an unknown continent? We discover it. An unsailed sea? We cross it. A mysterious jungle or desert or mountain peak? We journey to the ends of the earth to find and know them and make them ours. These things have come to seem to us almost as natural and inevitable a part of life as eating and begetting and building shelters against the cold. . . . That this is a Western attitude to the unknown bears underlying. The cross-legged Buddha was born into the world long before the wandering Faust. (Ullman 1964a, 17).

Even more abstract than the "cultural naturalists" have been those who, in moments of inspired imagination, have found a natural good not in the climbing of mountains but in the mere fact of their existence. They posit a kind of ultimate geographical causality. Gavin de Beer chronicles two such views. Scheuchzer philosophizes upon the good fortune that Switzerland is not a single mountain but several mountains separated by valleys, "for the mountains keep off the cold winds and enable fruit and corn to ripen and men to live in the valleys." Also, Leslie Stephen "has drawn attention to the old argument that mountains are useful in sending rivers down to the sea, and in providing crystals, pastures for cattle, and preserves for fur-bearing animals" (Beer 1967, 85). Shades of Dr. Pangloss![12]

But beyond these arguments of instinct, cultural traits, and geographical necessity—or nicety—lies another point of view often held by the climber. It is one in which the essential question "Why do men climb mountains?" is ignored. While nonclimbers may see mountaineering as ridiculous, some climbers view the continual questioning of their motives as absurd. As I said in the beginning of this section, most climbers are not particularly interested in the question anyhow. Such lack of interest among mountaineers in their own motives is clearly reflected in perhaps the best-known remark of a climber "naturalist." Ullman tells us how this famous comment came into being.

> During the winter following the [Mount Everest] expedition of 1922 George Mallory visited the United States on a lecture tour. One evening, after a talk in Philadelphia, a member of the audience approached him and asked the inevitable question: "Why do you want to climb Mount Everest?" Mallory considered a mo-

ment and gave his answer: "Because it is there," he said. (Ullman 1947, 385)

Perhaps this is as good an answer as that offered by the scientist for his research or the artist for his painting or the chess player for his game. But what do science, art, and games, and the persons who pursue them have in common? Can the climber be counted in this number? Answers to these questions may be found in the social psychology of play, the mechanism, character, and perception of enjoyment.

11
The Flow Experience

In the preceding chapter some of the answers found in literature about mountaineering to the question of why people climb were reviewed. If a single reason could be abstracted from those offered by climbers themselves, it would be safe to say that people climb because it is somehow fun—an enjoyable experience. But the essence of enjoyment sounds like a topic of study for philosophers, not social scientists. Fortunately, this need not be the case. Csikszentmihalyi (1974, 1975) has offered guidelines for the understanding of enjoyment which do much to clarify the position of the climber.

Csikszentmihalyi interviewed a number of subjects in diverse activities, including music composers, chess and basketball players, dancers, surgeons, and, related to the work here, rock climbers. He found the motive for involvement in all of these activities is the intrinsic reward they offer their participants.[1] When these activities are fully explored by their members, a kind of personal transcendence is experienced which Csikszentmihalyi calls "flow."

> Flow refers to the holistic sensation present when we act with total involvement. It is a kind of feeling after which one nostalgically says: "that was fun," or "that was enjoyable." It is the state in which action follows upon action according to an internal logic which seems to need no conscious intervention on our part. We experience it as a unified flowing from one moment to the next in which we are in control of our actions, and in which there is little distinction between self and environment; between stimulus and response; or between past, present, and future. (Csikszentmihalyi 1974, 58)

The French anthropologist Roger Caillois offers a classification of activities having the potential for intrinsic reward and flow. First is competition, including games and sports and religious or political contests where persons are pitted against each other. Second is chance, where the unpredictable is challenged, as in gambling, astrology, divining of spirits. Third is mimicry, where personal limits are transcended through fanstasy, as in the theater, dance, art. Finally, there is vertigo, involving the alteration of consciousness in purposely courted uncertainty in such activities as skiing, sky diving, mountaineering, and various forms of intoxication (Caillois 1961, 11–36). The last category, vertigo, is an obvious and direct reference to the mountaineer's world. Although I will not specifically elaborate each of the remaining classifications, it will be seen that competition, chance, and mimicry play their part in the climber's experience as well. But a classification system, however stimulating, does not tell us how the flow experience emerges, only where that experience is likely to occur. To develop a theoretical model of enjoyment we need to consider three elements which constitute and potentiate the flow experience. First, for flow to be achieved, it is necessary for freedom of choice among a wide range of uncertain outcomes to be possible. Second, the actor must creatively fashion from these myriad uncertainties some limited task within the limits of his or her perceived abilities. Third, he or she must achieve a level of involvement such that consciousness of the task at hand and the doing of it blend, that action and awareness become indistinguishable. Although these three elements represent a condensation of the six elements suggested by Caillois (1958, 9–10) and elaborated by Csikszentmihalyi (1974, 57–88), they give a broader view than the one found in these sources and permit considerable changes in it.

Freedom of Choice

Freedom

Flow occurs in the process of creativity, however that may be defined by the actor. For any experience to offer opportunities for creative expression, it must be one which is freely entered into, freely chosen. Such experiences are undertaken for the intrinsic rewards they offer, not because of any external constraint or internal compunction. In "Where the Action Is," Goffman (1967, 149–270) refers to this freely chosen, self-rewarding quality in his discussion of play and risk-taking. He uses the term "action" to describe the social and physical contexts in which Csikszentmihalyi's flow might occur. The two are complementary but not identical concepts. Flow may occur where the action is.

> By the term *action* I mean activities that are consequential, problematic, and undertaken for what is felt to be their own sake. . . . There are fateful activities that are socially defined as ones an individual is under no obligation to continue to pursue once he has started to do so. No extraneous factors compel him to face fate in the first place; no extraneous ends provide expediential reasons for this continued participation. His activity is de-

fined as an end in itself, sought out, embraced, and utterly his own. (Goffman 1967, 185)

Mountaineering meets this requirement of free entry and unrestrained exit. Those who find mountain climbing mandatory are the bizarre by-products of fateful circumstances—victims of plane crashes in the Andes, conscriptees in Hannibal's army, and the like. People choose to climb mountains; they are not chosen to climb them, or required to do so.

Rewards

What do climbers receive for their efforts? One scholar-mountaineer replies:

> The surest way *not* to understand a mountaineer is to suspect him of ulterior and practical motive. Certainly it is not money that impels him, for no fortune was ever made on a peak or glacier. Nor is it fame, for how many of even the greatest climbers are known by name to the general public? It is not power nor prestige, nor except on a Hollywood mountain—the hand of a heroine. . . . It is not an incidental, but fundamental aspect of mountaineering that it is, by pragmatic standards, "useless." That its end is neither money nor fame nor power nor knowledge nor even victory. That it is one of those rare and precious human activities that man performs for their own sake, and for that alone. (Ullman 1964a, 22)

Perhaps Styles (1967, 263) says it best of all: "One thing at least is clear: There is no material gain in climbing a mountain. The thing is useless, like poetry, and dangerous, like lovemaking."

The reward of climbing is climbing itself. Reaching the summit is not the culmination of the climb but a waypoint marking the end of upward travel. The remarks of several participants are illustrative. A rock climber:

> The justification of climbing is climbing, like the justification of poetry is writing; you don't conquer anything except things in yourself. . . . Climbing is the same: recognizing that you are a flow. It is not a moving up but a continuous flowing; you move up only to keep the flow going. There is no possible reason for climbing except the climbing itself; it is a self-communication. (Csikszentmihalyi 1974, 76)

Doug Scott, on reaching the top of the previously unclimbed Ogre in the Karakoram, Pakistan:

As I say, basically you come here for the climbing and we certainly had that. It had been a really interesting route, this. Engaged our attention the whole time, always exciting and interesting and that's what we were there for. It was the journey that mattered, not the arriving and so as soon as we got here—the summit—it was just a matter of turning around and hopping off back down. (Field notes, 1978)

And Jim States from the 25,645-foot summit of Nanda Devi:

I looked at John's face and the whole time the thing that's on your mind when you get there is, "Hey, now we can go home." That was the big issue. (Field notes, 1978)

So climbing is freely chosen and serves as its own reward. It has one other important related property, a quality of uncertainty.

Uncertainty

Flow occurs in the context of creativity. Such creativity can take place only where some new combination of ideas or images is made possible by vagueness, mystery, or imprecision in existing patterns. The sculptor does not create from preformed clay; the artist does not paint by the numbers; the chess player does not follow computer-generated moves. Similarly, the mountaineer does not ride to his summit in a helicopter or aerial tramway. Outcomes which are known in advance are not the medium of creative endeavor, not the realm of the artist, but of the technician or manager, Creativity requires a degree of uncertainty. But uncertainty is a broad concept, only a portion of which is applicable here.

The climber, on the mountain, is faced with two types of uncertainty, which I refer to here as danger and difficulty. (Other kinds of uncertainty are discussed in Chapter 12.) Danger refers to situations in which the probabilities of dire outcomes are not possible to estimate with any accuracy in advance; nor are those dire events within the climber's ability to surmount should they be met. Rock fall, snow, avalanche, and lightning are dangers encountered by the mountaineer. Difficulty refers to risks in which estimates of outcomes can be made by comparisons of the problem at hand and resources in terms of skill, experience, strength, equipment, and time available. Climbing a delicate rock pitch, setting a sound rappel anchor, relaying heavy loads at high altitude up a Himalayan peak are all difficult but not necessarily dangerous. The mountaineer eschews danger but enjoys difficulty within some limits.

Certainly the experience of mountaineering involves risk. Data from the American Alpine Club (1982, 70) indicate that during the three decades from 1951 through 1981, 2,658 persons were injured and another 961 were killed in mountaineering-related accidents in the United States and Canada.[2] These figures undoubtedly underestimate the extent of injuries, although the fatalities are probably more faithfully reported by the mountain rescue groups and clubs that supply these data. Personal injury to members of small climbing parties who handled such emergencies on their own would not be reflected here. Fatalities often involve formal search and rescue groups in attempts to save seriously injured persons or, as necessary and practicable, to recover bodies (see also Donnelly 1981a, 38–40).

Although perhaps not familiar with these statistics, the climber is nonetheless aware that accidents are an ever-present possibility. Yet he does not glory in the danger of his sport but continually seeks to limit dangerous circumstances to a minimum. Danger is avoided whenever possible; difficulty is prepared for by learning safety techniques, use of proper equipment, and careful planning. The attraction of the mountains lies in seeking and meeting difficulty to the limit of one's ability, not going beyond it. That the extent of the difficulty and the limits of personal performance are variable is the feature of uncertainty which potentiates the flow phenomenon. Mountaineering is not like Russian roulette, craps, or coin-flipping, in which outcomes and their proportions are foreknown but for the most part are unalterable through the player's skill.[3] Rather, it is more like painting or musical composition, in which skill and imagination determine the outcome within the broad known limits of the qualities of canvas and paints, the sounds producible by various instruments. Even success and failure are not as clearly delineated as one might think. As I suggested above, to reach the summit of the mountain is not everything. Indeed, sometimes it is the least important of objectives.

Rebuffat describes the mountaineer's attitude toward uncertainty:

> The real mountaineer does not like taking risks. It is stupid to scorn death. We are too fond of life to gamble it away. In my profession of guide, I have to accept some risks every day. I know them too well, I fear them too much to like them or seek them out. No, make sure you do the hardest and most daring things as safely as possible. The climber likes difficult pitches, even those which tax him to the utmost, but in such cases, it is as pleasant for him to feel safe, in his heart of hearts, as it is unpleasant to go beyond his resources, to run a risk or to incur some climbing hazard. . . . and yet the climber has sometimes to accept certain risks: the sudden onset of bad weather, storms, thunder, a hold which gives way although well-tested, a couloir exposed to falling stones which must be rapidly crossed, a melting snowbridge which must be negotiated, a pitch which the climber suddenly finds is beyond him but from which he cannot withdraw, once he is committed. In all these cases, a thrill runs through him, but

much too unpleasant a thrill for him to seek it out or enjoy it. We
are not "dicers with death." (Rebuffat 1957, 57)

Mountaineering is an uncertain enterprise. But the uncertainty which is
sought is the limits of one's skill and ability. The uncertainty of fateful
circumstance, of danger, is avoided and disavowed. The climber likes
solving problems; he does not like threats or gambles whose outcomes
are beyond his control.

This penchant for problem-solving and avoidance of risk is reflected
in the subjective assessment by rock climbers of their sport. Csikszentmihalyi (1974, 47) asked the participants in various activities he studied—
basketball players, dancers, composers, etc.—to rank eighteen acts (e.g.,
running a race, taking drugs, playing a competitive sport, watching a
good movie) according to the similarity of these acts with the respondents' chosen activities. The thirty rock climbers in his sample ranked the
experience of climbing as most similar to "exploring a strange place";
next, "designing or discovering something new"; third, "being with a
good friend"; and fourth, "solving a mathematical problem." Climbers
felt the least similarity between their own actions and "playing poker"
(rank 16), "exposure to radiation to prove your theory" (rank 17), and
"playing a slot machine" (rank 18).

For flow to occur, the activity must be one which is freely chosen and
which offers its own intrinsic reward. Freedom of choice also must exist
within the activity itself. This freedom implies an uncertainty of outcomes, defined by the actor as challenge, not necessity; as difficulty, not
danger. The difference between difficulty and danger, however, is not
always clear-cut. Might not the professional mountain guide find challenging some activities that the novice climber would find terrifying?
None of us has an unlimited capacity for uncertainty. None of us is totally
without resources to meet the unknown. These limits vary from one
person to another and, to a lesser extent, from situation to situation. The
next problem will be to discuss the ways in which danger is distinguished
from difficulty by actors, the ways in which challenges and uncertainties
are redefined and reduced to manageable tasks—the limiting of the
stimulus field.

Limiting the Stimulus Field

Freedom of choice is an important element of the flow experience. But
freedom of choice cannot be the universal condition. The person free to
choose in all aspects of daily experience is soon faced with a world so
unbearably problematic, so complex and unpredictable that he is likely to
become acutely anxious. While too much certainty brings boredom, too

much uncertainty engenders panic, a theme I shall return to later because it has important implications for another motive behind mountaineering. Indeed, some theorists have seen uncertainty and its attendant anxiety as being so pervasive in human experience that they are believed to constitute the motive for all behavior. From this viewpoint, we are continually seeking to satisfy instinctual drives, reduce tension, resolve dissonance, avoid pain. But these formulations, while stimulating, have not survived empirical review.[4]

> In any case, we know enough about anxiety and cognition to reject the extreme position that many philosophers and psychological theorists have held for centuries, that all cognitive needs are instigated by anxiety and are only efforts to reduce anxiety. For many years, this seemed plausible, but now our animal and child experiments contradict this theory in its pure form, for they all show that, generally, anxiety kills curiosity and exploration, that they are mutually incompatible, especially when anxiety is extreme. (Maslow 1963, 123)

Maslow further contends that uncertainty may be desirable for some people.

> Direct examination of psychologically healthy people shows pretty clearly that they are positively attracted to the mysterious, to the unknown, to the puzzling and the unexplained. This is noteworthy because it contrasts sharply with the psychologically sick person's tendency to be threatened by the unfamiliar, the ambiguous, the unknown. (Maslow 1963, 114)

Uncertainty, then, is sought by some persons in some settings. But when does curiosity become anxiety, difficulty become danger; when is action inhibited rather than enhanced by uncertainty in a given situation?

Atkinson (1957, 359–92) offers some seminal propositions regarding this issue in his article "Motivational Determinants of Risk-Taking Behavior." He discusses the interrelationships between the actor's motive to succeed or to avoid failure (two presumably exclusive statuses), the probability of succeeding, and the incentive value of a given task. Most simply, one cannot enjoy the thrill of a great accomplishment if the task is seen as a very easy one. Conversely, people do not experience only a minor sense of pride after some extraordinary feat against seemingly overwhelming odds. Atkinson argues that some persons are more motivated to avoid failure while others seek to achieve success. Those who are most concerned with failure-avoidance, if allowed to select their own tasks, will pick ones of either very high or very low probability of success: the former because of certainty of achievement and the latter because failure in a more difficult task is more easily accounted for by the nature of the task itself than by the actor's personal worth or abilities. Those motivated by a desire to succeed will choose tasks of intermediate probability of success. For these persons, incentive is greatest when the uncertainty regarding a given outcome is greatest, i.e., $p = .5$. Further, Atkinson proposes that if persons are required to perform a given task rather than to select one of the desired difficulty, all persons will be similarly motivated when uncertainty is maximized, $p = .5$.

Perhaps the best example of these principles in practice comes from one of the few pieces of social-science research on mountain climbers. I mentioned before that the social psychologist Richard Emerson was a member of the 1963 American Everest expedition. Emerson used the climbing-team members themselves as research subjects. He was interested in identifying the role uncertainty played in motivation, particularly motivation to climb mountains. Through a structured analysis of the team members' daily diary entries, tape-recorded conferences and radio communication, and other field notes, he found that uncertainty played an important part in motivating climbers.

When climbers were not under extreme stress, they managed the flow of information between themselves in such a way that uncertainty about the outcome of the climb was maximized. In general, Emerson found that when the environment provides largely pessimistic cues, when storm or avalanche threatens, when supplies are running low or barriers seem insurmountable, then the exchanges between climbers tend to be optimistic. Conversely, when events are proceeding smoothly, when the sun shines, the snow is firm, supplies are plentiful, and the way ahead apparently unhindered, then talk and diary entries become pessimistic. Likewise, if one team member expresses optimism (or pessimism) to another about the climb, then that other is likely to respond in opposite fashion with pessimism (or optimism). According to Emerson: "Communication offsets environmental information which might otherwise have led to premature pessimism or optimism (individual or collective). At the same time communication promotes maximum team effort" (Emerson, in Ullman 1964b, 398).

Mountain climbers purposely manage their definition of the situation to maintain maximum flux and uncertainty in the task at hand. In so doing, they illustrate Atkinson's "achieve success" condition.

Atkinson uses the "achieve success" and "avoid failure" typifications to identify personality types, basic and long-lasting, but this is not necessarily the case. Emerson observes that climbers attempt to maximize uncertainty of outcomes only when stress is not too great or, as I have put it, when uncertainty predominates only in a limited stimulus field.

These hypotheses about communication are stated with one qualification: they hold only if psychological stress is not too intense. Under stress, the challenge of uncertainty in achieving a goal is offset by the desire to escape from threat, and uncertainty may become intolerable anxiety rather than tantalizing challenge. (Emerson, in Ullman 1964b, 399)

We might reinterpret Atkinson in this fashion. When stress is high, persons will seek to avoid failure and will be motivated only by extremely simple or exceedingly difficult tasks.[5] When stress is moderate or low, a desire to achieve success will predominate. Maximum motivation emerges in situations defined as intermediate between the very difficult and very easy, between certain failure and certain success. It is possible for an individual or group to be oriented toward avoidance of failure at one time and toward achieving success at another, depending upon the degree of stress experienced in the challenge being faced. This shift in orientation from failure avoidance to success achievement can be seen in the developing novice mountain climber.

Persons first exposed to climbing often have a considerable fear of heights. Being far from the ground with only small holds to cling to is acutely distressing for novices although objectively they may be safely belayed from above. They think first about avoiding failure where the consequences of failure appear to them clearly detrimental. As they progress, are incorporated into the climbing fraternity, as they gain confidence in ropes and other protective devices, they begin to choose climbing tasks more intermediate in difficulty. The perceived dangers and attendant stress inherent in climbing have been reduced by training and experience. Beginners first seek to avoid apparent dangers by picking very easy tasks. As they advance in ability and understanding, they no longer fear for their immediate demise. Distress is reduced as they come to trust their tools and techniques and their own skill in using them. Thus, the need to be overly concerned with failure—falling, generally— has been reduced as the consequences of that failure are shown to be different from those expected. Caught by overhead belay, the beginning climber, although hundreds of feet above the ground, may suffer only scratches, not the quick death he visualizes.

A complementary example of the shift between orientations to achieve success and avoid failure sometimes occurs among more experienced climbers when they manifest what I call "summit fever." While the novice seeks to avoid failure defined in terms of falling from the mountain, the more skilled mountaineer may wish to avoid another kind of failure, failure to conclude the climb successfully. "Learning the ropes," overcoming a fear of heights, is a stressful time for the beginning climber, but stress is not reserved solely for that time and its circumstances. As the summit draws near, another sort of stress is generated for the experienced climber. The increasing desire to overcome final obstacles is also a potent motivation. The novice, in stressful moments, selects only simple tasks to avoid imagined hardship or harm. The experienced climber, under the press of a proximate and increasingly possible victory, may be motivated to accept increasingly difficult tasks.

As climbers come within sight of their goal, as the summit begins to look like an obtainable reality rather than an elusive dream, they sometimes abandon their carefully maintained balance of uncertainty in an all-out effort to clinch the victory and reach the top. A fine example of this process comes from the same Everest climb on which Emerson was collecting the data reported above.

Toward the end of the climb, a period of intense excitement and fevered activity occurred as chances of success grew greater. The summit was being approached in a two-pronged attack via the original South Col route and the unclimbed West Ridge. This bold plan envisioned two teams, one from each direction, meeting on the summit on the same day and retreating together to a support camp at the South Col. This would involve a traverse of the summit for the West Ridge climbers.

Emerson himself was part of the West Ridge team. As the day of the final summit rendezvous approached, personnel and equipment were being hurriedly rushed into position. The summit was in sight but not yet in hand. It was just at this moment of intense activity and rising expectations that Emerson's willing spirit and weakened flesh had a significant confrontation. While still low on the mountain, he was stricken with another bout of a recurring gastrointestinal illness (Emerson lost forty-eight pounds during the expedition). His companion was forced to leave him and forge ahead. Normally, under such circumstances, a climber might be expected to return to the advance base camp and remain there in shelter and security. But circumstances were not normal. The summit loomed tantalizingly near. Success seemed increasingly probable. The timetable clicked inexorably forward.

It was clear to Emerson that if he was to play a part in the final push for the top, it would be necessary to join the climbers far above on the West Ridge, with all due haste. To rest, to recoup, to regain strength were the safe and sensible choices, but with those decisions hope of taking part in the summit bid must be abandoned. ''For I knew . . . that if the West Ridge was going to move at all, it was going to be in the next few days, and if I missed out now, it would be forever'' (Emerson, in Ullman 1964b, 219). Sick, enfeebled, and alone, Emerson set out for the high camp.

In his weakened condition it was obvious that the next camp could not be reached before dark. That night, as he knew from the beginning he must, Emerson faced the very real danger of frostbite or worse, as he huddled in the bottom of an icy crevasse without tent or sleeping bag. A storm with winds of over 100 miles per hour raged around him.

This courageous effort is exemplary but not exceptional. As the chance of ultimate success grew larger, other climbers, too, made their own fateful commitments. On the eventual push for the top there was further need for heroism and another death-defying bivouac when, on their return from the summit, both climbing teams were cut off from their camp below by darkness.

These are not ordinary acts for mountaineers of even extraordinary courage and skill. Experienced climbers do not regularly risk the loss of life or limb to obtain their goal. Yet under these special circumstances three of the four successful summiteers, as a result of their extreme and committing efforts, did in fact suffer frostbite so severe as to require amputations. When the long-sought goal finally looms near, when the struggle has been protracted but success seems close at hand, then extra efforts are sometimes made to overcome final obstacles. This kind of motivation emerges most often when success appears to hinge on some imminent and final confrontation.

Atkinson and Emerson's assessment of the climbers' penchant for maximal uncertainty of outcomes is correct for most of the time encompassed by any climb, but uncertainty as an end in itself is enjoyed only so long. Ultimate mastery over oneself and the situation requires not only maintaining that delicate balance of uncertainty for a time but ultimately in achieving closure, in finally and definitely solving the problem. Thus, the climber may be brought to extraordinary efforts at the point where success is increasingly probable.

In this contrast between "summit fever" and the mountaineer's usual tendency toward maintenance of uncertainty we are reminded again that uncertainty is sought only within a limited stimulus field. Too much and too little uncertainty are conditions tolerable only for a time. The search for variety of experience and personal security are sometimes contradictory processes. Both are found in mountaineering.

The range of activity which is encompassed by mountaineering, the number of limited stimulus fields, is very broad. Uncertainty is of all degrees in the mountains. What is judged as challenging varies from one climber to another. "In mountaineering there is only one principle: that we should secure on any given day the highest form of mountain adventure consistent with our sense of proportion. All else is more a matter of practice than principle" (Young, cited in Ullman 1964a, 298).

Ullman continues concerning the diversity of mountaineering experience: "There are many fine peaks that can be climbed in a matter of a few hours, others which have been besieged for months on end, year after year, and still have not been won. There are ascents requiring the utmost in daring and acrobatic skill, others that are a little more than a stiff, uphill walk" (Ullman 1964a, 299). As I mentioned before, Mount Whitney, by the normal route, is a walk-up popular with adventurous backpackers, while the east face and buttress on that same mountain offer climbing of the highest technical order. Both routes lead to the same place. It's how one gets there that counts. Each person's "highest form of mountain adventure consistent with his or her sense of proportion" varies widely. Barnaby, in the final lines of Thornton Wilder's play *The Matchmaker*, says it well:

> The test of an adventure is that when you're in the middle of it, you say to yourself, "Oh, now I've got myself into an awful mess; I wish I were sitting quietly at home." And the sign that something's wrong with you is when you sit at home wishing you were out having lots of adventure. (Wilder 1956, 23)

It is possible that some persons may not find uncertainty at all in settings viewed by others as adventuresome. Such may be the case of the professional adventurer. Goffman notes: "Different individuals and groups have somewhat different personal baselines from which to measure risk or opportunity; a way of life involving much risk may cause the individual to give little weight to a risk that someone else might find forbidding" (Goffman 1967, 157). After all, those who make their living by dangerous jobs don't find them adventurous, except perhaps at first. Once they have mastered the work, they find it demanding and exacting, perhaps, but not adventurous. In fact, dangerous work is frequently described as tedious because it calls for such endless, painstaking routines and precautions.

> Many a lad goes to sea in expectation of a life of adventure, but pretty soon finds himself tied to the interminable tasks of watch-keeping, log-reading, safety-checking, measuring, recording, and dead-reckoning. People who climb for a living have much the same experience. Though they may derive some satisfaction from the awareness that other people regard their job as adventurous, to them it is just work. The only difference between it and more ordinary work is that it demands perpetual care and discipline. . . . Adventure . . . is really of the mind. What is an adventure to some, may be, to others, of more prosaic nature, an ordeal, or an imposition, or a nuisance, or a calamity, or even simply a bore. (Price 1974, 17)

So, freedom is exercised, necessary, and tolerable only in a limited stimulus field. The levels and types of challenge which fit this field vary widely according to the subjective interpretations of each individual. It is necessary that the actor feel in control of his actions but, as we shall see, not necessarily be aware of them. That blend of action and awareness becomes the next concern.

Uncertainty is maximized and motivating within this limited field when stress is not extreme. When stress is great, when outcomes are imminent and uncontrollable, then uncertainty is avoided. If success is near, unusual risk may be taken; if failure seems likely, exaggerated caution may predominate.

Action and Awareness Merge

A person in the midst of the flow experience is both keenly aware of his or her own actions and oblivious to that awareness itself. One rock climber remarks: "You are so involved in what you are doing you aren't thinking of yourself as separate from the immediate activity. . . . You don't see yourself as separate from what you are doing" (Csikszentmihalyi 1974, 64). Stimulus and response follow each other uninterrupted by conscious interpretation of events or purposeful manipulation of outcomes. There is neither need nor opportunity for calculated composition and testing of behavior, only action in answer to the pressing needs of the situation. Sensations of delicate balance and clinging grip, the unyielding downward pull of gravity, and the gritty friction between rock and boot rush urgently to the climber's consciousness, bringing about what Caillois (1961, 23) calls a "voluptuous panic," a fateful circumstance created by action and only resolvable through more action, immediate, unflinching, committed. To escape one's precarious circumstances requires movement to other unsure stances, yet certainty and a security of sorts are found in facing that challenge head-on. Goffman explains how fateful events are transformed into opportunities for concerted action, for problem-solving.

> Given the practical necessity of following a course of action whose success is problematic and passively awaiting the outcome thereof, one can discover an alternative, however costly, and then define oneself as having freely chosen between this undesirable certainty and the uncertainty at hand. A Hobson's choice is made, but this is enough to allow the situation to be read as one in which self-determination is central. Instead of awaiting fate, you meet it at the door. Danger is recast into taken risk; favorable possibilities into grasped opportunity. Fateful situations become chancy undertakings, and exposure to uncertainty is construed as willfully taking a practical gamble. (Goffman 1967, 171)

This transition is more than just a subjective one. Not only are difficulties redefined but new physical capacities emerge to meet them. In making this adaptation to the threatening circumstances around him or her, the climber prepares for an effort to overcome them, an effort not possible without the focused attention of the flow experience. Ullman describes this physical component of flow:

> One of the most remarkable developments in cragmanship has been the perfection of a technique known as balance, or rhythm climbing. It is based on the fact that equilibrium is much more easily maintained by a body in motion than a body at rest—a principle involved in many activities other than mountaineering. A dancer, skater, or bicyclist, for example, is frequently in off-balance positions which he can maintain only because he is in constant motion from one to the other; if he were to attempt to hold one of them without moving he would immediately fall. So too with rock-scaling. A tiny fingerhold or quarter-inch ledge, which would afford no support at all to a stationary climber, can yet be made to serve his ends if he uses them but momentarily, for friction on his way to another hold or ledge. Also the climber himself can maintain equilibrium in otherwise impossible positions, if, while he is in them, he is already on his way to a counterbalancing position. The result is that by constant rhythmic movement and the ingenious use of friction an accomplished cragsman can often master short stretches of vertical or near-vertical rock which would be insurmountable by the ordinary methods of "stop and go." (Ullman 1964a, 303)

While the climber's concentration is heightened in the flow experience, it is also focused on a narrower range of concerns—in space on problems literally at hand, and in time on the present. A university professor (cited in MacAloon and Csikszentmihalyi 1974) who climbs rocks illustrates the climber's limited time frame: "When I start on a climb, it is as if my memory input has been cut off. All I can remember is the last thirty seconds and all I can think ahead is the next five minutes."

Climbers may be acutely aware of kinesthetic sensations, of small, usually unnoticed muscular functions. They attend to each movement at every moment with intense concentration, yet other parts of experience may be obliterated. As an example, climbers in flow are seldom afraid. Fear is the luxury or the burden of those without urgent things to do. In the midst of the climb the mountain may pose precarious and problematic circumstances but the climber does not perceive them as such, only as challenges to be met. Fear is reserved for times of apprehension, or, as Goffman notes, reflection. "Much of the fatefulness that occurs . . . is handled retrospectively, only after the fact does the individual redefine his situation as having been fateful all along, and only then does he appreciate in what connection the fatefulness was to occur" (Goffman 1967, 170). The famous British mountaineer Chris Bonnington describes the role of fear in his own climbing experience:

At the start of any big climb I feel afraid, dread the discomfort and danger I shall have to undergo. It's like standing on the edge of a cold swimming pool trying to nerve yourself to take the plunge; yet once in, it's not nearly as bad as you have feared; in fact, it's enjoyable. . . . Once I start climbing, all my misgivings are forgotten. The very harshness of the surroundings, the treacherous layer of verglas [thin ice] covering every hold, even the high pitched whine of falling stones, all help build up the tension and excitement that are ingredients of mountaineering. (Bonnington, in Csikszentmihalyi 1974, 73)

Lucien Devies, then President of the Himalayan Committee of the French Federation of Mountaineering, shares a similar perspective.

In the extreme tension of the struggle, on the frontier of death, the universe disappears and drops way beneath us. Space, time, fear, suffering no longer exist. Everything then becomes quite simple. As on the crest of a wave or in the heart of a cyclone, we are strangely calm—not the calm of emptiness, but the heart of action itself. (Devies, in Herzog 1953, 16)

New England ice climber Laura Waterman describes her reponse to a very difficult climb: "Oddly enough I wasn't scared but in a state beyond fear. Our precarious situation was so patently obvious that I felt an immense calmness and clear-headedness that comes only when you know you are on the thin edge between living and dying" (Waterman, in Jenkins 1979, 29).

Perhaps the most significant experience which is absent during flow is a sense of self. Other writers describe similar states as a "loss of ego," "loss of self-consciousness," or "transcendence of individuality" (Csikszentmihalyi 1975, 42). Csikszentmihalyi (1975, 86) notes that when an activity is so encompassing that the person is involved completely with its demands for action, consideration of self becomes irrelevant. This brings a particularly valuable understanding to the social meaning of flow. Both Mead and Freud saw the concept of self as a mediating mechanism between the needs of the organism and the social demands placed upon it. A major function of the self is to integrate the actions of one person with those of others. This integration is a prerequisite of social life (Berger and Luckman 1967, 51, 72–73). Yet in activities where flow occurs this integrative function is superfluous, reflexive role-taking in Turner's (1956, 316–28) sense of the term is unnecessary. These activities

(such as games, rituals, art) usually do not require any negotiation. Since they are based on freely accepted rules, the player does not need to use a self to get along in the activity. As long as all the participants follow the same rules, there is no need to negotiate roles. The participants need no self to bargain with about what should or should not be done. As long as the rules are respected, a flow situation is a social system with no deviance. (Csikszentmihalyi 1975, 42–43)

The key to maintaining this selfless concentration lies in the simplicity of flow-producing activities. In climbing, reality places easily understood, noncontradictory demands for action on the participants and provides prompt and unambiguous feedback—find a safe anchor, get out of the storm, dodge the falling rock; if one foot slips, the other foot and the hands must not. These are not debatable issues like ethical principles but simple rules of survival.[6] For the climber the urgency of the immediate situation clearly distinguishes good from bad. Safe is good, unsafe is bad. Goals and means are logically ordered. People are not expected to do incompatible things on the mountain as they are in real life. They know, or believe they know, what the results of various possible outcomes will be.

In detailing the flow experience a better understanding of the enjoyment the mountaineer seeks and finds in climbing is gained. Flow is a special condition of intense energy outpouring, of maximum performance and minimum wasted motion. It is immediately and profoundly rewarding. But flow is not a continual experience for the climber. Extreme concentration cannot be maintained indefinitely. Relatively short periods of intense physical and mental effort are interspersed with interludes (from *inter ludes*, "between plays") of less focused activity (Csikszentmihalyi 1974, 62). In flow the climber devotes mind and body almost totally to the next set of moves, to reaching the belay anchor, the ledge, or the bivouac site, but with these achieved, the spell is broken. Heightened sensitivity to a narrow field of action gives way to a more global, less precise view of reality. Clarity is replaced with confusion, simplicity with alternatives to be considered, confidence with trepidation, selflessness with self-consciousness. What was moments ago unambiguous now becomes complex; decisions are not clear-cut; the way to go is uncertain. The conditions of the everyday world reimpose themselves on the climber's consciousness.

There is merit in looking at these everyday circumstances as well. So far, I have talked about mountaineering motives first in terms of accounts and in this chapter as a search for a psychological state—flow. But a third alternative is possible. If climbers are drawn to the mountains in search of the flow experience, might they not also be pushed from the lowlands by other, less desirable conditions? The attraction of climbing and the flow experience can be better understood by looking at the objectionable features of nonflow. Climbing may be both a quest and an escape. In the next chapter I will examine the special qualities of nonflow, a condition which, in other guises, has received considerable attention from sociologists.

12
Beyond Flow

Many, if not most, sociological analyses of sport have focused on sport per se, thus contributing to the sociology of sport. However, the ultimate goal of sociological considerations of sport is to develop sociology *through* sport, by drawing upon examinations of sport which contribute more generally to our understanding of the social world beyond the confines of the sporting life.

Donald Ball, "What the Action Is"

Flow, for the most part, takes place in avocational rather than vocational surroundings. Csikszentmihalyi (1974) point out that surgeons, professional musicians, and a few others may experience flow in their work experience, but these are exceptional occupations and individuals. Most people, most of the time, define their lives as predominantly nonflow situations. But what sort of experience is "nonflow"?

Flow occurs in the middle ground. We experience flow when a balance is achieved between our abilities and our responsibilities, when the skills we possess are roughly commensurate with the challenges we face, when our talents are neither underused nor overtaxed. Flow emerges in circumstances which are perceived as both problematic and soluble.

Beyond flow are two conditions. Both represent a state of imbalance between challenge and skill. When this imbalance is brief, temporary, or task-specific, we refer to the ensuing responses as boredom or panic. The impact of this short-term imbalance is minimal. But when imbalance is persistent and pervasive across many roles and occasions, when the world typically and in general presents challenges significantly greater than or less than one's perceived skills, when one is no longer free to choose, or when uncertainty spreads beyond a limited stimulus field, then social life itself takes on a predominately certain or uncertain quality, coloring definitions of both self and society. Short-term panic or boredom may characterize a portion of the climber's experiences in the mountains. More protracted certainty or uncertainty marks the day-today lowland existence of climber and nonclimber alike. The certainty or uncertainty of these routine social encounters influences one's interest in or avoidance of mountaineering and similar sports.

Boredom and Panic

Boredom describes a subjectively perceived condition wherein short-term tasks are simple, repetitive, undemanding, tiresome, but not troublesome. Faced with boredom, actors push on with their jobs, perhaps rarely inspired by an occasional interesting moment, a fleeting curiosity. Tedium is broken only infrequently. A climber on an extended approach-march confronts such a circumstance. The incessant plod up-hill and down along the dusty trail, burdened with a heavy pack, may be interrupted with an occasional glimpse of the distant peaks, the sight of columbine or shooting stars in bloom near streams close by, the rare appearance of a mountain goat on the horizon. The task itself is an onerous one, but the hope of future adventure or the distraction of other mountain pleasures keep the climber stolidly trudging along the track.

Panic ensues when an immediate and pressing task is perceived as being at the limits of one's ability, wit, endurance, and skill. When only faint hope remains of solving the pressing problem, action is taken, but it is more impulsive than considered—sporadic, sudden, ill-directed. The climber clinging by crampon points and ice-axe pick to a near-vertical pitch of rotten ice without protection of ice screws or other devices, a jumble of rocks below, arms and legs growing weaker, must act, but it is an act of desperation, not choice (see Chouinard 1977, 83 for a dramatic real-life example).

In flow, action and awareness merge. Both boredom and panic involve a similar though less pronounced blending. They are actions taken on the borders of consciousness. The panicked climber reacts to the urgings of fear rather than following considered guidelines of training or experience. The bored climber plods on in automaton fashion, only partially aware of the surroundings.

Certainty and Uncertainty

The final motive for mountaineering may be found in the climber's everyday experience in the mundane social world, typically but not exclusively Schutz's "world of working" (Schutz 1962, 226–29). Like everyone else, climbers have jobs, homes, families, and other interests that occupy the majority of their time and attention. In the enactment of these conventional roles, members may experience a recurring and pervasive certainty or uncertainty in social encounters, regular and frequent, "boredom" or "panic" in everyday affairs.

For some people, daily routines involve only slight and infrequent variety or challenge. They perceive the network of role relationships in which they are enmeshed as both comprehensive and constraining. The social world is not a question but a fact. The outcome of social encounters is easily and readily predicted on the basis of the interactants' relative positions in some inflexible social structure. Volitional action is neither required nor encouraged. Goals are subjugated to a tyranny of permissible means. Most personal skills and resources are superfluous.

For other people, daily routines frequently pose urgent and difficult problems. Capacities are routinely overstressed in the attempts to perform necessary tasks. The social world is more mystery than entity. Social encounters produce confusing and contradictory outcomes seemingly unrelated to efforts to predict or control them. Existing skill and personal resources are inadequate, the means for meeting basic needs unclear.

The key and common feature in both of these extremes of experience is the degree of certainty or uncertainty with which the results of action in one's social world can be predicted. The terms alienation and anomie may be used to represent the polar states of certainty and uncertainty concerning these predictions.

It will be necessary to broaden the definitions of certainty and uncertainty over those used in Chapter 9. Before, Atkinson and Emerson spoke of uncertainty as an assessment of task difficulty midway between two known conditions—certain success and certain failure. This usage made two assumptions that are inappropriate here: that the task was simple and limited and that it engaged actors' capacities in only one or a few peripheral roles. It is only when tasks are simple or familiar or when actors are in sufficient control of the situation that probabilistic guesses about outcomes can be meaningfully made. Estimating chances of success or failure is possible because the task itself is already relatively familiar. Simple physical manipulations or cognitive tasks of the kind often found in laboratory experiments are of this sort. Likewise, sport actions such as climbing a particular technical pitch on a mountain call forth practiced abilities. Atkinson's usage is appropriate only when discussing action within narrow limits, when problems are not only simple and familiar but are faced within a limited stimulus field, when one is playing a peripheral role. Self-conceptions are only slightly influenced by the outcomes of laboratory experiments—Milgrim's obedience research and a few others being exceptions. Likewise, one's prowess on the mountain has little bearing on lowland identities.

Here the use of certainty and uncertainty goes beyond limited and tangential circumstances to define pervasive qualities of the actor's social world experienced across many roles and relationships. When the individual's internalized normative structure is articulated only at limited points with the behavior of others in interaction, when one's daily experience of the social world does not match existing expectations in any consistent fashion, then social life assumes ever-increasing uncertainty. Following Atkinson, one might say that actors in these circumstances come to be "certain of the uncertainty" of the behavior of others, but it seems simpler to talk about a continuum of social experience from predictable certainty to unpredictable uncertainty. The latter usage will be employed henceforth.

Alienation and Anomie

Alienation is one of the oldest concepts in the social sciences, derived from yet earlier notions of original sin. This longevity, however, has not contributed in any significant way to a simple definition of the term. Anomie, more recently arrived on the sociological scene, nonetheless shares with alienation a considerable diversity of interpretations.

Alienation and anomie have been used to describe such wide-ranging psychological and social conditions as loneliness, powerlessness, isolation, despair, depersonalization, ruthlessness, apathy, aggression, self-estrangement, normlessness, anxiety, meaninglessness, and hopelessness. Among the social categories said to be alienated or anomic in varying degrees are blacks, women, blue-collar workers, white-collar workers, migrant farm-workers, artists, college professors, the mentally ill, drug addicts, the aged, the adolescent, the poor, the newly rich, voters, victims of prejudice, the prejudiced, political conservatives, political radicals, physically handicapped, immigrants, exiles, bureaucrats, beatniks, and recluses (Josephson and Josephson 1962, 12–13). The Josephsons observe that, even taking into account possible duplications, this list includes a sizable proportion of the persons found in any industrial society.

In the face of this apparent ambiguity and vagueness in the definitions of alienation and anomie, some scholars have called for these terms to be abandoned entirely (Israel 1971, 289; Feuer 1963). However, in the light of the continued, albeit diverse, applications of these concepts, it appears that they are here to stay. A more reasonable enterprise than simply trying to make them go away may be to contribute to their meanings. In an attempt to accomplish clarification, I argue here that alienation and anomie can be treated usefully as distinguishable aspects of a single dimension of social experience. That dimension in turn may be usefully applied to a number of social situations, bringing a variety of theory and research into some common ground. It is possible that reducing the meanings of alienation and anomie to points along a single dimension poses the disadvantage of eliminating some of the richness and subtlety inherent in previous interpretation and application. On the other hand, it avoids their use as what Kaufmann calls "bargain words," ones that require little or no thought and "can be used in a great variety of contexts with an air of expertise" yet signify little or nothing (Kaufmann, in Schacht 1970, xlix).

Efforts to organize the melange of meanings applied to alienation and anomie have been made before. Seeman in his early article (1959) catalogues alienation according to five usages in the literature: powerlessness, meaninglessness, normlessness, isolation, and self-estrangement. Feuer (1936, 137), in a more structural view, divides alienation into six types: (1) the alienation of class society, (2) the alienation of competitive societies; (3) the alienation of industrial society; (4) the alienation of mass society; (5) the alienation of race; (6) the alienation of generations.

Scott (1965) describes alienation in regard to its sources as four kinds of inadequacies of social control: lack of commitment to values, absence of conformity to norms, loss of responsibility in role performance, and deficiency in control of facilities. Barakat divides alienation into three stages rather than a set of variances: "(1) sources of alienation at the level of social and normative structures; (2) alienation as a psychological property of the individual; (3) behavioral consequences of alienation" (Barakat 1969, 134). Johnson (1973, 370–80) distiguishes five types of alienation according to level of association: segmental encounters, primary relationships, institutional relationships, mass associations, and reified (projected) relationships.

These schemes, while stimulating, have themselves been fraught with confusion. Classifications overlap and are paralleled by other categories. This is not to demean the work which has been done. The confusion which inheres in these terms must in large part be attributed to their extremely broad, and often casual, application rather than to inadequacies in the schemes that propose to organize them. I will suggest another way in which alienation and anomie may be understood and related, one which integrates a portion of Marx's and Durkheim's work.

Marx is often credited with bringing the concept of alienation into sociology. Certainly he did much to popularize it. His notion of alienation focused upon the individual's position in the economic order. He saw workers in a capitalistic system as being required to sell their labor to those who own the means of production. In so doing they are stripped of any meaningful relationship to the goods they produce and become alienated from their labor. Marx's concept of labor is similar to the idea of meaningful work that offers opportunity for creative self-expression. Production, labor, is a vital process of self-actualization.

Production, for Marx, is "the direct activity of individuality." Through the production of objects the individual "reproduces himself . . . actively and in a real sense, and he sees his own reflection in a world which he has construed." This "reproduction of himself" constitutes an actualization of his otherwise implicit "self" or personality in the realm of objectivity. . . . In other words, the kind of production considered by Marx to be man's "life activity" is motivated by nothing more than the need to create, to express oneself, to give oneself extended embodiment. (Schacht 1970, 85–86)

Alienation, according to Marx, is the experience of work without opportunity for self-directed creativity; work for some end exterior to the working itself. Such employment no longer has intrinsic value but becomes a burden, a noxious but necessary drudgery.

In what does this alienation of labor consist? First, that the work is *external* to the worker, that it is not part of his nature, that consequently he does not fulfill himself in his work but denies himself, has a feeling of misery, not well-being, does not develop freely a physical and mental energy, but is physically exhausted and mentally debased. The worker therefore feels himself at home only during his leisure, whereas at work he feels homeless. His work is not voluntary but imposed. . . . It is not the satisfaction of a need, but only a *means* for satisfying other needs. (Marx [1844] 1956, 169)

For Marx, the antithesis of alienation is gratifying and meaningful work through which creative self-expression is possible.

Hegel used "alienation" in two ways (Schacht, 1970). Marx focused upon the first of these when he wrote of alienation as "surrender" to alienating work, a giving up of one's time and effort in order to obtain some future remuneration—be that a paycheck or salvation. For Hegel, this "surrender" was also the solution to a more unendurable condition. Alienation is, in Hegel's second sense, a "separation" from the social substance, suggestive of what Durkheim ([1897] 1951) referred to as anomie.

For Durkheim, the cause of anomie lay not in repressive or unrewarding work but in a breakdown of normative constraints concerning economic aspirations. It is not a lack of creative opportunity but a disturbance in the social order which leads to anomie, and anomic suicide. This is not necessarily because objective conditions worsen. "Every disturbance of equilibrium, even though it achieves greater comfort and a heightening of general vitality, is an impulse to voluntary death. Whenever serious readjustments take place in the social order, whether or not due to a sudden growth or unexpected catastrophe, men are more inclined to self-destruction" (Durkheim [1897] 1951, 246).

When persons are no longer constrained by a stable economic order, "human activity naturally aspires beyond assignable limits and sets itself unattainable goals" (Durkheim [1897] 1951, 247–48). Uncertainty about the appropriateness of desires leads to disorientation, confusion, a sense of normlessness some resolve through suicide. Although Durkheim was aware of a condition in direct opposition to anomie where "excessive regulation" and "oppressive discipline" overly restrict individual action, he granted this circumstance little importance. It receives mention only in a footnote followed by the qualification that "it has so little contemporary importance and examples are so hard to find . . . that it seems useless to dwell upon it" (Durkheim [1897] 1951, 276).

My use of alienation borrows from Marx, and that of anomie from Durkheim. Unlike either of these authors, however, I see alienation and anomie as the opposite poles of a continuum of certainty or uncertainty in experiencing social life. Figure 12.1 illustrates these relationships. The idea that alienation and anomie fall at polar extremes of a continuum of certainty or uncertainty is not entirely new. Cooley (1912), for example, discussed two opposed extremes of experience he called "formalism" and "disorganization," which correspond roughly to my uses of "aliena-tion" and "anomie." Formalism he identified as "mechanism supreme," disorganization as "mechanism going to pieces."

> The effect of formalism upon personality is to starve its higher life and leave it the prey of apathy [and] self-complacency. . . . Dis-organization, on the other hand, appears in the individual as a mind without cogent and abiding allegiance to a whole and without the larger principles of conduct that flow from such allegiances. (Cooley 1912, 343)

Formalism or alienation leads to stifling of creativity and apathetic accept-ance while disorganization or anomie leaves people confused, without direction, uncertain.

Parsons conceptualized anomie as the opposite of "full institution-alization."

> The polar antithesis of full institutionalization is . . . *anomie*, the absence of structured complementarity of the interaction process or, what is the same thing, the complete breakdown of normative order. . . . Just as there are degrees of institutionalization so are there also degrees of *anomie*. The one is the obverse of the other. (Parsons 1951, 39)

Figure 12.1 Relationship between Anomie, Flow, and Alienation

Anomie	*Flow*	*Alienation*
Prevailing uncertainty		Prevailing certainty
Ability < Responsibility	Ability ≈ Responsibility	Ability > Responsibility
Subjective experience	*Subjective experience*	*Subjective experience*
Confusion-disorientation	Competence	Frustration-repression
Normlessness	Self-as-cause	Powerlessness
Isolation	Action and awareness merge	Self-estrangement
Motive for action		*Motive for action*
Social and economic		Personal freedom,
Security, stability,		Creative self-
Certainty		expression, challenge
Comprehension, control		Recognition, creativity

Others have suggested pairings of similar concepts. Coburn (1975, 214), in discussing the relationship between work conditions and health, identifies three possible "demands-individual ability" conditions: demands exceed capabilities; demands and capabilities match or are congruent; capabilities exceed demands. He labels the first condition work pressure and the third worker underobligation and argues that both of these types of job-worker incongruences have negative consequences for mental health.

French and Kahn (1962) describe the condition in which abilities exceed demands as frustration; the situation where abilities and demands are congruent as self-actualization; and where work demands are greater than capacity as role overload.

Barakat (1969), while recognizing, but not incorporating, anomie in his framework, divides the term "alienation" into conditions of overcontrol, powerlessness and undercontrol, and normlessness. He subsumes anomie under his own definition of alienation, arguing that alienation arises from two sources, which he identifies as states of overcontrol and undercontrol in social structures.

> Overcontrol is defined here as a state of over-integration or great emphasis on moulding individuals into the society and/or the social systems of which they are members. . . . Thus among instances of overcontrol are: 1) states of powerlessness; 2) depersonalized relationships; and 3) demand for conformity. . . . Simply, undercontrol refers to states of disintegration, permissiveness, and lack of restraints . . . normlessness and disintegration in interpersonal relations. (Barakat 1969, 4–5)

In using the terms alienation and anomie, I refer to subjective states experienced by individual social actors. Although it may be possible to speak stereotypically of categories of persons as being alienated or anomic, as in "Blacks are alienated" or "workers are anomic," it is more accurate to focus on the individual's perception of his or her social circumstances. Only if persons link their races, occupations, genders, etc., to the quality of their social relationships is it of interest here, although, as will be suggested, this may well be the case for some who climb mountains. For me, alienation and anomie are conscious states. I reject the idea that individuals may be alienated or anomic from some standpoint of which they are not aware (see Schacht, 1970, 154–59). Perceptions are realities for purposes of understanding social relationships. "If men define situations as real, they are real in their consequences" (Thomas 1928, 572). For me, reality does not precede its defining.

Anomie

Anomie is experienced when uncertainty about behavioral outcomes extends to the greater part of social interactions met by the individual. When new social encounters are largely unrelated to previous social experience, unpredictable by known rules, unstructured and foreign, when the behavior of others in interaction and the effect of one's own acts upon those others remain uncertain, the individual experiences anomie. The social world appears fleeting, irregular, insubstantial. In the world of work the lives of confidence-game artists, secret agents, and race-car drivers, and the whole existence of the lone shipwreck victim in a foreign land provide a high degree of uncertainty about behavioral outcomes. They may also engender anomie. This anomie expresses itself in three ways.

When the world becomes too uncertain, unpredictable, when one is anomic, a sense of normlessness, meaninglessness, or isolation may obtain. One experiences normlessness when known rules for social behavior are inapplicable or ineffective, meaninglessness when understandable purposes for action are absent, isolation when social support from one's fellows is inadequate or undependable. The anomic individual finds himself unsupported by significant others, free to choose from meaningless alternatives, without direction or purpose, bound by no constraint, guided by no faith, comforted by no hope. The uncertainty of outcomes elevates the taken-for-granted to the problematic, the routine to the traumatic, the normal task to the major test.

Anomie motivates a search for social stability, security, and certainty. The goal of anomic persons is the restoration of stable social interaction, escape from pervasive uncertainty, reintegration into an understandable and predictable social order. In response to anomie people seek a state where the demands placed upon them to achieve are in rough equilibrium with their capacities. Using the limited case of economic achievement, Merton (1938, 1957) explains several types of deviance in terms of people's efforts to adapt to anomie, to alter their life experience in the direction of increased predictability and control. Not everyone, however, is in want of security, stability, and certainty.

Alienation

Alienation emerges when certainty about behavioral outcomes extends to the individual's anticipations of his or her own actions. When people can predict their own behaviors on the basis of the social order in which they are situated, when they perceive their world as constrained by social forces, bound over by rule and regulation at every turn to the extent that personal creativity and spontaneity are stifled, when they know what they will and must do in a given situation regardless of their own interests, they experience alienation. The alienating social world is omnipresent and repressive. Meaningful mobility is forlorn, the stability of relationships renders self-directed change elusive; security, stability, and certainty are no longer experienced as desirable or even tolerable. Life in the concentration camp, prison, or on the assembly-line provides a high degree of certainty about behavioral outcomes. It may also be alienating. This alienation expresses itself in two ways.

When the social world becomes too certain, the individual feels powerless and self-estranged. Powerlessness is sensed as one's own behavior proves insufficient to bring about outcomes sought in the social world. Action produces an inadequate effect. Self-estrangement grows from a social life lacking rewards in the here-and-now. Action is without autotelic character. Social tasks are undertaken and performed for rewards outside those activities themselves. The certainty of outcome reduces interaction from challenge to drudgery, from a novelty to a necessity.

In sum, the lives of social actors can be described by use of a dimension based upon their perceptions of the predictability of social outcomes. This dimension is bounded by alienating certainty at one extreme and anomic uncertainty at the other. In between is a common and desirable condition sought by alienated and anomic persons alike.

Competence

The goals of the alienated individual are both different from and similar to those of anomic persons. They differ in that alienated individuals, in searching for occasions to utilize their perceived abilities, may purposely seek out problematic and puzzling circumstances, or actively encourage continued instability in some areas of their social lives.

More important than the differences, however, are the similarities between alienated and anomic social actors. Both are seeking ways of bringing into balance their perceived abilities and the responsibilities

confronting them. Both endeavor to match the challenges they face with
the resources they possess. Both attempt to move toward a state of
equilibrium between what they perceive themselves capable of doing and
what they are allowed or required to do as a result of their positions in the
social structure. Achievement of this balance renders activity intrinsically
rewarding, enjoyable, "fun." It becomes leisure in the classic sense (de
Grazia 1962, 11-25).

In neuropsychological terms, organisms are motivated to alter environmental inputs, reducing stimulus variability when too much is
present, increasing variability when stimulation falls below some optimal
level (Berlyne 1960; Hebb 1955; Hunt 1965). Social-psychologically, role
expectations are met with appropriate and adequate role performances.
Persons are motivated to achieve what White (1959) refers to as competence, a sense of personal worth, self-as-cause, efficacy in interaction
with others. Sociologically, normatively prescribed success goals are
articulated with socially legitimated structural means.

Competence grows from the process of recognizing one's abilities
and applying them meaningfully and completely. Competence means
assessing oneself as qualified, capable, fit, sufficient, adequate. Competence emerges when a person's talent, skills, and resources find useful
application in meeting a commensurate challenge, problem, or difficulty.
In sum, the competent individuals' perceived abilities are roughly equal
to their perceived responsibilities.

A sense of competence is a prerequisite to flow. Flow comes when the
mountain is steep and demanding, the hand-grip firm, and the muscles
well conditioned; when the route is complex and the eye keen and
discovering; when the load is heavy, the air is thin, and legs and lungs are
strong and efficient. Flow is found in using a full measure of commitment, innovation, and individual investment to perform real and
meaningful tasks that are self-chosen, limited in scope, and rewarding in
their own right. Flow is the "opposite" of both alienation and anomie. In
terms of social actors, motivations, and aspirations flow is not some
stressless lacuna but a balanced, dynamic tension.

Alienation, Anomie, and Avocations

How the everyday social world is experienced affects the selection of
avocational pursuits. Feelings of overstress or underutilization of skills
and abilities, perceptions of life as going on within a superordinate social
structure or a tenuously constructed subjective reality, experiences of
prevailing alienation or anomie, lead to different kinds of recreational
activities. Generally, avocations contrast with and sometimes comple-
ment routine affairs. They do not duplicate them. Although it need not be

the case, for most persons an essential feature of their reaction is its separation from everyday life, discontinuity from normal action-frames. (Ball 1972, 124–25). As Goffman notes, adventures are not to be found within but beyond common routines. "Ordinarily, action will not be found during the week-day work routine at home or on the job. For here chance-takings tend to be organized out and such as remain are not obviously voluntary" (Goffman 1967, 194–95).

If daily routines are threatening, uncertain, if existence in the world is insecure, then recreation will be sought in another realm—in situations where outcomes are not influenced by players' efforts, where actors are largely freed from the necessity of choice. In this sort of recreation, strategy and skill are inapplicable. All that is required or desired in play is the passive acceptance of variability in fateful circumstances. Such people fulfill the prediction of Dostoyevsky's Grand Inquisitor. "I tell thee that man is tormented by no greater anxiety than to find someone quickly to whom he can hand over that gift of freedom with which the ill-fated creature is born" (Dostoyevsky 1972, 42).

When everyday activity is constraining, routinized, invariant, overly structured, when experience of the world is one of excessive regulation and oppressive discipline, then people seek variety and personal challenge in their recreation. They search out occasions for creative self-expression, more puzzling problems, and difficult tests. They yearn for freedom of choice, for situations where outcomes hinge on the volitional control of players. Resources are purposely limited to decrease the probability of success and ensure that the uncertainty of these outcomes is maximized.

In short, those who experience a surplus of certainty in their daily lives, i.e., those who are alienated, will seek uncertainty in play. On the other hand, those who view the world as mainly uncertain, i.e., anomic persons, will seek certainty in recreation.

Donald Ball (1972) supported these arguments in his article "What the Action Is: A Cross-Cultural Approach." He noted that recreational activity falls along a continuum of action in which participants have greater or lesser degrees of control over the play. In some action situations, such as mountain climbing, players are "control oriented." By virtue of their skills and strategies, they exercise considerable influence over outcomes. In other situations such as "fair" dice games, participants have little control, are more "acceptance oriented." Ball argues that the type of action sought by players depends on the amount of perceived risk or uncertainty experienced by them in everyday nonplay affairs—"*control oriented* action is positively associated with sociocultural units where regularly perceived risk is low . . . [and] *acceptance oriented* action is positively associated with sociocultural units where the regularly perceived risk is high" (Ball 1972, 126).

To test these hypotheses, Ball used data from Murdock's (1967) *Ethnographic Atlas* and Textor's (1967) *A Cross-Cultural Survey*. He identified seven indicators of potential risk, including scarcity of food supply, degree of urbanization, and several measures of political integration, leadership, and organizational complexity. These indicators were compared to the games most popular and prevalent in four hundred societies/cultures indexed by Textor, dichotomized as control-oriented versus acceptance-oriented activities. In general, these data support his hypotheses and he concludes that the "Type of action is a function of risk, and more specifically, that deliberate risk-taking [control orientation] is associated with the absence of perceived risk in everyday life. Action is searched for where and when it is not likely to be found; when it is extraordinary rather than ordinary" (Ball 1972, 134).

This effort at cross-cultural validation is as laudable as it is unusual for sociological research, but it provides only a gross understanding of the climber's everyday circumstances. With Ball in mind, one would predict that mountaineering would be most prevalent among members of those societies where safety and stability characterize routine affairs. Robin Campbell, in his address to the British National Mountaineering Conference, March 1974, guessed a similar relationship. "I suspect that a case could be made for the view that a strong interest in mountaineering only arises in countries where the people are denied the opportunity for meaningful work, where they live lives relatively free from personal danger, and where they are obliged to live in squalid surroundings in large cities" (Campbell 1974, 31). In support of these predictions, observe that there are relatively many mountaineers from Britain, France, Germany, Switzerland, Japan, and the U.S.A., while there are relatively few from Uganda, Ethiopia, Turkey, Peru, Pakistan, Nepal, Vietnam, and Cambodia.[1] But the sociocultural unit is a bit ungainly for my purposes. It might be stated correctly that Americans climb mountains, but which Americans? Certainly the majority do not. Control- and acceptance-oriented actions are both readily available in this country. Los Angeles residents can reach the peaks of the Sierra Nevada and the gaming tables of Las Vegas with similar ease. Why do some choose the mountains and others the gambling casinos?

Ball's argument can be applied to persons within a given sociocultural unit. In modern, highly industrialized societies such as the United States, risk will be experienced differentially. Some will find their circumstances routinely more threatening and tenuous than others. Who would be likely to face such regular risk and uncertainty?—those persons who have hazardous, low-prestige occupations, insecure employment, less education; the politically disenfranchised; minorities and other stigmatized groups that have less than average control over their own life space and experience. This is the segment of the population that would be expected, following Ball's hypothesis, to seek high-certainty recreational activity in contrast to the unpredictability of their daily affairs. Climbers emerge from the obverse of this group.

If Ball is correct, mountaineers will be found in circumstances where certainty and security is normal, risk and uncertainty improbable, in safe and prestigious occupations with secure employment; hence, they will be well-educated, white, middle- and upper-class individuals. The climber's everyday affairs should be characterized by stability and permanence in both interpersonal relations and institutional position. How well do those anticipations fit the empirical reality of the mountaineer?

Attributes of Mountaineers

Two sources of information are available to help answer this question. The first is a sketchy but intriguing description of early British climbers; the second, survey data from a sample of Southern California mountaineers.

Arnold Lunn assembled a list of the first members of the British Alpine Club, the prototype for mountaineering organizations. He included those who joined between the club's foundation in 1857 and 1863. These early mountaineers are described as follows:

> Of the first 281 members, 57 were barristers and 23 solicitors; 34 were clergymen, 15 dons and 7 schoolmasters. . . . There were 5 scientists, 4 professional authors, 4 artists, 2 architects, 2 librarians, and 1 lecturer. The Civil Service was represented by 12, the Army by 7, and the Royal Navy by 2 members. There were 2 publishers, 5 engineers, 6 printers, stationers, and engravers, 8 barbers, 4 insurance agents, 2 railway directors, 2 estate agents, 5 stockbrokers, 18 merchants. The club included 3 professional politicans, 13 rentiers, 19 landed gentry, 4 foreign members, and 7 whose professions cannot be ascertained.
>
> Of the first 281 members not more than 3 belonged by birth to the old aristocracy. The social structure of the club was predominantly middle or upper-middle class. Most of its recruits came from city dwellers. (Lunn 1957, 43–44)

Apparently Ball's framework is adequate to account for the characteristics of the early British mountaineers. They were, as anticipated, in occupations indicating economic success, safety, and security, better education, and community respect. A look at contemporary Southern California climbers offers further support for this argument.

In the spring of 1976, an opportunity arose to obtain demographic information from a sample of Southern California Sierra Club mountaineers. Respondents were the teachers, leaders, and other staff of the club's Mountaineering Training Committee (MTC). MTC activities include the training and certification of Sierra Club trip leaders and the teaching of the Basic Mountain Training Course (BMTC) to 1,000 would-be climbers in Los Angeles and Orange counties each year.

My own position within the MTC was that of "data analyst." In this capacity I was responsible at that time for the ongoing program of information-gathering and interpretation designed to monitor the progress and development of the Basic Mountaineering Training Course and students. This entailed the solicitation of students' suggestions for improvements and evaluation of student competence via various questionnaires and objective examinations. Incidentally, but importantly, the data analyst attended MTC planning meetings, and I was thus provided a legitimate role through which interaction with MTC staff could be maintained.

In discussions with the MTC chairperson and other key committee members it was decided that a more complete knowledge of staff members' demographic makeup, experience, abilities, and a polling of their opinions regarding issues or course curriculum would be of use for long-range planning. The data reported here are a result of a questionnaire mailed to all of the committee's 149 members. Respondents were cooperative and enthusiastic.[2] With due consideration for the validity problems of any fixed-or-limited response category, paper-and-pencil survey research (see Phillips 1971), these data can be considered a reasonably faithful reflection of the characteristics of the respondents being evaluated.

It was noted previously that not all climbers are associated with or participate in club activities. Some prefer the company of a few of their friends to the less intimate companionship of a club-sponsored climb. Others prefer to plan their own trips with the freedom to establish their own goals, priorities, and paces. To the extent that these individuals predominate among mountaineers, the sample utilized here is not representative of the climbing population as a whole. But, estimating the size of this unaffiliated group is difficult.[3] It is my clear impression that a majority if not most climbers are associated with climbing clubs or organizations at least at the beginning of their mountaineering careers.[4] Climbing mountains is far too serious a business to be learned directly from instructions or by trial and error. Most would-be mountaineers seek formal instruction through school- or club-sponsored classes, and the Sierra Club offers one of the largest programs of climbing-oriented instruction in the country. That the MTC represents a core element in the Sierra Club's climbing cadre is less questionable. MTC members are some of the club's most active and enthusiastic mountaineers. Their dedication to the sport is further underlined by their willingness to expend considerable time, energy, and money as volunteers in training BMTC students and trip leaders and performing other instructional and evaluative tasks. At a minimum, the data here came from respondents who speak for the most dedicated component of an important climbing organization.

The 108 climbers who participated in the survey had the following characteristics. All respondents were Caucasian: 94 (88 percent) were male, 13 (12 percent) female. They ranged in age from 15 to 58, with a mean and median age of 38 years. Regarding marital status, 27 percent were single; 60 percent married or living with someone; and 13 percent widowed, divorced, or separated. The married/living-together group had been together with spouse/lover for an average of nine years and had an average of 1.1 children. Almost all respondents (96 percent) had some college training. Half held college degrees and had done some postgraduate work. About one-quarter (26 percent) held graduate-level degrees; 7 percent had doctorates or the equivalent.[5]

Occupational choices of the respondents showed an interesting and significant bias in favor of the applied physical sciences. Fifty of 108 respondents, or 46 percent of the total, identified their work as aerospace design or production, applied mathematics, electronic and phototechnical tasks, computer programming, and the like. Of this group, 34, or 31 percent of the total, explicitly listed their occupations as one form or another of engineer. By comparison, less than 1.6 percent of the 1970 work force was classified as engineers (U.S. Department of Commerce, Bureau of the Census 1973, Table1). Academia accounted for 18 percent of the respondents, with 7 teachers, 3 university professors, and 9 students, again, primarily in the physical sciences. Business and sales pursuits occupied another 14 percent: 5 persons in finance and accounting, 7 in retail sales, and 3 in commercial-art design and decorating. Another 9 percent were in various managerial and administrative positions, four of which were in aerospace or electronics. Two respondents were in law, one retired, and the remainder did not respond with sufficient data to allow classification. The noteworthy proportion of applied-science occupations in the sample is fortuitous. The experiences of applied scientists serve especially well to illustrate the effects of a growing rational-scientific world view in industrialized nations. However, these effects are not limited to doers of practical science, especially in a narrow sense of particular occupational categories such as "engineer." While examples of the scientist-technician are used in the discussion to follow it is with the caveat that many other persons with professional skills and training are similarly influenced.

In summary, a typical MTC mountaineer is a male Caucasian about thirty-eight years of age. He has been married about nine years and has one child. He is a college graduate and is employed in some aspect of applied physical science, most frequently as an engineer in the electronics or aerospace industry. The results indicate that the mountain climbers surveyed come from stable social surroundings, enjoy economic security, and have considerable education and occupational prestige.[5] Confidence in these demographic data is increased by comparing them to the results of another survey of mountain climbers. Bratton, Kinnear, and Koroluk (1979, 55–57) obtained demographic descriptions of 266 members of the Calgary Section of the Alpine Club of Canada. Although their questionnaire items and response categories were not entirely comparable to my own, the similarity between the results of the two surveys at a number of points is striking. Respondents from both groups of climbers were similar with regard to sex distribution, age, marital status, education, and length of time involved in climbing (see table 12.1).

Ball's contention that those in social environments characterized by relative certainty will seek control-oriented uncertainty in their recreational activities would seem to be correct. Those with minimal likelihood of experiencing uncertainty in their daily affairs—white, middle-class, married males in established and respected careers—are also those found pursuing mountaineering and similar avocational activities.

Table 12.1 Comparison of American and Canadian Club-Climbers

	Groups Surveyed	
	Angeles Chapter of the Sierra Club, Mountaineering Training Committee (N = 108)	Calgary Section, Alpine Club of Canada (N = 266)
Sex	Male, 88%; female, 12%	Male, 80%; female, 20%
Age	38 (mean, median)	30–39 (most frequent response category)
Marital Status		
Married	60%	57%
Married with children	41%	40%
Education		
Some college or technical school training	96%	89%
College/university degree	62%	62%
Graduate school training	47%	27%
Doctoral degree or equivalent	7%	6%
Length of time respondent has participated in mountaineering:	3–5 years (most frequent response category)	3–5 years (most frequent response category)

The reader may feel a commonsensical contradition beginning to emerge here. If the notion is accepted that alienation, especially in the world of work, motivates a search for control-oriented risk, then why is it that engineers, technicians, and other professionals climb mountains? Surely assembly-line workers, keypunch and telephone-switchboard operators, theater ticket-takers, mail sorters, and a whole range of other clerical personnel must also find their work alienating, confining, bereft of opportunity for creative self-expression, to an equal or greater extent than scientists, technicians, and the like. In fact, are not today's engineers and technicians, for example, viewed as special sorts of skilled and respected craftspersons? Are they not the elite who, guided by the principles of science, wield the powerful and sophisticated tools of technology in creating a better world for all humankind? Is their work not inherently purposeful, meaningful, and challenging? So many people believe.

The problem lies not in the absolute but the relative deprivation experienced by scientists, engineers, technicians and similar others. While clerks, laborers, and assembly-line workers may encounter few opportunities for creativity and self-expression, they often expect no more. Many of these workers have already abandoned the quest for personal creativity as a capacity beyond them or inevitably denied them and leave it at that. A job is a job, they say; what matters is the pay and security. "The average manual worker and many white collar employees may be satisfied with fairly steady jobs which are largely instrumental and non-involving, because they have not the need for responsibility and self-expression in work. They are relatively content with work which is simply a means to the larger end of providing the pay checks" (Blauner 1970, 96).

Walter Kaufmann reminds us that modern education misleads many persons concerning their creative potential and the opportunities before them, ultimately resulting in their abandonment of a search for creative outlets altogether.

> Nobody is creative all the time, and nobody is creative none of the time. Unfortunately many people approximate the latter extreme, especially as they grow older. But this is due in part to two great errors. Their education gives them far too romantic an idea of creativity and then persuades them that they are creative in its wholly exceptional sense. Most men discover soon enough that they are not, and then give up. In effect, they swallow the false notion that there are two kinds of men, and their resignation is often poisoned by resentment against those who do not give up. (Kaufmann, in Schacht 1970 lii-liii)

But not everyone abandons the search for creativity. Some, in fact, are given little choice in the matter. It is expected that scientists and their pragmatic helpers, the engineers and technicians along with some other skilled professionals, will actively seek creative self-expression in their work. While the assembly-line laborer may abandon this elusive hope, the scientist or successful businessman may not. He is driven to succeed in this search, not only by his own unrealistic training but by the opinions of others regarding the proper enactment of his role.

The scientist, engineer, and technician again provide clear examples. Throughout their training these professionals are inculcated with the idea that their chosen work in life will be contributory, creative, and meaningful. They come to believe that science, through the rational study and manipulation of a physical universe, presumably governed by predictable and immutable laws, will advance humankind toward a better understanding and control of the world. Proper science, good science, science well done will lead incrementally but inexorably toward freedom from toil and travail by the creation of more and better machines and technologies. But the realities they encounter in the world of work do much to undermine this positivistic hope. They soon discover that much of what they are called upon to do on the job is less than helpful and more than a little dull, particularly for the applied scientist, technician, or other professional. These persons in particular experience a considerable schism between their academic preparation and actual work experience. Their training consists of learning broad theoretical principles, but that knowledge is often put to use in narrow, pragmatic circumstances. The structural engineer may imagine a career building great bridges or skyscrapers and wind up designing door knobs for iceboxes. The chemist looks forward to making dramatic research breakthroughs in alternatives to fossil fuels and finds himself monitoring gauges at an oil refinery.[6]

Certainly, many students find that their life's work is poorly articulated with the ideals that they developed during their school years. But the applied scientist, technician, and a few others—the professional symphony musician, for example—are not given leave to temper these ideals with reality. He or she differs from others who make a similar discovery following the completion of their education. These special professionals are still held *by others* to be creative individuals. Applied science, for example, is presumed by nonscientists to be by definition the search for creative solutions to real and important problems. Work as a symphony performer, it is believed, must reflect the highest form of musical artistic expression.

The facts may be otherwise. The work of designing and building modern bridges and buildings is highly differentiated. In such projects the role of the individual engineer is sharply limited and often of much less importance to final outcomes than that of bankers, promoters and other money manipulators. The company research scientist may be limited in his or her investigations to the development and refinement of products designed to exploit markets, not to solve larger technical or social problems. A few are employed even more narrowly in amassing proofs of product purity and otherwise meeting the challenges of government agency inspectors and consumer advocates. The symphony orchestra is also a formal organization. Musicians learn that technical accuracy, punctuality, and obedience are more stringent requirements for continued membership than individual creative expression in star solo performances. These realities of the scientists, technicians, and other professionals' lives are often obscured from persons outside these occupations. As far as the latter are concerned, the scientist or professional still is and must be a creator and they act toward him or her accordingly. Scientific and professional work must be meaningful, even if theirs is not, they say; the scientist must be engrossed, fascinated, inspired. Thus, scientists and similar others experience recurring social encounters where they are expected to take their work seriously; to act, at least outwardly, as if it were rewarding and purposeful. They are not allowed the luxury of self-indulgent bitterness toward their disappointing jobs. Rather, they are continually reminded of what their work ideally entails and are called upon to demonstrate enthusiasm for these ideals.

Against this steady pressure for an outward show of purposefulness and creativity, particularly scientists and technicians may be all too aware of Thomas Kuhn's (1962) well-made point that advances in science are revolutionary, not accretive. They may realize that such revolutions are few and far between, requiring the inspiration of an Einstein and the messianic gumption of a Martin Luther King. These qualities of extraordinary perception and zeal are perhaps the very ones that were suppressed during one's training in favor of methodological rigor and classical grounding.

Underutilization of talent and limited scope of action are not the only causes of alienation for professionals. Obviously not all engineering and related work is inherently meaningless. Yet, even when the job being done is important as well as stimulating to the doer, it may still pose problems in everyday interaction with others, problems which lead to experiences of alienation. A sociologist with a marriage and family-counseling practice in Southern California put it this way:

> I have many engineers . . . as clients. Two quite different elements often lead to feelings of alienation on their parts. (1) They often work on such technically specialized projects that it takes them weeks to explain to colleagues and superiors what they are doing at work—it frequently isn't worth the effort since really those people are more interested in the results than in the way

they are obtained. As for wives, family, neighbors, forget it! (2) Becoming accustomed to security clearances (either due to fear of industrial piracy or government secrecy) these guys get out of the habit of talking to *anybody* about *anything*—I suspect the same habits affect socializing and recreation. (Lasswell 1979)

During the 1979 Pacific Sociological Association meetings, in a section on "Alienation in Work and Leisure," a similar point was made by a member of the audience, a former engineer turned sociologist. He pointed out that engineers often do see themselves as solving important problems. The frustration they feel, the alienation they experience, comes from a failure to see those solutions adopted and implemented in practical circumstances. The product of the engineer's labor, he argued, is not just ideas but ideas with tangible applications in the real world. When the translation of concepts into concrete realities is delayed or distorted or denied by political or economic or even ethical concerns, engineers, according to this person, experience their work as remaining incomplete, as being less than fully meaningful. Another engineer, quoted by Tracy Kidder in *The Soul of a New Machine*, expresses similar sentiments. "Ninety-eight percent of the thrill comes from knowing that the thing you designed works, and works almost the way you expected it would. If that happens, part of *you* is in that machine" (Guyer, in Kidder 1981, 273). Kidder argues that gratifying experiences of this sort are usual for many engineers.

Engineers are supposed to stand among the privileged members of industrial enterprises, but . . . a fairly large percentage of engineers in America are not content with their jobs. Among the reasons . . . are the nature of the jobs themselves and the restrictive ways in which they are managed. Among the terms used to describe their malaise are *declining technical challenge; misutilization; limited freedom of action; tight control of working patterns*. (Kidder 1981, 273)

While engineering work may be unsatisfactory, it is not atypical in that respect of the work of a large segment of professionally trained persons today. Instead of finding creative self-expression in work, and because that work stimulates others to remind them constantly of what that work could, should, and ought to be, applied scientists and professionals are alienated to a greater extent than others. In that alienation lies a motive for mountaineering. The mountains offer an alternative arena to the world of work and other routine life-experiences, an arena in which meaningful and creative self-expression may realistically be found. To the mountaineer, the mountains offer the antithesis of alienation; they offer the potential for flow.

Summary

In discussing the motives for mountaineering, I have suggested that persons are both drawn to the mountains in search of flow and driven to that search by alienating circumstances in their occupations and other central role experiences. In discussing alienation and anomie, I have met one of the principal objections raised by Kaufmann (in Schact 1970, xxiv) that it be specified from *what* one is alienated. It is my contention that alienation and anomie are more simply viewed as end points in the continuum characterized by greater and lesser certainty about the outcomes of interaction. The midpoint between these two extremes, the goal which is sought, the "opposite" of alienation and anomie is the holistic experience Csikszentmihalyi (1974) refers to as flow. In the climbing of mountains, participants find great opportunity for flow.

Some persons, especially in work, come to perceive their circumstances as predominately of alienating certainty or anomic uncertainty. Ball (1972) demonstrated at the sociocultural level that prevailing uncertainty or anomie leads to a search for acceptance or a fatalistic sort of avocational risk-taking, such as gambling. On the other hand, prevailing perceptions of certainty or alienation engender an interest in control or volitional risk-taking, such as mountaineering. Applying Ball's scheme to members of given sociocultural units, we observe that those who enjoy financial security, interpersonal stability, and prestige, those whose life experiences are characterized by certainty and predictability, are the same ones who seek control-oriented sport. Barbara Zeller, a Colorado mountaineer, describes the relationship between perceived social conditions and climbing in this way:

> Most people today are secure, financially and socially. . . . We have all the conveniences and comforts, but it's like living in an elaborately decorated cell. . . . There is nothing mystical about the way we are controlled and over-governed by rules and systems. Others control you. You are like a puppet; you don't make your own moves. . . . Sure, [climbing is] an escape, but it's escape from the control of others. . . . If it is escape, it's escape from others back to yourself. You get yourself back again for awhile. (Zeller, in Jenkins 1979, 20)

In a survey of Sierra Club mountaineers, it was noted that professional persons, especially engineers, tehnicians, and other applied scientists, were prevalent. It was argued that these persons experience significant relative deprivation in work. Unlike people in other occupations, applied scientists and similar professionals are subject to frequent and ongoing pressure from others to act as if their work were creative and meaningful in spite of its often routine and mundane qualities. This continual pressure leads to a heightened sense of alienation in work and a search for flow in recreation.

Finally, all of this takes place amid a vague public acceptance of mountaineering. The Appendix outlines the results of a nationwide poll of nonclimbers' impressions of mountaineers. Americans appear to know little about the climbing world, but what impressions they do have are more positive or neutral than negative. If people choose to climb, their efforts are more likely to receive impetus than impediment from the community. If flow can be found in mountaineering, then nonclimbers are likely to accept and even encourage that search (see also Catton 1969, 123–26).

The issue of climber motivation will be examined again in the concluding chapters in the context of the broader social phenomenon of rationalization. For now, it is time to sum up, to bring together the themes of climbing process and climber identity and motive in a concrete example of mountain adventure.

13
Benuzzi's Tale

To set the scene for some final remarks and to underscore many of the topics discussed throughout this book, I would like to offer one extended example of mountaineering action. This takes the form of a story, an account of three climbers and a climb, drawn from a single source. It is not a fanciful tale constructed for purposes of illustration. The events described are part of a very real mountaineering adventure carefully documented in the fine book *No Picnic on Mount Kenya,* written by one of the principals, Felice Benuzzi (1952). In order to condense Benuzzi's rich and subtle report into a manageable length, it is necessary to abbreviate some events and add occasional emphasis to others. At all times I try to convey the spirit of the action as an ongoing social experience, without misrepresenting significant facts. This story is not well-known, even among ardent climbers, being contained in one thin volume of limited circulation now long out of print. It is worth retelling to any audience interested in the process, motives, demands, and rewards of climbing mountains.

Felice Benuzzi knew it would happen. Standing at attention before the camp commandant, he heard his sentence pronounced. It was what he expected. For escape: twenty-eight days on bread and water in the vermin-infested high-security block of POW camp 354. Benuzzi did not really mind. Others had fared worse. Most never got away at all. Beside, he had always intended to come back—as soon as he climbed the mountain.

In 1941 the world was torn by war. Benuzzi entered the service of his country. His classical education, multilingual abilities, fame as an international-class swimmer, and distinguished career as a lawyer made him well-suited for the diplomatic corps. These talents were soon recognized and he was assigned to an important post in Africa. As fighting raged across that continent, he was captured by the enemy in Ethiopia and declared a prisoner of war. He and hundreds of his countrymen were sent, packed into cattle cars, to an internment camp "for the duration of hostilities." It was there that the suffering began.

Physical privations were not the worst part of camp life. To be sure, there were shortages, discomforts, and sometimes rough treatment. The dusty clay compound, baked by the equatorial sun, held ten thousand prisoners, living crowded together in tin sheds. Ever-watchful, armed guards looked down from towers along the double rank of barbed-wire fencing. Food was limited and dull, personal items in short supply, privacy nonexistent, camp rules strictly enforced. Yet, for most prisoners, camp 354 was not a place where bodily pain and want were keenly felt. The keepers were not intentionally cruel men, only indifferent ones.

Far worse than physical need was the despairing monotony of daily routines, the ever-present reminders of personal failure and uselessness. The prisoners were no longer treated as feared and respected adversaries. Rather, they were dealt with like dependent children, kept living in a dream world by their grown-up captors who were busy elsewhere with the grim reality of life. The camp smothered them. They were engulfed by the terrible hopelessness of unending, certain sameness. Tomorrow would be like yesterday, and today—reasonably safe, absolutely secure, utterly maddening.

Time was the true enemy. How long would the war go on? Unlike ordinary prisoners they could not mark the days till the ends of their sentences. How long must these able men endure enforced idleness? How long must they live without purpose or direction, without meaningful tasks to engage the mind and body? Benuzzi reflects:

> Forced to endure in the *milieu* we seemed almost afraid of losing our individuality. Sometimes one felt a childish urge to assert one's personality in almost any manner, shouting nonsense, banging an empty tin, showing by every act that one was still able to do something other than to wait passively. . . . The past was finished; there was nothing more to think about, to grasp. A normal life in the future seemed so far off, so impossible. . . . Only the present existed, unavoidable, overwhelming. For me, Time stood still. It was easy to understand how people go mad. . . . A prisoner of the last war wrote in his memoirs: "At the front one takes risks, but one does not suffer; in captivity one does not take risks, but one suffers." In order to break the monotony of life one had to start taking risks again, to try to get out of this Noah's Ark which was preserving us from the risks of war by isolating us from the world, to get out into the deluge of life. (Pp. 24, 25–26; this and all subsequent quotations in this chapter are from Benuzzi 1952).)

At camp 354, many longed to escape, but to get away, at least in the conventional sense, was nearly impossible. Getting past the barbed wire and guards would be difficult but it was beyond the perimeter that the greatest obstacle lay—Black Africa. Outside the camp, the only white Europeans at large were enemies. A prisoner might flee, but not far. He could not blend inconspicuously into crowds, fabricate a credible identity, travel undetected. The prisoners were condemned by their language and skin color to a perpetual and glaring foreignness.

Benuzzi, too, longed for freedom, to return to the world of action, to usefully engage himself in the business of living, to work at determining his own fate.

> As I approached my barrack I heard the noise of hammering. I wondered who was busy at that hour of the night and what he was doing. A strange sense of envy crept into my mind. The prisoner had set himself a task, whatever it was. For him the future existed for presumably he intended to finish the job. For the moment he had found a remedy against captivity. . . . I was thinking "The future exists if you know how to make it. . . . It's up to you." (P. 25)

Benuzzi realized that only by making a concerted effort toward some self-selected goal could he rescue himself from the slow, sinking suffocation of the camp. But what goal? The answer came on a brief walk one evening at sunset. He stopped for a moment and looked up, beyond the compound, into the darkening sky. There, wreathed in angry clouds eleven thousand feet above him, rose the glacier-studded blue-black rock summit of 17,058-foot Mount Kenya. He had found his challenge.

At that moment a bold plan was born. Benuzzi would escape camp 354, but not to reach some distant neutral land, carry military information to his superiors, or rejoin the combatants. Benuzzi sought freedom in another way. He would escape a prisoner-of-war camp to climb one of the great and beautiful mountains of the world. With that inspiration, the draining hopelessness of camp life began to fall away. With this newfound purpose, he was free again, to create, imagine, strive, prepare, build, achieve. The mountain gave him back himself. He was grateful.

The obstacles to overcome were awesome. Even supposing the barbed wire could be breeched and the guards evaded, other hazards lay beyond. Both the mountain's flora and fauna were, at best, unfriendly. The camphor forests ringing the base of the peak were blanketed by six-foot stinging nettles. In the zone above, giant Lobelia and groundsels grew in a rain-drenched near-vertical bog dotted with four-foot-high grass and earth tussocks which made footing difficult and tiresome. Benuzzi learned that elephant herds had been seen grazing at 11,000 feet; groups of water buffalo had attacked a previous climbing party, only being driven off by rifle fire that killed two of the beasts. In another instance, a water buffalo in a rage was observed to kill a male lion. Higher on the mountain, he knew he would face cold, wind-driven sleet and snow at subfreezing temperatures. Avalanches might thunder down from above while gaping glacial crevasses opened at his feet. Finally, in the thin air of high altitude, he must meet the last challenge, the ice-sheathed ramparts of the summit pyramid. It would not be an easy climb, but a worthy one. It would take eight months of planning, preparation, saving, negotiation, conditioning, sacrifice, and effort before his plan could be tested in reality.

For Benuzzi's adventure to succeed he needed companions. This posed an initial problem for he could not openly announce his intentions in order to locate other interested parties. It required many weeks of dropping hints, seemingly casual references to the mountain and moun-taineering, making guesses, tentative offers, and finally negotiation be-fore two willing accomplices were found. Giuan was a physician and a climber himself. He joined the enterprise in its early stages and helped in many of the important preparations. Enzo was recruited just prior to departure. In spite of frail health and recurring bouts of malaria, he proved to be a loyal and hard-working supporter. But companions alone were not enough to overcome the mountain's defenses. Food, clothing, maps, ropes, and related climbing paraphernalia must also be assembled. Meeting these needs posed other problems.

How do people get ready, in secret, inside the walls of a prison camp, to climb a major mountain? Some examples of their patient resourceful-ness are enlightening. Benuzzi quit smoking. His weekly ration of cigarettes was then used as cash in the prison economy to purchase needed items, particularly food scraps. The camp tailor was bribed into sewing a warm jacket from remnants of Benuzzi's only blankets. He fashioned other pieces of material into mittens and a hat himself. Jogging, callisthenics, and soccer aided physical conditioning. The camp cobbler surreptitiously restitched their boots, studding the soles with nails for traction. Mutton fat from the kitchen provided waterproofing for the leather. Sixty paper arrows were trimmed from discarded newsprint and painted red with stolen supplies. These were to serve as markers showing the way back off the mountain to high camp, in storms. For a map they had only the picture label from a meat-ration can that used Mount Kenya as a logo. For climbing ropes they pressed into service seventy feet of aging sisal cord that supported their bed mattresses.

Using bits of steel from the mudguards of an abandoned truck and pieces of the barbed wire fence that encircled the camp, they fabricated crampons to fit their boots for travel on hard snow and ice. The essential climbers' tools, ice axes, were fashioned from stolen hammer heads secretly reworked at the camp forge and ingeniously fitted to steel-tipped hardwood shafts. A worn tarp was restitched into a tent-shelter. Sewing together remnants of colored cloth, Benuzzi even constructed a small flag to raise upon the summit. Special rock-climbing shoes were made using unraveled sisal bags, an old tarpaulin, and many hours of hard labor. As completed gear and supplies were assembled, they were smuggled out and buried in the furrows of a vegetable garden that was tended by a few prisoners just outside the main gate.

In these and a myriad of other creations they more or less prepared themselves for the challenges of the mountain. There remained, however, one major uncompromising obstacle. To climb the mountain they must first escape the camp. This problem was solved in an ingenious and straightforward way.

The main gate to the encampment was overseen by native guards in nearby towers. From time to time this gate would be unlocked by one of the wardens, and trustee prisoners, singly or in small groups, would be sent to perform outside errands or work on the camp vegetable plot. It was easy for the guards to distinguish between the European prisoners and their keepers by their dress. Prisoners wore shirts with large emblems on the backs, indicating their inmate status; compound officers wore khaki shorts, socks and shirts, and, of course, carried the keys to the gate.

Benuzzi's plan called for the combination of some masterful fabrications and a simple ruse. First he needed a duplicate key. After months of patient watchfulness the compound officer left his keys unattended on a table. Benuzzi quickly made impressions of the needed key in a piece of tar he had carried for that purpose. A deft mechanic in the camp was able, after considerable and painstaking labor, to produce a handcrafted duplicate, which, following several "fittings," proved to be a success. Thus, the gate could be opened at will. But the problem of the guards remained. Here Benuzzi replaced stealth with bravado.

Umberto, a friend and fellow prisoner of about the same physical build as the compound officer, was recruited and dressed in officerlike attire—shorts and khaki shirt. A few moments after the genuine officer had retired for lunch, Umberto marched authoritatively to the gate, key in hand, followed by the apparently deferential Benuzzi, Enzo, and Giuan. The latter three carried gardening tools. Opening the gate with the bogus key, he ordered the prisoners to "Come on! Quick!" and ushered them outside as if on some legitimate errand. Umberto then relocked the gate and calmly walked away.

The escapees feigned garden work until the tower sentries were changed. They were then able to slip away and hide themselves until it grew dark. That night they unearthed their buried gear and supplies and entered the jungle.

Just before leaving the camp, Benuzzi had performed an action that must be judged thoughtful and stylish by any prison-escape standards. He wrote a note to the compound liaison officer as a gentle jibe at his captors and in the hopes of sparing his barracks mates any recriminations.

> Sir,
>
> We have not previously informed you of our intentions, sure that you would try to dissuade us. We are leaving the camp and reckon to be back within fourteen days. Then you will know and certainly approve of our action. We assure you formally that in escaping we have not misused our passes [to work outside the perimeter] given to us. . . . In order to avoid any such suspicion, we hand over to you herewith the above mentioned passes bearing our names.
>
> We regret causing you this bother, and remain, Sir, etc., etc. (P. 70)

By the time this note was read the next day, Benuzzi and his companions hoped to be far away, three escaped prisoners of war on their way to climb a mountain.

After two days of narrow scrapes with the enemy and thirsty thicket-crawling in the hot, dusty, populous lowlands, the trio at last reached the lower fringes of the mountain wilderness. It was a time of rejoicing.

> We had passed the zone in which we might have been seen by men and recaptured. Other dangers were undoubtedly in store for us but not from mankind, only from nature. "More honest dangers" we qualified them.
>
> So hungry for adventure and hazard were we, so convinced of our good luck that joyfully and happily we went on . . . toward the lovely equatorial peaks, into a world untainted by man's misery and bright with promise. (P. 95)

They entered the jungle and set up their evening camp. Adventures were not long in coming.

Spilling the nightwatch coffee on the fire terrified Benuzzi. Now it was dark. Only a memory of flame kept the circling leopard at bay. Furious fanning of the smoldering, soggy bamboo produced no more than steam and splutters. Memory grew dim; the animal crept closer. Sometimes-sensible Enzo awoke just then. He took the situation in at a glance and thought he knew what to do. After all, he had read many adventure stories of brave travelers meeting wild beasts. Some were even true stories, thankfully. Catching up the metal cooking pot and cups he banged them together with enthusiasm. The din shattered the predawn jungle quiet, sending the irritated leopard sliding back into the bush in search of quieter and perhaps fatter prey. Momentarily Giuan joined them by the reborn fire. Each tried to conceal his shivering, for it was not at all cold. Another day on the mountain had begun.

Traveling was not easy. Their intention was to follow a streambed up through the jungle forest to a climbing base camp near the great glaciers above. From the beginning this route was more than they had bargained for. The way was steep and slippery, over moss-covered stones along the watercourse, with diversions around waterfalls and cliffs. These side trips were fraught with special difficulty. The stream was edged with high, steep slopes of rotting vegetation, slippery with ooze. They struggled upward by clinging to loose bamboo shoots and standing on small tussocks of crumbling earth. Vines and creepers ensnared their feet and clung to their heavy packs, pulling them backwards. The rocky streambed, sometimes a hundred or more feet below, beckoned threateningly.

At night they searched for open space to construct their camp where fire and watchfulness could be maintained against wandering animals. Leopards were not their only problem. Rhino were frequent in the area. A bull elephant wandered by within twenty yards. To penetrate the dripping, clogged undergrowth required much hauling, hacking, pushing, and mutual assistance. Without adequate food, they were soon exhausted by this regimen. Their travel time fell to little more than three hours a day, slower than they had hoped, woefully slower than their supplies allowed. Even under the best circumstances they would have had too little food, only five days' worth by modern scientific standards. They planned to stretch it twice that far, but in the end the trip was to take much longer. Starvation as well as mountain summits lay ahead. Wearily they pushed on.

On the seventh day they left the forest jungle. The transition was abrupt. Cacophonous steaming green gave way suddenly to silent gray stone and heather. Here they felt the power of the mountain. Their enchantment had begun. "Everything seemed more sedate in this new world, almost solemn as though there was a spell in the air" (p. 124).

Giuan and Benuzzi climbed a small knoll to scout for a camping place. As they stood atop the hill, a mist enveloped them. The spell grew stronger.

> A gentle breeze rose from the mountain, and passing through the thousand needle-like leaves of the heather, played on them a tenuous, soft, weird music. It started *piano* like a tune on a flute and it increased, *mezzoforte, forte,* till it resembled a magic harp concert. We looked at each other and listened fascinated. The arpeggio rose and fell, . . . accompanied by a deeper music which started like the fluttering of wings and strengthened to the sound of a double-bass, caused by branches of heath-trees rubbing one

against the other. I have never listened to anything so eerie, so
unearthly. We felt both very humble. Were we worthy of hearing
this wondrous music? (P. 124)

The spell passed as quickly as it came. Mysterious music was replaced
by mundane misery. The sky burst forth with the torrential rain that only
equatorial storms provide and a cold wind set in, the cold that blows only
at 11,000 feet on a mountain. They had no time to erect the tent but
huddled together, clutching it about them like an ungainly cloak, trying
to shelter their rucksacks and a few sticks of wood for the hoped-for fire. It
was no use. The rain drove under the edges and soon people and
possessions were completely soaked. The storm continued for hours.

The mountain world is one of contrasts, of delight and disappointment, hope and despair, cynicism and faith. Climbers may celebrate their
liberation and curse their lonely frailty in close order without contradic-
tion to the larger meaning of mountaineering. These contrasts reflect
upon each other and sharpen the cutting edge of perception. Sometimes
the mountaineer trembles and aches and remembers the life left below.
After the storm, Benuzzi awoke from fitful exhausted dozing.

I realized where I was. It was a hideous reality I had to face, as a
damp cold penetrated by clothing and a heavy weariness was
about to drag me into the depths. . . . What unpardonable stu-
pidity to have made the escape and to have left my warm snug
bunk and blankets in order to come up here into this cold. (P. 86)

As the sky cleared, the plains of Nanyuki could be seen spreading out to
the west from the base of the mountain. In the rain-scrubbed air the
distant prison camp was clearly visible. The mood began to change. At
first they were silenced by the sight. Then Benuzzi had other recollections. He remembered

All the hours, days, months, years spent in doing just nothing
but trying to keep oneself sane and clean as possible; and all that
amid the most sickening pettiness and meanness of human nature, as is inevitable in the confined artificial life of people of all
ages and conditions, on the wrong side of the wire. How remote
that life seemed, and was! (P. 127)

The contrast between the camp and their present circumstances caught
them up, heightened their sense of liberation. They were more than
physically free now, they were transformed. The prison was behind them
and so, for a time, were their prison identities. When Benuzzi exclaimed
"Look there! Isn't that the railway line? . . . And further on . . . Yes, it is

our camp!" Giuan quickly corrected him. "You're wrong. It is not *our* camp that you see. It is the camp where we *were* prisoners" (p. 127). They grew animated, chattering to each other excitedly, pointing out various details of the compound. As it grew dark, they laughed and joked and built a huge bonfire visible, they reckoned, to everyone in the prison. With their last few drops of home-brewed pineapple brandy, they toasted their good fortune and turned in for the night. Tomorrow would be their final hiking day. After that came the climb.

Enzo, unconscious, lay gasping on the ground. Giuan, the physician, turned the limp body over and put his ear to his companion's chest. Benuzzi had gone ahead but now came rushing back, breathless. "Is Enzo's heart bad?" he asked. "Yes," answered Giuan in a harsh voice. "Make some coffee please. Quick." (p. 135). The 14,000-foot altitude had almost claimed a victim. They were making good progress through the heather when disaster struck. On a short rest-break, impetuous, middle-aged Enzo left his pack and ran chasing after a bird. His tired, under-nourished body was no match for his youthful spirit and he collapsed after a short dash. Now the coffee was ready. Giuan poured a few drops onto Enzo's pale lips. The patient stirred, swallowed, opened his eyes, and smiled weakly. He would recover, but for Enzo this was the end of the line. He could go no higher. For better or worse, this was to become their climbing base. While Enzo rested they set about improving the campsite as best they could. It was not an ideal location, that much they knew, too low to give them a good start on the main summit, Batian, too far away from the secondary peak, Point Lenana. There was much more about the mountain they did not know. They would learn the hard way.

Ignorance is not always a bad thing. As Benuzzi and Giuan sat studying the mountain, it is probably better they were not aware of the full history of the peak. They had not perused guidebooks nor read the details of previous ascents in journals. Mount Kenya had been climbed before, they knew, but that was all. In fact, a few years earlier the illustrious British climbers Tilman and Shipton had scouted the mountain from the side where the camp now lay and quickly realized "the hopelessness of trying to tackle the ridge from Northerly Glacier or of gaining it higher up the north face" (p. 148). Far easier routes lay on the other side of the peak, but of those or the opinions of experts the adventurers had not an inkling. Nor were conditions well-suited for their attempt. When the British aces climbed the peak, it was summer. The rock had been warm and dry. Now it was February, the dead of winter. The escaped prisoners were about to attempt one of the most difficult routes on the mountain in the most contrary conditions. The cold rock would be glazed over with treacherous ice and plastered with snow. Hand and footholds would be scarce and tenuous. Their homemade equipment would be marginal for the task ahead, their physical condition and supplies woefully inadequate.

Ignorance of the conditions before them was perhaps their greatest handicap, at least from the point of view of material achievements, but,

> From the spiritual point of view, which is of far greater importance to the true mountaineer, it was in the nature of a gift from God. Every step led to new discoveries, and we were in a state of amazed admiration and gratitude. It was as though we were living at the beginning of time, before man had begun to give names to things. (P. 151)

The future was unknown, but that left hope.

It was the end of the beginning. The long march was over. After half a day of prowling, sketching, and scouting, they chose a route. They rested and repaired their gear. Now only the final test remained. Above them loomed Batian, named for the greatest of all Masai kings, the 17,000-foot-plus main peak of Mount Kenya. It was too high, too far away, too difficult, to be a realistic goal. But climbers must at times be dreamers as well as practical men. Batian, above all, was too beautiful to pass by without giving one full measure of commitment, one honest try. Tomorrow it would have its due.

At 3 A.M. the climb began. Only starlight framed the crags above. The land was locked in still-frozen quiet. Ice in small depressions cracked beneath their boot nails and tinkled down over the rocks. In the dark, giant groundsels, like sleepy sentinels, seemed to rise ghostlike from the heath as the climbers drew near, then faded behind. Warm breath froze instantly into sparkling fairy dust and clung about their hoods and clothing. Following a small stream, they passed by two pitch-black pools. Now, far above the camp, they stopped to rest.

> The water was so still that we could see the stars of the zenith reflected motionless in it. We lay down and solemnly, as if performing a strange ritual, we drank in small, slow draughts the ice-cold black and starry water. (P. 165)

As they continued steadily up a long scree slope, small loose stones rasped beneath their weight with a soft grinding sound. They worked toward the top of an intervening ridge that blocked their view of the main peak. What lay beyond they did not know. As they drew closer, the massive bulk of the mountain lifted above them, a solid black wall inking out the sky.

At the equator dawn is not protracted. Dark and light are divided by but a momentary line. Other changes may come as quickly. So it would be this day. They moved the last few feet up the slope, the sun and wind rose together, and, without warning, they stepped into a maelstrom.

Violent winds churned the clear air into a raging gale. They were stopped, stunned by the cold. Inside their packs the water bottles froze solid. Cowering down behind rocks they tried to renew their strength. Fingers withdrawn from a mitt to hold a nibbled biscuit turned stiff. Escape from the wind was urgent. They pushed on. Below the ridge the wind suddenly abated. It had only been a warning. They could continue.

They began a long traverse across a sheer face. Fist- and foot-sized holds shrank to tiny nubbins and nitches. Giuan led, Benuzzi belayed with their frail sisal rope. The rope worried them. The coarse double strand between them seemed to be forever kinked and tangled or snagged upon some rocky protrusion. In event of an accident, it would be strong enough to jerk an unstable belayer from his holds, too weak to stop a falling leader if the belay held. Both outcomes were now real possibilities. Their route turned upward toward new obstacles: an ice-filled gully, a vague ledge, a smooth crack overcome only by the strength-sapping counterpressure of arms and legs pulling in opposition on the crack sides. Now, at over 16,000 feet, their lungs labored to sieve precious oxygen from the rarefied air. The hours slipped by but the climbers did not notice. They slipped into a flow of events fixed in an urgent and encompassing present. As their senses sharpened, the mountain's subtleties of texture seemed to leap into clear relief while their bodies responded with delicate control of movement and balance. The sky remained clear, but when possible Benuzzi left a paper arrow to mark their return route in case of storms. It was a wise precaution.

Progress slowed. Giuan inched upward, clearing the rock in search of hoped-for purchase. So smooth was the face that it was no longer possible to belay. "We were already risking too much. . . . Had Giuan fallen he would have dragged me with him and vice versa." The Italians have an expression for acts like this. They call it "pulling the Devil by his tail" (p. 171). In a masterful display of climbing art, Giuan led on, centimeter by centimeter, until at last he stopped. Benuzzi waited. Minutes passed, then a quarter of an hour. Still the ropes curling upward did not move. It was now past noon. Numbed with cold, Benuzzi looked about. What he saw coming was the beginning of the end. "To my horror I noticed rags of mists coming from the south . . . while other tongues blown by an increasingly strong wind condensed on our side of the mountain" (p.172). The temperature plummeted. In a few moments the clouds enveloped everything. The storm reared and beat against them, the force of whistling sheets of snow and hail threatening to fling them into space. Looking up through the mists, Benuzzi could see Giuan's ghostly figure creeping down the rock. They shouted, but their words were garbled by the wind. Still, they understood each other. The message of the mountain was clear. Retreat or die.

The snow fell more steadily and more thickly. Snowflakes whirled round us, snow heaped on every irregularity of the rocks and plastered the wool of our caps, jackets and trousers with an icy crust. . . . Clinging to my small holds I peered down into the fury of the elements, trying to locate a red arrow in all this white hell. At last I saw one, a welcome sign of life in this dead world. Slowly and with great effort we reached it.

Our fingers were frozen from continuously clearing the snow from off our holds. The sisal ropes were as hard as iron rods and their icy fibers stung our hands likc needles. (P. 173)

The retreat went on for hours. Visibility was sometimes only a few yards. They groped down from one arrow marker to the next. Exhaustion reached every muscle and nerve yet to fail in strength or concentration was to fall, and that they must not do. Soon it would be growing dark. Slowly, almost imperceptibly at first, the angle of the rock eased back from the vertical. Holds became larger, more numerous. A solid knob to grasp, a small ledge to stand on, then scrambling on all fours, until at last they could stand up and walk without clutching the wall for balance. They paused briefly to rest. As they looked back the way they had come, the clouds parted.

Batian stood far above them, giant against the darkening sky. It was a magnificent sight. The lower ramparts of rock were still hidden in mists but toward the summit a fresh coating of snow blushed in the setting sun. They stood silently staring upward, oblivious of their own condition, enthralled by the beauty before them. Here was a superb peak, a climber's dream, and they rejoiced at having stretched their hands toward such a worthy goal. Success or failure meant less just then than the exhilaration of knowing that they had dared to do a great deed. With few resources but much courage, creativity, and will, they had come to climb this wonderful mountain. It was a moment of inner consummation, of self-fulfillment, of pride. Eight and half months of planning, deprivation, and struggle had given them the chance to measure themselves against these eternal stones. They were pleased with the accounting.

The clouds returned and they set off once more on the weary way to camp far below. Stupified with fatigue and cold, Benuzzi began to hallucinate. Characters from novels spoke to him and to each other; bells clanged nearby, in his feverish imagination. Repeatedly they slipped and fell on the slick heather and mud. Sometimes they crawled on hands and knees for a distance before they could rise. In the dark and fog they wandered, lost, searching for the route. After eighteen hours of almost continuous climbing, they stumbled into camp, half-frozen, starving, numb. Giuan crawled into the tent and with a word to Enzo fell instantly asleep. Benuzzi followed. He was at the end of his strength. "I tried to take off my puttees, sodden with water inside and covered with a crust of frozen mud outside. Puttees, hands, legs, all together trembled and shook. It was the last hard job of the day" (p. 180). He took his pack off. The neatly trimmed flag-pole sections protruded a few inches from the rucksack top, their carefully handcrafted flag still furled about the shaft. At the bottom of the bag lay the brandy bottle sealed with wax, containing a brief note and their names. These tokens had been intended for the summit. Something would have to be done about them before this adventure was finished. But now it was time to rest.

"Simple" is perhaps too much of an understatement but the climb of Point Lenana was not difficult by comparison with the challenge of Batian. After a day of rest, Benuzzi and Giuan again started early. By midmorning their flag pole was firmly guyed in place, with banner flying, on Mount Kenya's secondary summit. It was a proud moment, of course, especially to prisoners of war long denied the sight of their country's colors, but one tempered by their empty stomachs and by other hungers. They studied the view and searched for souvenirs around the cairn, but with equivocal enthusiasm. They were weak from lack of food and saddened by some of what they saw before them. Their weakness was easy to understand. For days they had been on short rations. Now their supplies were nearly gone. Attempts to catch the rats scampering near camp had failed and they were denied even those morsels. The main meal of this climbing day was breakfast. It was not much. "On the last flickering flame of the boiler Enzo melted the lump of ice which had formed in the cooking pot. In the warm water Enzo washed the inner side of the bags which had contained Ovaltine . . . added the four teaspoons of sugar, a few leaves of tea and served almost cold" (p. 181).

Sitting atop Point Lenana they could look across at the magnificence of Batian, the summit of their dreams, the mountain they had come to climb. One final time it threw them a challenge. They could now see that the main summit was much more easily approached from this side than from the north where they had made their attempt. The most difficult section, if not less severe, was certainly shorter and the start of actual climbing 2,000 feet higher. All they needed was a bit of food, a good night's rest, and they could try again, perhaps this time with success. It was a bitter test they now endured. The peak was so close, so possible, if they could just have another chance, just a little nourishment and shelter. They could also see that everything they required was within their grasp but outside of the rules of the game they played.

The tin hut was in plain sight a few hundred feet below. It was a climber's refuge like many found throughout the Alps. They knew from experience that it probably contained tinned rations, perhaps blankets, candles, matches—the things a climber needs to rest and fuel himself before going on the summit. Only these things were not theirs to use.

Mountaineering is least of all getting to the top of outsized piles of ice and snow and stone. It is foremost the search for a moral balance between the climbers' resources and the uncertainty he faces. To climb is first to set limits, establish rules, define acceptable and unacceptable acts, and then to live within these self-imposed restrictions. Without rules the enterprise has no purpose. Each climber sets his own limits and within these plays out the game.

Benuzzi and Giuan were escaped prisoners of war but they were also mountaineers with their own stern climbing code. For them the hut and its contents were out of bounds, forbidden. They came to climb on their own terms, with their own resources, however meager these might be. To accept this unanticipated aid would be a violation of that commitment and would tarnish and hollow their victory. Better that Batian be left inviolate. With a last admiring look at this handsomest of peaks, they turned and plunged down into the rising mists. The ambivalent march began. Each step led nearer to sustenance and security; each step brought them closer to captivity. Five days later they arrived.

14
Rationalization and Leisure

What makes them do it? While several chapters of this book have been directed to that question, it is worth one final examination. This question is both obvious and suggestive. It is obvious: most people's lives offer little that parallels the climber's experience; mountaineers are special people worthy of special attention. It is suggestive as well: how does mountaineering contrast with routine social life? What does climbing offer that cannot readily be found in the everyday world? Danger? Coal miners and police daily face greater hazards. Physical prowess? Many active people are as fit and capable as climbers. Prestige, wealth, power? Playing golf with the boss is probably a better way to obtain all three.

Everyday experience pales by comparison with mountaineering, fundamentally because daily routines seldom offer the encompassing, profound gratification climbers clearly enjoy. Climbing is fun, and, thus, a puzzlement. Mountaineers gain elation and fulfillment from what looks to nonparticipants like tiresome and demanding hard work. In a society where work and enjoyment are not commonly associated, the climber's actions are curious. Mountaineers seem to perform an improbable alchemy. For them, strenuous effort becomes fun, necessity offers opportunity, labor is leisure.

The study of mountaineering highlights more general social processes. Many persons seek creativity and meaningful expression in their lives. By examining what climbers have found, one can glimpse what others may yet gain. Similarly, the barriers that create the climber's alienation are part of broader dissatisfactions; segmentation in the spheres of life, a loss of encompassing enchantment and purpose. This chapter examines the cultural roots of these dissatisfactions and their impact on leisure. Rationalization is a central theme.

Flow and Everyday Life

There are rewards in the act of climbing that participants anticipate and that color subsequent experience. The key concept, the desirable condition, the sought-after goal of climbing is the social-psychological condition of flow. The mechanisms of flow were examined earlier relative to the mountaineering setting, but what of other less exotic social action? Is it possible to find or create the climber's enthusiasm and gratification in more common encounters?

The answer is a tentative yes. Csikszentmihalyi (1975, 140–60) argues that it is possible to conceive of flow and its contradictions as microphenomena sprinkled throughout daily routines and encounters. Conversation, for example, is sometimes embarrassed and halting when the roles of participants are unclear or the definition of the situation is unresolved. At other times, talk may be stifled by rules of order or other proprietary considerations so that only a vestige of one's ideas is communicated (Lyman and Scott 1970, 132). There are also times when conversation progresses comfortably, when ideas are exchanged directly, emotions are shared, and participants feel both understanding and understood. In a more general interpretation of the concept, Glaser identifies flow as "the basis for tremendously varied compulsive, addictive or engrossing activities, including much avid religious study and practice, the pursuit of sexual orgasms, the search for optimum alcohol or drug intoxication and many other types of yearning for dramatic moments" (Glaser 1981).

Those who are successful in finding flow-producing action in one area of social life may find other areas permeated by it as well, turning ordinary events into rewarding encounters. The flow to be found in climbing certainly is not limited to a few hours of fateful grappling high on a mountain. Climbing is more than an assortment of esoteric technical maneuvers. It is a complete social act in Mead's (1938, 3–25) sense of the term, extending from impulse to consummation, from first imagination of mountain adventure to final fleeting memory of the deed. In Benuzzi's example, mountaineering provided a lively purposefulness and direction to months of plans and preparations. With the challenge of Mount Kenya ahead, quotidian camp life took on new meaning. Crafting tools and clothing from bits and scraps, gleaning information, plotting routes and means of escape offered repeated opportunities for intense concentration and gratifying imaginative use of a full spectrum of available talents. These were animated and engrossing times, filled with demands for creative ingenuity and thoughtful problem solving, hopeful anticipation, and profound hard work. These were times rich with opportunities for flow.

If flow is presumably available in such a wide range of action, especially in leisure, why is it not a more frequent experience? After all, a seemingly sensible notion of many social scientists and lay people alike is that ordinary lives lack even the remotest parallel with experiences like climbing a mountain. This notion is only partly correct, it is more descriptive than prescriptive. Flow is possible in everyday events. However, there are cultural factors that discourage the discovery of flow and diminish the range and frequency of interactions with high flow-potential, especially in conventional leisure and sport. The process of rationalization is at the heart of these factors.

Rationalization

Viewed from a historical perspective, Western civilization is now in the throes of a great realignment of social and economic patterning. Max Weber called this process of change "rationalization," the infusion of scientific method, technological improvement, and rational management into all areas of human endeavor. It is manifested in the West through the religious ethic of Protestantism (Giddens 1971, 169) and the economic form of capitalism. Rationalization connotes more than guidelines for the organization of production or the generation of practical knowledge; it reflects an underlying value, urging the injection of calculation and method in meaning patterns at all points in life (Schlucter, 1979:14–15). Rationalized society is characterized by increasing capacity to predict and control natural phenomena in the external world. It is also accompanied by a rejection of the impractical and spontaneous in favor of the measured and purposeful. Rational life is not merely utilitarian and sensible, it is desirable and proper.[1]

Rationalization has left in its wake three sorts of deficiencies in social experience; linguistic restrictions on expression of leisured states, a paucity of meaningful challenges, and disenchantment at the loss of unifying myth. Climbing is in part a response to these deficiencies and in part a reflection of them.

Linguistic Restrictions

Why is flow not a more frequent experience? One partially correct answer is to counter that it does occur more than conventional wisdom suggests but is simply overlooked. Csikszentmihalyi (1981) argues that many social scientists are so convinced of the supremacy of extrinsic rewards in motivating human behavior that flow-like experience is ignored or regarded as insignificant. Flow may be hard to find simply because so few are looking for it or are prepared to identify and discuss it once found.

Robert N. Wilson elaborates this idea. In an eloquent essay, "The Courage to be Leisured" (Wilson 1981, 282–303), he argues that our language itself works against a full grasp of the flow concept. Rephrasing the Whorf hypothesis, Wilson reminds us that it is only possible to perceive and take action toward those objects and processes that can be expressed through available linguistic frames. Like a window latticework, the structure of language provides sharp clarity and definition to parts of the experiential universe while obscuring or occluding others. According to Wilson, our language is dominated by what Suzanne Langer calls discursive symbolism; this is the language of scientific and technical reports, textbooks, and instruction manuals. Discursive language is more useful in getting things done. It is deliberate, analytic, purposeful; if you will, left-hemisphere-dominated. "It is instrumental in the double sense that it assists in . . . shaping our mundane actions and also that it is predominantly a means to an end, a pointer or reference to objects and events outside itself" (Wilson 1981, 292).

Other means of expression, what Langer calls presentational language, are needed to articulate the flow phenomenon. Such means are hard to find. Caught as we are in a "rational linguistic trap" (Wilson 1981, 289), we find these presentational elements often unfamiliar or inaccessible. Presentational language is reserved for infrequent efforts to express the soft, fragile subjectivism of artistic appreciation, mystical wonder, religious spirituality, and other elusive sentiments. These are neither common nor comfortable topics for many people.

Presentational language is not efficient and linear but rich, intuitive, profound, filled with the delicate tension of emerging thought and subtle shading, the degrees and qualities of human experience. It is the language of growing possibility, not obdurate fact. Poets, dreamers, children, and true scientists could not do without it. But poets and dreamers are a danger to conventional, ordered society; they see and know too much. Wilson recalls James Joyce's dictum that the proper strategy for the artist is "silence, exile, and cunning." A French observer even advances the notion that certain of our definitions of insanity are designed to "keep poetry out of the streets" (Wilson 1981, 291), to suppress curiosity and reflective interpretation lest official definitions of reality be undermined. Presentational language therefore is not encouraged.

Conventional, discursive language is well designed for themes of action, direction, order, but ill suited for understanding and discussion of the leisured playfulness that is flow. Trapped in a restrictive language frame, flow-searchers are like artists off to capture the sunset with hammer and nails, compose songs for pulleys and levers, choreograph a chemical reaction. Flow seems rare and ephemeral to those half-blinded by incomplete perception, slow to emerge into full consciousness as a significant component of daily life. Rationalization creates other effects that separate flow from routine experience and that lead some to seek compensation in an isolated and distinct leisure pursuit.[2]

Separation

The bright promise of applied science as a solution to human needs has yet to be fully realized. On the success side, technology has made available a variety of effort- and time-saving devices. Throughout the

Western world and notably in the most heavily industrialized nations, persons in an expanding middle class find themselves increasingly free from subsistence labor, in circumstances of growing economic security and social stability. These persons are no longer preoccupied with an anomic struggle for marginal existence; no longer concerned exclusively with escape from economic uncertainty, the urgent construction of some understandable and predictable social order. However, such gains have been obtained only at a price.

A key social-structural component of rationalization is progressive differentiation. Adam Smith (1776) and Durkheim ([1893] 1947) called this process the division of labor, the development of new roles and units of organization in society, each devoted with greater intensity to the performance of some narrower function than those it replaced (Glaser 1978, 16–17). Differentiation produces a separation in the spheres of life. Functions formerly served by the primordial institution, the family, are now performed by a variety of specialized organizations: the school, factory, church, and so on. Within each of these institutions, individuals enact varied roles and hold different statuses to which they attach variable importance.

The differentiated organization of labor segments work and leisure, allotting separate times and places for each. In the name of efficient production, workers are discouraged from singing, laughter, or other playful behavior on the job. Such nonwork activity in the employment setting is considered deviant, "goofing off." The opportunity for play is institutionalized in the form of paid vacations and holidays, and persons are expected to use these "life spaces" (Parker 1971, 25) in their designated ways, for leisure (Biggart 1980, 34).

Weber drew particular attention to the separation between institutions meeting instrumental needs and those meeting expressive needs. He believed this division makes possible the exclusion of personal desires, affective attractions and distractions from the pursuit of efficient enterprise (Coser and Rokoff 1974, 491). Thus, in segmented society, instrumental failure or expressive denial may be role-specific, not comprehensive but limited. It then becomes possible for dissatisfactions in one area of life to be compensated for in another. Specifically, the emotional or creative shortcomings of work may be assuaged by fulfilling leisure. This is a key proposition of the "compensatory hypothesis" proposed by Wilensky (1960) and refined by Kando and Summers (1971), wherein leisure behavior is linked directly to negative or positive attributes of work.

The mountaineer has already been proposed as an illustration of this compensatory action. Differentiated labor is more efficient but not necessarily more gratifying. Persons within newly segmented roles may find the range of individual responsibility and scope of permissible action narrowed, their stable, ordered, and productive work reduced toward meaningless tedium. When work is perceived as overly regimented and routine and aspirations for creative expression are unabated, some workers turn to climbing in search of a direct, uncompromising challenge to the full spectrum of their abilities. On the mountain, rationalization is held in abeyance. Alone or in small groups the climber ventures to awkward and demanding places where competence in the tasks at hand is mandatory, differentiation is minimal. Even if each participant does not lead, belay, navigate, establish camp on every trip, some measure of these and other skills is considered prerequisite for all. Mountaineers pride themselves on their comprehensive independence as much as on their technical climbing ability.

Yet climbers and those with like avocations are a minority. Others in rationalized society respond to their confining circumstances with greater emphasis on the tasks at hand in the hope that increased effort will somehow produce greater and more abundant satisfactions than the paltry ones now available. That faith is ill founded.

Enchantment

The ultimate disappointment in rationalization is not its shrinkage of complex and commanding tasks to be done but a more fundamental malaise. What is missing finally from rationalized society is not action but purpose, a sense of belonging to a unified, animated, spiritually encompassing world.

Weber was fond of Friedrich Schiller's phrase the "disenchantment of the world" (Gerth and Mills 1946, 51). According to Weber, disenchantment was the inevitable, if lamentable, negative by-product of rationalization. The rationalized world increasingly becomes the artificial product of human manipulation, estranged and separated from a conquered nature.

Change created by scientific and technological progress is always possible and, in the disenchanted world, it is rationally obligated. As a result, present circumstances are perceived as perpetually unsatisfactory, untidy, incomplete. Leisure pursuits offering intrinsic satisfaction in existing conditions are shunned in favor of utopian striving for a promised world offering greater improvements in external conditions, although the form of these improvements remains nebulous.

As rationalization progresses, much information is generated through scientific techniques, yet these facts do not constitute knowledge in the sense of a better understanding of our way of living. The streetcar passenger may understand something of schedules and tokens but has little grasp of the design, construction, and operation of the device he or she rides (Weber, in Gerth and Mills 1946, 139). At the supermarket or drugstore, consumers buy any number of products without knowing what they actually contain (Freund 1969, 20). By comparison, "primitives" living in the bush know infinitely more about the conditions under which they live, about the tools they use, and the foods they consume.

Rationalization does not increase actual understanding but reflects a touching belief by human beings in the possibilities of their own works.

> The increasing intellectualization and rationalization do *not*, therefore, indicate an increased and general knowledge of the conditions under which one lives. It means something else, namely, the knowledge or belief that if one but wished one *could* learn it at any time . . . that one can, in principle, master all things by calculation. (Weber, in Gerth and Mills 1946, 139)

But principle and reality do not coincide. Much must be learned and time is short. Only a few things can be fully mastered, so these are given special emphasis, touted as truly important, while much else is reduced to dilettantish trivia. The remainder is dismissed, without total conviction, as "common sense" and not worthy of much effort to comprehend. In disenchanted society, existence is no longer encountered holistically as a unified spiritual experience, a world of shared definitions and clear consequences. Knowledge of things is gained, but understanding of life is lost.

Enjoyment that is available here and now is judged unimportant by imagined future standards and rejected as a distraction to the cause of the rational perfection of the world. The dilemma of rationalization is this: happiness is postponed until the important work of scientific restructuring is complete. Yet science is a process of continual bringing into question without definable limits, leaving gratification postponed indefinitely. For human happiness to be achieved, science and technology must continue to make necessary improvements, yet it is not within the scope of science to offer the ethical guidelines needed to identify the form and direction these improvements should take. Ideal science is value-free and, as such, moves blindly. The rationalized world is one of imperative and urgent means, without comparably clear goals. When the value of all but rational-scientific action is demeaned, humanity is left with efficient and effective ways of living but without a reason for doing so.

> Increasing rationalization and intellectualization have had one decisive consequence on which Weber laid great stress: they have disenchanted the world. With the progress of science and technology, man has lost his sense of prophecy and above all his sense of the sacred. Reality has become dreary, flat, utilitarian. (Freund 1969, 23–24).

The biblical Abraham lived in a time of great mystery, powerful magic, and encompassing myth. He died an old man, satiated with life, having seen and done all there was to experience. In today's rationalized world, men and women simply wear out, frustrated in their inability to achieve through technological means an elusive goal they cannot comprehend (Weber, in Gerth and Mills 1946, 140).

Weber (1958) noted that it was the Puritan's fervent desire to work in a calling, to both achieve and demonstrate grace and virtue. Building the new industrial order was simultaneously a challenging opportunity for creativity and confirmation of abiding religious conviction. But for those who came after, born into an already rationalized world, work was not a calling but a necessity. Weber recalls the theologian Baxter's view that "the care for external goods should only lie on the shoulders of the 'saint like a light cloak, which can be thrown aside at any moment' " (Weber 1958, 181). The results of rationalization are otherwise for "fate decreed the cloak should become an iron cage." (Weber 1958, 181). The work ethic remains, undiminished in potency but stripped of the sacred religious qualities that gave it an adjoining life purpose.

Once again mountaineering offers participants what they may be denied in other realms of experience. Climbers are never satisfied in simply overcoming technical problems. Theirs is most importantly a social act structured by a myriad of self-imposed restrictions, rules, and limits. Mountaineering involves the active construction of proprietary guidelines for the use of various apparatuses and techniques and the constant critical assessment of one's own behavior against those standards. In a rationalized world of amoral inconstancy mountaineers find in their avocation the purpose and direction that science and technological improvements fail to offer.

The source of climbers' ethical parameters and understandings is significant. Climbers frame their own social order as part of the joyful creation of meaning in self-chosen leisure. The genesis and power of climbing-rules reside in no higher authority than the participants themselves. After eight months of toil and anticipation Benuzzi rejected the food and shelter of the climbers' refuge he found high on Mount Kenya. Those aids might ensure success but not in the way he had chosen to play the game. No external legacy imposed rules, demanded compliance, guided his footsteps away from the hut. Constraints on the scope and style of climbing action are in the end manifestations of a personal convenant between self and referent others. Each climber on every climb decides personally and anew how the climbing will be done.

Climbers do not merely follow rules, they make them. In so doing they infuse a portion of life experience with a sense of quality and rounded wholeness. Rationalization finds many solutions but poses few meaningful problems. The mountains demand much, and mountaineers allow themselves only simple aids to augment their full measure of commitment. Rationalization provides control. Mountaineering, for a time, enchants the world and gives meaning to the climber's place within it.[3]

The Metamorphosis of Leisure

Rationalization strips life of spiritual vitality, creates linguistic limits and structural barriers to the experience of flow in ordinary events. But what of these segmented activities specifically set aside for play? Even these are influenced by rationalization, and thus flow potential is further restricted. Leisure in a rationalized world has special qualities. As society is permeated by the perceived need for ever-increasing scientific guidelines and calculated control, the form and content of play itself is profoundly affected.

Guttmann, mincing no words, has described the European criticism of rationalized sport:

> Sport is not an escape from the world of work but rather an exact structural and functional parallel to the world of work. Sport does not offer compensation for the frustrations of alienated labor. . . . It seduces the luckless athlete and spectator into a second world of work more authoritarian and repressive and less meaningful than the economic sphere itself. (Guttmann 1978, 69)

What causes this mutation of institutionalized leisure from the joyful spontaneity of flow toward less desirable states? A reexamination of the constituents of flow reveals a variety of rationalization-effects, each distorting or diminishing flow potential in leisure.

Paidia and Ludus

Play is characterized by two qualities Roger Caillois (1961, 27–35) calls paidia and ludus. Both are present in leisure action but in varying proportions according to the type of activity. Paidia is the expression of the spontaneous, impulsive, inner-directed self, a self similar to what Mead ([1934] 1970, 137–48) called the *I*. Paidia is curiosity, exuberance, a desire to touch, taste, smell, combine, order, manipulate, and disrupt, to explore one's capacities for becoming a cause in the world at hand. It is the infant's fascination with his rattle; the child's delight at stacking blocks one upon another and then knocking them down, the joy of walking balanced on a railroad track or going for a stroll on a rainy day or running through the lawn sprinklers on a hot one, the satisfaction of singing in the shower, sounding the car horn while driving alone through a tunnel, and blowing bubbles in a milkshake through a straw. To borrow Wilson's fine phrase, it is "the unrestrained capacity to toy with the stuff of existence, to juggle the modalities of sensation, perception and judgment, of cognition and feeling" (Wilson 1981, 300). Play in which paidia predominates is idiographic, changeable, expressive, intrinsically rewarding, creative, and relatively independent of others' behavior.

In rationalized society, play, like other forms of human endeavor, is presumably amenable to scientific refinement, but paidia is not well suited to calculation and patient testing. Something else is required, some means by which performances may be evaluated and compared, incremental change charted, improvements noted, and extraneous variables controlled. Limits must be placed on play and action, and actors must be standardized within these limits. Ludus is the response to these needs. It is the structured, ordered, rule-governed aspect of play, one manifestation of the *me*, the internalized perspectives of the generalized other (Mead [1934] 1970, 173–78), although certainly not all internalized attitudes are rational. Ludus is not the inspiring or motivating of play but the balance and regulation of it, the identification of boundaries and development of evaluation schemes.

Initial, player-generated and dictated ludification is a convenience to flow. When players agree among themselves on parameters and procedures for play, limits are placed on the stimulus field, uncertainty of outcome is bounded within a manageable frame. But in rationalized society this stage is quickly passed. Testing of managerial strategies becomes more important than individual expression. Spontaneous paidia loses ground to predictable ludus.

> The rationalization of these leisure activities leaves little room for the spirit of arbitrary invention or the disposition to leave things to chance. Risk, daring, and uncertainty—important components of play—have no place in industry or in activities infiltrated by industrial standards, which seek precisely to predict and control the future and to eliminate risks. . . . Prudence, caution, and calculation so prominent in everyday life but so inimical to the spirit of games, comes to shape sports as they shape everything else. (Lasch 1978, 102, 123)

As rationalization efforts increase, planned strategy and methodical training must be isolated from natural ability or physical advantage. Players are matched in number, sex, age, weight, and other characteristics, according to the game, to render each as nearly equal to the other as possible. Advantages in the fields of play themselves must likewise be neutralized. The length and breadth of the field or court or arena become standardized along with the height of the grass, the goal-post or basket, the weight, size, and shape of bats, balls, and other equipment. The benefits of sun, wind, direction, and other subtleties of the playing arena are homogenized by a periodic exchange of positions, ends, sides. Turns at play are governed by standardized procedures and divided into downs, serves, and moves within preestablished time frames: periods, innings, rounds, games, and seasons. Player conduct and game procedures are regulated by stipulating fair and foul play, with appropriate penalties for infractions.[4]

As rationalization accelerates, even these efforts at balanced equality prove inadequate. The need to unambiguously establish the supremacy of one technique over another becomes paramount. Scientific knowledge, the ability to reject null hypotheses, is not enough. Rationalization implies not simply a growth in knowledge but utilitarian, functional application and control. The value of some plan of play ultimately rests on its comparison with other plans, in success or failure, triumph or defeat. Judgments about the quality of play shift from nebulous reports of intrinsic satisfaction to more reliable externally observable criteria such as the number of hands, baskets, points, goals, or runs that are scored, hit, won, or earned. These increments of success can then be easily aggregated to arrive at game and season totals and a variety of individual and team statistics.

Pragmatism in rationalized play has other corollaries: pecuniary profit in much of the West and political prestige world-wide. Rational play not only seeks to demonstrate the practical usefulness of some method or scheme but to apply those schemes to the winning of purses, playoffs, prizes, and pennants, to generating support from paying fans and media advertisers or praise for national ideologies.

Effects on the Elements of Flow

Flow is made up of a limited number of essential elements. For flow to occur outcomes must be significant and determined by individual volitional action; the act must be intrinsically rewarding, occasioned by a merging of action and awareness, an absence of self-consciousness; and action must take place in a limited stimulus field. Rationalization aids achievement of only the last condition. Each of the other components is variously diminished or eliminated to the extent that leisure is rationalized. Commercialized leisure provides useful examples of these effects, although certainly not all such activities are bereft of flow potential.

Flow is possible only when real, meaningful, fateful outcomes are dependent upon the volitional action of participants. Activities which are trivial in substance or beyond the control of actors do not facilitate flow. Grappling with raging rivers, hunting wild carnivores in the bush, and going on mountain pack-train expeditions would seem to offer much fateful experience, but as these activities are rationalized, outcomes are

no longer personally controlled. Outdoor adventure enthusiasts on commercial white-water raft journeys, big-game hunts, and the like, find that
much of the significant action is prescripted by the professional staff and
that they are relegated to the role of largely helpless incompetents, of
glorified baggage. For example, on some Colorado river raft trips no more
is required of customers than a willingness to get wet and some effort to
remain in the boat. Planning, logistics, scouting, route selection, boat
management, camp setup, cooking, and even fireside entertainment are
provided by guide service personnel. Outings such as these are clearly
fateful encounters, but the participants have little to do with the outcomes.

Lasch echoes Huzinga's concern that as games are rationalized and
lose their sacred ritual qualities they deteriorate into trivial recreation and
crude sensationalism (Lasch 1978, 109). Such is the case in other commercial leisure activities where actors retain control but the significance of
play results is sharply reduced.

Hockey, baseball, basketball, football, tennis, and a host of other
games have been miniaturized and simplified so they can be played with
electronic images that are projected on a video screen and are controlled
by subtle wrist and finger motions. The experiences of torpedoing enemy
ships, destroying alien invaders, Grand Prix auto racing, even intergalac-
tic war and other improbable activities are available for a small sum at
nearby amusement arcades or through home video equipment. These
ersatz games disregard the energy, skill, and determination required for
their full-scale counterparts. The violence, brutality, injury, even death
that actual participants would face are trivialized into machine-made light
flashes and noises. To a large extent actors determine outcomes in these
games but the results are hardly fateful.[5]

Mass-produced replicas of sign equipment allow actors to create the
impression of mountaineering ability or presumed experience in other
fateful, volitionally controlled action, but without the need for actual
participation of any kind. "Go Climb A Rock" T-shirts were originally
sold only to graduates of the Yosemite Mountaineering School. Now they
are available in tourist curio shops. Likewise, "Go Climb A Glacier" shirts
from Glacier National Park and "Go Climb *The* Mountain" from Rainier
Mountaineering, Inc., a guide service, may be purchased and worn
without any prerequisite climbing. To become a Swiss mountain guide
requires years of training, testing, and apprenticeship; yet the distinctive
red and white sweaters identifying the members of this prestigious and
highly skilled profession are available in Zermatt sports shops and are
sometimes purchased by visitors as props for "barroom mountaineering."[6] Identity claims based solely on such items may allow nonparticipants to experience some of the climbers' lowland social encounters but
not the mountaineering process itself. Reality shrinks to the bounds of its

own metaphor. Life becomes solely a dramatic performance. Fateful climbing fades to nothing more than an imaginative construction.

For an event to offer the potential for flow experience it must be perceived by actors as intrinsically rewarding, satisfying in its own right. Rationalization occasions a shift in many forms of play from the achievement of immediate enjoyment to the earning of ultimate success, from means to ends. Competition becomes the dominant form of play and winning the preeminent goal. Intrinsic gratifications are replaced by the extrinsic rewards of prestige and profit. This shift, in turn, alters other components of flow.

In flow experiences, self-consciousness is eliminated. Action and awareness are tightly and reflexively intertwined, merging together. It is this quality that provides the concept with its strongest sociological roots. It is possible to locate this blending of action and awareness in what Mead ([1934] 1970, 273–381) identified as the fusion of the *I* and the *me*. When the impulsive, spontaneous, nondirectional *I* urges behavior in correspondence with the expectations, definitions, and guidelines of the incorporated other, the *me*, flow may occur.

Thus the social act, as Mead (1938, 3–25) defined it, is abbreviated in flow. Initiating impulses give rise directly to consummatory action without need for focused perception or constructed manipulation. In flow, conscious mediation between the individual and society is unnecessary. In the special circumstances of flow, behavior is at once personally satisfying and socially appropriate yet requires neither rehearsal nor correction. In Caillois's terms ludus encompasses paidia but does not constrain it. Flow is a condition without deviance. Action and attention are focused exclusively in the present. Actors neither apprehend their deeds nor reflect upon them; they lack both fear of the future and guilt for the past.[7]

In contrast, rationalized play is eminently self-conscious and fraught with potential deviance. As concern shifts from playing to winning, as games become more competitive and especially as external rewards grow in importance—when scholarships, prizes, bonuses, and political advantage ride in the balance—the temptation to rule deviation grows. "Transposed to reality, the only goal of *agon* [competition] is success. The rules of courteous rivalry are forgotten and scorned. They seem merely irksome and hypocritical conventions. Implacable competition becomes the rule. Winning even justifies foul blows" (Caillois 1961, 54). Cheating must be minimized. Making decisions about the conduct of play becomes too critical to remain in the hands of players themselves. While participants might be fair judges of their own enjoyment, this is a matter of diminished significance. Other theoretically unbiased specialists emerge who are charged with the duty of detecting rule transgressions, noting legitimate accomplishments, and assigning appropriate rewards and punishments: judges, referees, umpires. Overall, regulation of games becomes the duty of boards and commissioners who evaluate the impact of new developments and who structure rules to insure that technical or strategic innovations do not disproportionately favor some players or groups over others.

Finally, rationalized specialization extends beyond play to participants themselves. As players are subdivided and the rules of interaction refined, certain activity-specific qualities grow in importance. Persons who possess or develop those attributes are selectively recruited into these games. Players within each activity come to approximate each other but are increasingly differentiated from the general population. Physically adapted and temperamentally suited players are chosen and trained to be best at a single game. Their talents are not usually transferable to other kinds of play.

In the case of popular sport, it is easy for most Americans to examine the specialized qualities of these players. Their reflexes, moves, muscle mass, speed, reach, endurance, and emotional responses under stress are broadcast over the nation's television airways with color closeups and instant replays. In comparing their capacities and performances with his or her own, the viewer is invariably left wanting in some vital component. They are not like us. Possessed of a superior ease, these rare individuals accomplish with apparent nonchalance deeds of balance, dexterity, energy, and savagery at the very borders of imagination. We may marvel at the fluid strength of a tiny woman gymnast, the massive power of a 280-pound football lineman, or the bounding grace of a seven-foot-tall basketball center, but it is difficult to identify with these people. Yet their standards are often the ones by which our own actions must be measured. The intensive media coverage given these special people makes them a primary basis for evaluation of performances for much of the population. Persons who do not play a particular game often come to judge those who do by these highly elevated standards. Such comparisons are almost invariably invidious for the casual athlete.

As a result, those leisure activities with the strongest cultural mandate, the most rationalized sports, have the least potential for flow. Rationalization drives people from the field of play all together. Self-consciousness grows extreme. The stakes have gotten too high. Winning is of such importance, competition is so keen, players are so specialized, the chances of an average individual performing adequately are so remote and of being criticized are so likely that it is no longer worth the risk. Losing imparts a stigma, becomes a sign of inferiority, irrationality, lack of commitment. It becomes easier to join the bystander-analysts than to continue a halting and unappreciated participation. Actual play is abandoned in favor of discussion and comparison of others' performances. Finally, the last vestige of volitional control is given up. For some, sport undergoes a last transformation into a game of chance, a gamble, where onlookers in no way influence the action but wager on outcomes in the office football pool or at the local bookie.[8]

The metamorphosis nears completion. Through the process of rationalization, play is transformed. Ludus replaces paidia. Rules expand. Impulsiveness, individual creativity, are discouraged; regimentation, precise execution, and routine are demanded. The purpose of play shifts from the achievement of immediate enjoyment to the earning of ultimate success, from means to ends. For those few who remain in the game the genuine laughter and authentic tears of spontaneous play are replaced by smug gloating over success or foul muttering in defeat. Self-consciousness is heightened, action and awareness divided. In an urgent effort to regain some valued but intangible aspect of life, the disenchanted ones search for flow experience in less than encompassing ways. They look where other people structure the action, make decisions, take risks for them. Partial commitment offers only partial fulfillment. Others are drawn to the shallow, frantic allure of synthetic play in which they may find endless electronic distraction but little lasting satisfaction. Flow continues to elude them.

15
Conclusion

The elusiveness of flow should be taken seriously. As Csikszentmihalyi (1981) points out, the significance of enjoyment is not trivial. It is vital to the survival of society. In the long run a boring system cannot last. An essential quality of any social order is the way opportunities for expressive experience are institutionalized.

> Are they segmented into leisure activities that eventually preclude enjoyment because they become ruled by instrumental goals? Are intrinsic rewards available in adult roles—in jobs, in the family, in schools, and communities? These are the questions that disclose the essential structure of a social system. It is important to know how a society produces its means of subsistence, but it might be more important to know what pleasures it can give its members. (Csikszentmihalyi 1981, 339)

Society without play grows stilted and stunted. When members are discouraged from spontaneous expressivity in play they may overlook other possibilities. Elemental play and scientific curiosity stem from a common source, a generous hospitality toward newness, puzzlement, the untried difficulty, the emerging unknown. Creative acts of whatever order, in play or art or scientific inquiry, call for a willingness to follow the flight of hazardous processes, to surrender the self to forces beyond one's control. Creative life, which is to say a vitally experienced and satisfying life, is not led easily or safely (Wilson 1981, 302). It is demanding, challenging, stressful.

Stress is a key term. Stress may be defined as a social-psychological condition of perceived urgency, importance, or significance associated with some set of persons or events. A stressful situation is one that matters, one that is real, meaningful, and commanding. Stress is simply and essentially stimulation.[1] Genuine leisure—flow, that is—is not possible without it.

Leisure is sometimes conceptualized commonsensically as the antithesis of stress, as a respite from the burdens of demanding work, home life, and other responsibilities. This notion of leisure as being stress-free is problematic. It is predicated on assumptions about social life that are only partially tenable in modern industrialized countries.

There is a popular if unsubstantiated notion that in today's rapidly changing world additional stress of any sort is too much. This belief holds that most persons are already faced with nearly unbearable demands in contemporary social life and that, for them, stressful leisure would be neither desirable nor tolerable. The image of the ulcer-ridden, heart-attack-prone executive fighting his way up the corporate ladder comes to mind. Surely such individuals have little capacity for further stress, nor do other categories of persons we might imagine—men at war, those under pressure of pain and extreme deprivation, individuals whose work loads are overwhelming or who face constantly shifting social requirements. Perhaps for these persons that utterly unstimulated condition which Freud once sketched as the epitome of neural bliss is a tenable if not ideal leisure objective. But these are extreme examples and special instances, conditions encountered only infrequently except by the fictional heroes and heroines of afternoon soap operas, prime-time cop shows, and late-night spy thrillers. The growth of the modern industrial social order in which many of us live has brought with it a different sort of challenge to human adaptive abilities: not an increase in demands but a diminution of opportunity for personal expression, creativity, and self-guidance.

Gone are the days of rugged individuals eking out a subsistence on the wild frontier. In modern America more than half the nation's employees work in monolithic corporations and government bureaucracies, the institutions that combine economy of scale, massive capitalization, and scientific management to produce the relatively cheap and plentiful goods and services that make ours the highest standard of material living in the world. These organizations protect and insulate their members. They provide retirement programs, health plans, civil service, tenure, all of which combine to offer job security, economic stability, and social certainty, but at a price.

In the name of rational efficiency, work activity is stripped of complexity and novelty, streamlined, standardized, routinized. Following the ghost of Frederick Taylor (1923) the occupation has been simplified to a set of logically related tasks, the individual reduced to an assortment of roles and statuses. This process is not limited to clerical or assembly-line jobs but is beginning to influence all categories of work. Engineers, chemists, computer programmers, and other professionals are likewise affected. Far from increasing stress, these organizations at all levels function to isolate people from sensation and varied experience, minimize their decision-making domain, limit options, cloister and confine.

Numerous psychological experiments have demonstrated that humans and animals alike seek out and are rewarded by moderate complexity, uncertainty, novelty in their environments (see Fiske and Maddi 1961; Harris 1972). Maximum motivation is reached and gratification for accomplishments potentiated when a balance is achieved between our abilities and our responsibilities, when the skills we possess are roughly commensurate with the challenges we face, when our talents are neither underused nor overtaxed. But for many persons enmeshed professionally in modern large-scale organizations, this relationship between task and talent, between ability and responsibility is woefully skewed. Many in our society feel this imbalance and curtailment in their range of actions and creative potential. Some are willing to forego intrinsic rewards in exchange for material plenty and economic security.[2] People who climb mountains are not.

The executives, scientists, and businessmen who constitute the majority of contemporary mountain climbers are highly imaginative and creative persons. Although diverse in background they share a common perception of their life opportunities. The mountaineers studied in this work see themselves as capable, even exceptional persons whose talents are in part repressed by bureaucratic regulations and organizational regimen. When creative people find their best abilities stifled by overly restrictive social structures they may express these capacities in other ways. Some may purposefully search out stressful situations in their leisure activities. Climbing mountains offers such opportunities. Mountain climbers are not looking for greater security, stability, and certainty in their lives. Typically, these qualities are seen as being overabundant. Rather they are seeking in leisure a test of their limits in a gratifying no-compromise situation where their behavior is meaningful and outcomes depend upon their own self-directed action. For them stress is an essential ingredient in leisure experience. Mountaineers and certainly others who engage in risk avocations demand a challenge to the entire spectrum of their perceived capacities. Complete expression of personal creativity and freedom is only possible when the activity tests the individual to his or her fullest. For these people leisure without stress is unsatisfying and incomplete. In what they perceive as a homogenized, sterilized, rationalized, and rule-governed social world, climbers and their ilk seek a raw encounter with an environment that can only be met with a full measure of personal commitment, innovation, and investment.

To be without stress is to be eddied in the stream of life-experiences, cut off from stimuli, noxious or otherwise. Less is required of the person and less is possible. The opposite of stress is not celebration, satisfaction, or tranquility. It is a state of reduced awareness and diminished capacity, of torpid disinterest as found in drug-induced stupor and, when logically extended, in coma and quintessentially in death. Only by the distortions of Orwellian doublethink can such stresslessness be judged a desirable leisure goal.

Civilization protects us not just from real dangers but sometimes from the full possibilities of our humanity. Society is not Benuzzi's prison camp nor are we its unwilling captives, but instructive similarities exist. The perceived scope of available meaningful tasks in the modern industrial world is for some persons as restricted as Benuzzi's limited range of camp-life opportunities.

Science and technology provide facts and leverage but offer no global understanding or inclusive moral order. They strip life of mystery and spirituality. Rationalized play loses its iconic meaning and autotelic reward. But there are solutions. We are not shut up forever within the iron cage; it is of human design and we can escape from it. Benuzzi showed a way this might be done.

The transition is not complete. Play and other enjoyable actions are not all rationalized away. The immense possibilities of human spirit are not yet flattened to the dehumanized outline of two-dimensional man. While the vital reaffirmation of self in flow comes only from stressful engagement, we are capable of that effort. Flow is to be found in the climbing of mountains. This book attests to that. But for some the mountains may be far away or otherwise unreachable. Perhaps the most important thing learned from a study of climbers is the potential of flow in daily life.

Invisible mountains surround us all. They are hidden in stamp collection albums, in paints and brushes, in the well-written lines of a letter to a dear friend or an irritating politician, in making a fine soufflé, in delivering a convincing speech, or in performing delicate surgery. Flow is not reserved for leisure in the limited sense of sport or recreation but is possible whenever unswerving commitment, energy, and will find meaningful and effective application in the world of social experience.

For those who will climb there is this reminder. While looking for happiness and fulfillment, some of us find mountains. If, in climbing them, we feel and become more than was possible before, let us not forget whom to praise. It is not the stones that make us happy. They provide no memories or sense of completion. Whatever we find in the mountains we took there in the first place. In the end the mountains do not care what experiences we make of them. They are nothing but wrinkles on a shifting crust, frozen water upon water, dust upon dust—nothing—until men and women come and give them meaning.

Appendix
American Attitudes
Toward Mountaineering

In order to develop a consistent and comprehensive view of self, social actors build up in imagination a composite "generalized other" from whose standpoint they evaluate their own behavior. This generalized other frees the individual from the confusion of ever-shifting local and present expectations. He or she is emancipated from the peculiarities of immediate situations, the pressures of proximate others. This is not to suggest that the impact of others upon the self becomes homogenized, that all are equal as points of reference. There are special qualities required of those used as evaluators of our performances. But the generalized other remains a common background of attitudes, definitions, understandings, and expectations with which each new social situation is met. In Mead's ([1934] 1970, 154) words, "the attitude of the generalized other is the attitude of the whole community."

Understanding how the "whole community" views mountaineering provides further insight into the climber's motive. If mountaineering is generally well thought of, the climber will receive encouragement and respect. If it is viewed as objectionable, he or she might be belittled or defamed, and turn, perhaps, to other avocations. Knowledge of generally held attitudes toward mountaineers is useful in estimating the support or discouragement climbers may expect to receive from the nonclimbing public. But, first, it is important to stress that opinions concerning avocations are not trivial.

In America, occupation remains the dominant factor in determining social status, but that dominance is diminishing. Shorter work-hours, an improved standard of living, increased early retirement, and longer life-expectancy have combined to create more interest, opportunity, and participation in leisure activities. Leisure occupies an increasing proportion of our time, energy, and consumer dollars. Likewise, knowledge of people's leisure-time pursuits increasingly guides the way others judge them. Initial estimates of people's social prestige, life-style, and even personality may be made on the basis of the sports, games, and hobbies they enjoy (Clark 1956; White 1955; Burdge 1969). For example, it is sometimes claimed that only introverts collect stamps and butterflies, while intellectuals play chess, and "real men" go hunting. Golf is presumably a game for stockbrokers, doctors, and bankers, while up-and-coming executives play tennis or racketball at a private club. Further assumptions are that playboys sail yachts, blue-collar workers go bowling, and hoodlums play pool. Of course, these are not always accurate stereotypes, but still they are used, particularly in initial acquaint-anceships and superficial encounters. People's avocations as well as their occupations influence the tenor of emergent interaction.

Most mountaineers have known moments of misunderstanding, even persecution, when their sport was revealed to a hostile audience. Woodrow Wilson Sayre provides an illustration:

> But I was not prepared for open hostility. In some quarters there was an almost undeclared war against me and the project [climbing Mount Everest]. . . . I remember, for instance, a woman who was a perfect stranger coming up to me at a cocktail party.
>
> "Are you the man who's going off to climb mountains?" she demanded. And then, without waiting for an answer, she continued, "Well, I think it's absolutely irresponsible. You have no right to leave your wife and children, and go running off on such a harebrained adventure. Why don't men ever grow up?"
>
> She was angry and hostile and very serious, and she talked for quite a while. (Sayre 1964, 30)

At other times, being identified as a climber may elicit praise and admiration. "You climb mountains? Wow! You must be awfully strong and brave!" is an example of the affirmative remarks climbers sometimes hear. How typical are each of these remarks? How often does the public censor or celebrate mountaineering? What is the attitude of the "whole community" concerning people who climb mountains? Relevant survey data are available to answer some of these questions.

Methods

Under my supervision, a quota sample of 1,032 adult male and female Americans was interviewed individually by professional market research personnel in twenty cities across the country. Cities were selected on the basis of size and geographic locale to represent both the large metropolis and small community in the South, Northeast, Midwest, and West. Within each city, interviews were conducted in both central and sub-urban locations.

Interviews took place in: Kalamazoo, Michigan; Chicago, Illinois; San Francisco and Los Angeles, California; Washington, D. C.; Boston, Massachusetts; Atlanta, Georgia; Albuquerque, New Mexico; New York, New York; Fort Lauderdale, Florida; Kansas City, Missouri; Cincinnati, Ohio; Boise, Idaho; Seattle, Washington; Davenport, Iowa; Omaha, Nebraska; Portland, Maine; Dallas, Texas; and Charlotte, North Carolina. Actual field interviews were conducted by affiliates of Facts Consolidated, Inc., Los Angeles. Data were obtained on the respondents' age, sex, and marital status. Then they were asked "What is the first word that comes to mind when you think of people who climb mountains?" The results of that survey offer a glimpse of what the whole community, the generalized order, thinks about the mountaineer and mountaineering.

Results

Responses were coded initially into twenty-two categories. These categories, in turn, served as the basis for two kinds of subsequent analysis. The first of these was accomplished by condensing the response categories into seven distinct major headings.

"Good" Climber

As the question was worded, one might expect the preponderance of responses to describe the personal qualities of climbers or, if the respondent identified with the role of mountaineer, to describe the climbing experience itself. To a large extent this was the case. What was not anticipated was the sizable proportion of complimentary descriptions. Almost half (46.9 percent) of all responses characterized the climber as a good individual possessed of valued and respected personal and physical qualities, pursuing a satisfying and valuable activity. He or she was described as "adventurous" (14 percent); "brave" (8.4 percent); "strong," "athletic" (7.8 percent); "ambitious," "determined," "striving" (7.3 percent); or "beautiful," "good" (3.7 percent). The climbing experience itself was seen as being "happy," "fun," or "free" (5.7 percent).

"Bad" Climber

Not everyone who responded was enthusiastic about climbers and climbing. About one-fifth (20.2 percent) of the total responses took a decidedly unflattering view of mountaineers, describing them and their sport as "crazy," "stupid," "dumb," "nuts," or otherwise demonstrating a lack of sanity or wisdom.

Climbing Environment

About one out of every nine respondents (10.8 percent) took the question as an occasion to describe the climbing environment. This included remarks on altitude or height (4.4 percent); the presence of cold and snow (2.7 percent); geology and flora, with such comments as "rocks" or "flowers" (1.5 percent); and the fauna presumably found there, "snakes" and "goats" (.8 percent). Still others made mention of the climbers' equipment, "ropes," "boots" (1.4 percent).

Climbing People and Places

The small number of responses (6.3 percent) in this category indicates the relative obscurity of mountaineering in the minds of the American public. Only 15 (1.5 percent) respondents mentioned actual persons whom they associated with climbing. These included a mixture of real and imagined mountaineers: Hillary, basketball player Bill Walton, the skier Jean Claude Killy, the Colorado singer John Denver (author of the popular song *Rocky Mountain High*), and actor Clint Eastwood (star of *The Eiger Sanction*, a spy thriller in a mountain-climbing setting). Other respondents made reference to groups of people associated with mountainous environments, such as hikers, skiers, and Sherpas (2.5 percent). For some the question brought to mind not persons who climbed but places where climbing goes on: Colorado, Mount Everest, the Alps, Switzerland, and the World Trade Center (after George Willig's much publicized ascent of one of the center's twin towers) (2.3 percent).

Climbing Hazard

For a small number of respondents (3.7 percent), climbing mountains was identified as a hazardous or even fatal undertaking as indicated by such descriptions as "danger," "falling," and death."

Existential Climber

A small (3.0 percent) but interesting group of respondents saw mountaineeeering as a transcendental, spiritual, or holistic subjective experience, indicated by responses like "God," "Jesus," and "serenity."

No Knowledge/No Answer

For one out of every eleven respondents (9.1 percent), being a mountain climber was apparently beyond personal experience or imagination. For this group the question tapped no reservoir of surplus meaning, and they answered by simply rephrasing or repeating a portion of it. Thus when asked, "What is the first word that comes to mind when you think of people who climb mountains?" they responded with "mountain climbers," "climbers," or even "mountains" (5.2 percent). Still others could produce no image of climbers at all and answered "none," "nothing," or simply failed to respond (3.9 percent). Again, one is reminded of the limited interest and knowledge of mountaineering possessed by typical Americans.

To facilitate further analysis, responses were reclassified into three categories—positive, neutral, and negative—indicating the valence of the respondents' remarks toward mountaineering. Positive comments corresponded closely to the good-climber category and include those personal qualities and situational characteristics presumably valued or enjoyed by Americans—"brave," "strong," "freedom," "smart," "nice," "outdoor sport," and the like. Comments were classified as negative if they demeaned the climber or described the climbing environment as hostile, for example, "cold," "breathless," "danger," "stupid," "dumb," "solitude," "loneliness," and "death." Remarks were classified as neutral if they were ambiguous or without clear valence. Remarks about known climbers and climbing places, partial rephrasing of the original question; other mountain travelers, such as hikers and skiers; and existential references were all classified as neutral. Classification of responses was the result of the collective judgment of four individuals: two climbers and two nonclimbers. Responses were assigned to categories only when agreement had been reached among those four concerning the appropriate valence. Classification was not done independently, so measures of intercoder reliability are not available. Subjective impressions suggest that agreement would be quite high, as little disagreement was evidenced between judges. Classified in this manner, responses were 46.6 percent positive, 26.1 percent neutral, and 27.3 percent negative. Again, mountaineering appears to be viewed more favorably than unfavorably. But how might the age, sex, or marital status of the respondent affect these attitudes?

Age

Respondents were selected for interviewing on the basis of age. They ranged from 18 to 65, with a median of roughly 30. These respondents were divided into six age-categories. Age had little bearing on the proportion of positive responses made. The 18–21 group made positive remarks about as often (49.5 percent) as those in the 51–65 group (45.3 percent). However, the proportion of negative commentary increased with the respondent's age, from 26.3 percent for the 18–25 group to 43.8 percent for the 51–65 group. With increasing age, respondents tended to make fewer neutral comments and more negative ones, although the proportion of positive remarks within each age group remained fairly constant.

Sex

Women respondents were slightly more supportive of climbing in their remarks than men. They made positive comments more often (47.7 percent) than men (45.4 percent). They were neutral slightly more often (26.6 percent) than men (25.5 percent), and they commented less negatively (25.6 percent) than men (29.2 percent). In general, the responses by

Table A1 Positive, Neutral, and Negative Comments about People Who Climb Mountains, by Age of Respondents (N = 1,029)

	Age Group					
	18–21	22–25	26–29	30–35	36–50	51–65
Positive comment	49.5%	50.0%	47.3%	44.6%	42.6%	45.3%
	(94)	(110)	(70)	(90)	(80)	(29)
Neutral comment	23.7	28.2	25.7	28.7	27.1	10.9
	(45)	(62)	(38)	(58)	(51)	(7)
Negative comment	26.3	21.8	27.0	26.7	30.3	43.8
	(50)	(48)	(40)	(54)	(57)	(28)
Total	100%	100%	100%	100%	100%	100%
	(189)	(220)	(148)	(202)	(188)	(64)

both men and women should be marked for similarities rather than differences.

Marital Status

Noticeable differences were evident between persons who referred to their marital status as living together and those who indicated they were separated. The married, single, and divorced respondents made similar proportions of positive, neutral, and negative comments intermediate between the separated and living-together groups. Separated persons commented negatively more than twice as often (34.8 percent) as those living together (15.4 percent). Separated respondents remarked positively in 43.5 percent of the cases, while those living together made positive comments 51.9 percent of the time. The small number of respondents in the separated and living-together categories would suggest caution in interpreting these figures.

Table A2 Positive, Neutral, and Negative Comments
about People Who Climb Mountains,
by Sex of Respondents (N = 1,030)

	Male	Female
Positive comments	45.4%	47.7%
	(235)	(244)
Neutral comments	25.5	26.6
	(132)	(136)
Negative comments	29.1	25.6
	(151)	(131)
Total	100%	100%
	(518)	(511)

Table A3 Positive, Neutral, and Negative Comments
about People Who Climb Mountains,
by Marital Status of Respondents (N = 1,005)

	Married	Single	Divorced	Separated	Living Together
Positive comments	46.5%	48.1%	44.4%	43.5%	51.9%
	(238)	(162)	(36)	(10)	(27)
Neutral comments	25.2	26.7	24.7	21.7	32.7
	(129)	(90)	(20)	(5)	(17)
Negative comments	28.3	25.2	30.9	34.8	15.4
	(145)	(85)	(25)	(8)	(8)
Total	100%	100%	100%	100%	100%
	(512)	(337)	(81)	(23)	(52)

Table A4 Positive, Neutral, and Negative Comments
about People Who Climb Mountains, by Region (N = 1,030)

	Far West	Midwest	South	Northeast
Positive comments	43.5%	40.2%	49.0%	52.1%
	(135)	(80)	(103)	(162)
Neutral comments	35.5	25.6	21.9	19.9
	(110)	(51)	(46)	(62)
Negative comments	21.1	34.2	29.0	28.0
	(65)	(68)	(61)	(87)
Total	100%	100%	100%	100%
	(310)	(199)	(210)	(311)

Region

Opinions expressed by respondents were not uniform in all areas of the nation. Of the four regions delineated by the study (Far West, Midwest, South, and Northeast), midwesterners were the most negative in their comments toward mountaineering. Respondents in the Far West made neutral or ambiguous remarks more often than the interviewees in other regions. Positive comments were more prevalent in Northeastern cities than in other areas. Responses from the South were quite similar to those from the Northeast but somewhat less positive and slightly more neutral and negative. The data from a few cities were especially noteworthy. Omaha respondents led the nation in negative comments about mountaineers, while Boston and Portland, Maine, tied for the city with the highest proportion of positive comments. San Franciscans showed the greatest tolerance toward, if not outright support for, mountaineering, with the fewest negative comments of any city and the highest proportion of neutral remarks.

In summary, it would appear that respondents know very little about climbing and climbers, but the attitudes they do have are more supportive or noncommital than antagonistic. Older respondents and those separated from their spouses viewed climbing more negatively than younger persons and those living together, but in all cases positive responses predominated over negative ones. The sex of the respondent made little difference in the valence of comments. From the mountaineering people, places, and circumstances reported, one can infer that the media and entertainment industry shaped respondents' impressions of climbers more than firsthand knowledge. Attitudes varied considerably by region with the most affirmative or accepting views expressed in the Northeast and West.

Notes

Preface

1. U. S. Department of Health, Education and Welfare, Public Health Service, National Center for Health Statistics, *Vital Statistics of the United States*, 1973, vol. 2. Cited in *Social Indicators 1976*, U. S. Department of Commerce, Bureau of the Census, Office of Federal Statistical Policy and Standards, table 5/1, "Life Expectancy at Birth, by Race and Sex: 1900–1974" (1977), p. 190.

2. *New York Times*, July 10, 1977. Cited in Beth B. Hess and Elizabeth W. Markson, *Aging and Old Age* (Macmillan: New York, 1980), p. 193.

3. U. S. Department of Health, Education and Welfare, Public Health Service, National Center for Health Statistics. *Vital and Health Statistics*, Analytical Studies, series 10, nos. 1, 5, 13, 25, 37, 43, 52, 60, 63, 72, 79, 85, 95, and 100. Cited in *Social Indicators 1976*, table 5/12, "Incidence of Acute Conditions, by Type of Condition: 1957–1974" (1977), p. 198.

4. *Social Indicators 1976*, table 8–26, "Paid Vacations of Plant and Office Workers, by Length of Vacation and Years of Service: 1959–1974" (1977), p. 388.

5. U. S. Department of Commerce, *Bureau of Economic Analysis, Benchmark Revision of National Income and Products Accounts: Advance Tables*, 1974. Cited in *Social Indicators 1976*, table 9–25, "Personal Consumption Expenditures, by Type of Product and Service: 1946–1974" (1977), p. 471.

6. John P. Robinson, "Changes in America's Use of Time, 1965–1975," *Report of the Communication Research Center* (Cleveland State University, 1976). Cited in *Social Indicators 1976*, table 10/1. "Average Hours per Week Spent in Major Types of Activity by Selected Urban Population Groups: 1965 and 1975" (1977), p. 509.

Chapter 1

1. The bouldering (climbing on small rock-outcrops) at Fontainebleau outside of Paris approaches these conditions of foreknowledge. In the king's wood adjacent to the famous palace, once a summer retreat for French monarchs, are scores of hard sandstone boulders, each one marked on a map available from the local tourist office. On weekends and holidays thousands of metropolitan-area climbers of all ages and both sexes come to enjoy the climbing there. "I never imagined that bouldering could be such a family sport; but then I never imagined an area where each [climbing] problem was numbered and color coded for difficulty with little arrows painted on the rock, and where out-of-bounds handholds were so literally marked off by dotted lines, nor could I have imagined an area so heavily used" (Matous 1980, 34).

2. Although this example is drawn from the experience of a group of ski-mountaineers on a tour, the principle is equally applicable and the illustration appropriate for the mountain climber.

3. There is at least one notable exception. One NASA engineer (now retired) who was stationed near Mojave, California, took advantage of perhaps the ultimate weather forecasting system. At the base where this engineer worked, were four F104 fighter planes for the use of those military personnel also employed there who wanted to keep their combat-ready status. Before an upcoming climb, this engineer would request an overflight and visual inspection of the area he intended to visit in the Sierras. A jet would then be "scrambled," flown to the proposed climbing area, and the pilot would give a firsthand report on the weather, snow conditions, etc. (Field notes, November 1978).

Chapter 2

1. The names of Reinhold Messner, Herman Buhl, Cesare Maestri, and Walter Bonati will always be identified not only with great mountaineering achievements but with solo climbing. Many other names could be added to this group. For a review of soloing history, ethics, and techniques in Britain and the Alps, see Alan Rouse's article "Two's a Crowd" in *Mountain* (1972, 28–31). John Cleare's (1975, 72-81) subjective impressions of his own solo climb of the Disgrazia in the Alps also provide useful insight.

Solo ascents in the 1980s are becoming more common and their objectives more demanding. The north face of the Eiger was Europe's last great climbing problem and stymied the world's best mountaineers for years between the wars. Siege tactics and appalling risks were accepted practices. Success was gained in 1930 but at the cost of many failures and much loss of life. By contrast, the British climber Eric Jones climbed the Eiger alone in September of 1980 in a straightforward yet skillful demonstration of modern big-wall climbing techniques. Even more impressive was Reinhold Messner's solo ascent of the North Col/North East Ridge of Mount Everest, the route of many prewar British attempts. Accompanied only by a single woman companion, Messner established an acclimatization camp during the monsoon season of 1980 and waited for a change in the weather. His chance came. From his advance base, Messner moved upward, alone, unsupported by other climbers from below, without supplementary oxygen. In three days he had climbed the highest mountain in the world. The summit photo of Messner standing beside an aluminum flagstaff placed by an earlier climbing team demands reflection. It is a simple photo of a man dressed in warm clothing standing on a small snow hummock surrounded by clouds. But what went into that picture? A lone human had come to the highest point on earth with a minimum of technological aid and only the imagined presence of others. In this loneliest of places, a few yards from the summit, he drove his ice axe in the snow and fixed his camera to it, activating the self-timer. He then turned uphill and in the seconds remaining, *ran* back toward the top of Mount Everest. Empty-handed, he looked down on the rest of the world. (See Dyhrenfurth 1980, 39.)

2. As an example, the Mazamas, a Portland-based climbing club, sponsored a guided group-climb of nearby Mount Hood on July 9, 1936. On that trip the leader, Lynn Darcey, led a single-file line of 401 climbers to the summit and back (Grauer 1975, 216). Regular Sierra Club and Mazama Club climbs are less monolithic yet routinely include twenty-five members.

3. Perhaps I exaggerate. After all, some of us may freely and with little thought get into an automobile for a journey on urban freeways with drivers of only casual acquaintance, without much consideration of their skill. Yet that skill is crucial in ensuring survival among the hostile hordes of commuters, hot-rodders, drunks, and the plain inattentive or uncoordinated. The fact that this experience is commonplace does not make it any less objectively dangerous; yet one's climbing companions are selected with greater care than those with whom we drive. Danger may be an acceptable, even unnoticed, attribute of daily life but in mountaineering it is avoided with study and care. (I personally never met a mountaineer who did not wear a seat belt as a hedge against the dangers of the highway.)

4. In extreme instances expeditionary climbing organizations may become more stratified and differentiated. A large, costly Japanese expedition went to the north side of Everest
in April–May 1980. On that assault, weather forecasting, the establishment of general
climbing schedules, personnel deployment, and summit attempts were planned and
directed from the climbing leader's headquarters in Tokyo via a satellite telecommunications
system and relays through Peking. Messner's climb in August of one of the same routes
attempted by the Japanese is in striking contrast (see n.1 above).

5. This commonality of effort and purpose is not universal among expeditions
although it remains an essential characteristic. Climbers on expeditions do have their
disagreements, sometimes serious ones. Such rifts are deleterious to the overall climbing
project, and leaders and group members alike strive to achieve harmony among themselves
whenever possible. Until relatively recently no public recognition of strife between climbers
on a major expedition was recognized in the books which summarized expedition deeds and
adventures or, for the most part, in the accounts presented in fund-raising slide shows
following these climbs. Strife with Sherpas, porters, and other climbing parties might be
given passing comment but intragroup relationships were depicted as blissfully convivial.
In the 1970s this tradition began to break down, as can be seen in some examples: Galen
Rowell's *In the Throne Room of the Mountain Gods* (1977a), Snyder's *The Hall of the Mountain
King* (1973), and Rick Ridgeway's *The Last Step: The American Ascent of K2* (1978). Even though
these and other expedition accounts describe dissension, disagreement, and tension between team members, they are atypical. They do serve, however, to offset the somewhat
Pollyannaish style of earlier works of this genre. In the final analysis, climbing, especially
expedition climbing, remains a cooperative act of persons sharing more or less a common
goal. Without such a source of direction and mutual commitment the enterprise becomes
impossible.

Chapter 4

1. The results of a survey of Sierra Club climbing instructors indicate that the average
altitude gain to camp from the roadhead on a typical weekend climb was 3,024 feet, and from
camp to the summit 2,244 feet. If the climber was a 170-pound male carrying a 40-pound
pack to camp and a 10-pound pack from there to the summit, he would perform 1,038,960
foot-pounds of work on the way up. A 1967 Volkswagen "bug" weighs slightly less than a
ton, and a standard building story is about 10 feet high.

2. The variability of climbers' approaches to physical conditioning is also illustrated by
the results of a survey of members of the Calgary Section of the Alpine Club of Canada.
Among climber-respondents, 46 percent indicated that they never participate in a fitness
program, 35 percent responded that they participated one or more times per week, and 11
percent exercised daily (Bratton, Kinnear, and Koroluk 1979, 56).

3. A few impressions of my own conditioning routine may also add meaning to the
reception mountaineering receives in the community at large.

The public has grown accustomed to the sight of exercisers jogging in parks, on local
school tracks, and around the block but is generally unprepared for the mountaineer-in-
training, whose dress and action do not meet their physical expectations. Joggers wear
sweat shirts and pants or more stylish warm-up suits along with appropriate running shoes.
They carry nothing more than perhaps a handkerchief or stopwatch. Wearing shorts and old
tennis shoes, I frequently used to don a filled backpack and walk a mile to the local high
school where I ascended the bleacher steps over and over again, simulating the actual
altitude-gain of climbing. This act sometimes puzzled onlookers, who substituted some
more understandable motive for repeatedly carrying a heavy burden up and down flights of
steps in the center of a major metropolitan area.

Onlooker: "Getting ready for the fire department test, eh?"
RGM: "Nope. I'm getting ready for hiking."

Evening Sports Director: "I hope you're doing that to get ready for hiking, not the
Marine Corps."
RGM: "Yes, it's for hiking."

The term "hiking" is used advisedly. Repeated experience in these kinds of exchanges
has shown that detailed responses confuse the issue. The public associated packs with
"backpacking" or "hiking," both of which go on in the "mountains." When I explained my
activity as preparation for "mountain climbing," questioners would often ask where this
climbing would go on. For some time I attempted to answer as completely and factually as
possible: "Where ya going mountain climbing?" RGM: "We are going to do a west face route
on Florence Peak out of Mineral King." Blank stares, then "Where?" Finally, RGM: "In the
Sierras." After this, some statement of recognition and sympathy usually follows. "Oh
yeah. I was in the Sierras," or "My brother was in the Sierras last summer" or "I want to go
to the Sierras," etc.

Another common misunderstanding is to identify people wearing backpacks and
walking down city streets as hitchhiking travelers. "Hey hitchhiker, where ya going?" This
is a more difficult situation to deal with. When people ask in open and seemingly honest
curiosity, "Where are you coming from?" or "Where are you going?" they expect to hear a
brief recounting of at least a modest journey. They are obviously dissatisfied when I tell
them I have not been anywhere except to the local high school and that I am not going
further than a few blocks to my house. The spirit of vicarious travel and adventure is lost,
and people turn away without asking why one would go to the local high school carrying a
fully loaded pack. The hitchhiker for some people is the contemporary urban replacement
for the much romanticized hobo. And a stay-at-home hobo without a story to tell is a sorry
disappointment.

Chapter 5

1. The fact that more climbers meet with accident or injury along the freeway than in
the mountains is an observation climbers are quick to point out in defense of their sport. This
is not surprising, considering the disproportionate exposure to hazards of the road experienced by the weekend climber. While ten hours of driving for a single climb is typical for the
Southern California mountaineer, ten hours of technical climbing, potentially the most
dangerous phase of the climbing process, would be more than might be expected on a
two-day trip.

2. In fairness to the climber, the principal offender in misuse of the backcountry is
another sort of wilderness user, the fisherman or woman. An acquaintance in the U.S.
Forest Service (Field notes 1976) supports this contention with the following observations.

The Palisades encompass an eight-mile-long stretch of the eastern escarpment of the
Sierras. They are considered by many to be the most spectacular mountaineering area in
California (see Roper 1976, 187, for a glowing description). They are liberally appointed with
imposing granite peaks to tempt the climber, including five of the eleven 14,000-foot peaks
in the entire range. Numerous climbing parties are thus attracted to the area throughout the
year. By contrast, lakes and streams to interest the fisherman are conspicuously absent. As a
result of this reduced pressure from fishing fans, the Palisades remain one of the cleanest,
most well-preserved mountain areas in the state.

The implied damnation of the fishermen, in this example, of course fails to take into
consideration the relative number of climbers versus fisherfolk. Fishing is one of American's

most popular outdoor participant sports while mountaineering attracts only a tiny minority of outdoor recreationalists. Rendering an area unattractive to fishermen, therefore, probably ensures a proportionate reduction in use greater than the increase attendant on encouraging climbers to visit that same area. Climbers may be as sloppy in the wilderness as their fishing counterparts; there are just fewer of them. Certainly, climbers are not entirely blameless. Whatever group or groups are the ultimate worst offenders, the automobile plays a key role in bringing about the desecration of the backcountry.

3. Norms of this sort are applied according to the objective of the climber. Those who ascend summits by their easiest or most popular routes generally include more of the nontechnical approach in their definition of mountaineering than those who seek out more difficult routes. The latter may show little concern for methods of approach but be highly critical of the means used to overcome technical portions of the climb. Peak-baggers on their way to the top by less technical routes take pride in their ability to meet all of the mountain's demands, including long approach hikes and scrambling, if need be.

4. This vast retinue of porters was erroneously credited as being in support of the Japanese Ski Expedition in the film *The Man Who Skied Down Everest*. In fact, the ski party was only a minor part of the Japanese climbing effort, which included attempts on the difficult and then unclimbed South West Face as well as the traditional South Col route.

5. Ski-mountaineers and cross-country skiers might also be added to this list. Both ski-mountaineers and climbers may employ common techniques and share a common territory. Whereas the climber emphasizes the ascent as the central purpose for climbing, the ski-mountaineer climbs in order to access the downhill run through the wilderness snows. Some of these runs are over terrain so steep that it may require technical climbing techniques to ascend. A small but avid group of Southern California mountaineers devote their summers to the climbing of challenging peaks and their winters to skiing that same territory in places where the grade is not quite as steep. Other climbers use skis as a means of access to base camps when they must travel over snow for some distance on the approach. The author is an avid and experienced cross-country skier. This traditional Nordic sport has recently enjoyed a resurgence of interest. Skiers with sophisticated and light skis and boots are capable of wilderness travel in a variety of terrain and might be likened to winter backpackers. I have used Nordic skis and three-pin bindings and boots to ski three times across the Sierra Nevada, on a month-long crossing of the Monarch Icefield in British Columbia, and on numerous mountain trips in the Oregon and Washington Cascades.

Chapter 8

1. The award system within the Sierra Club is paralleled in other climbing and outdoor activity clubs. The Portland-based Mazamas has a similar program of awards and recognition. Some modest reputation as a climber accrues to one who simply becomes a member of the Mazamas, for membership is predicated on at least minimal mountaineering experience. "Who can join? Any person of good character who has climbed to the summit of a mountain peak on which there is at least one living glacier is eligible for membership" (Mazamas membership information brochure, 1979). Beyond simple membership, the Mazamas member may earn awards that signify various levels of climbing achievement. The brochure identifies three.

> Guardian Peaks. An award given by the Climbing Committee for successful ascents of Mt. Hood, Mt. St. Helens, and Mt. Adams on official Mazamas climbs.
> Seven Oregon Cascades Peaks. An award given by the Climbing Committee for successful ascents of Mt. Hood, Mt. Jefferson, Mt. Washington, Three-Fingered Jack, North Sister, South Sister, and Middle Sister.

Sixteen Major Northwest Peaks. A bronze plaque awarded for the successful ascent of all peaks in the previous awards plus Mt. Shuksan, Mt. Baker, Glacier Peak, Mt. Stuart, Mt. Olympus, Mt. Rainier, and Mt. Shasta.

In Russia, an award system exists, but climbers there have much less choice about participating in organization-sponsored climbs. Russian climbers are restricted in the mountaineering activities they may participate in until they have demonstrated considerable ability and have amassed a good deal of experience in organized climbs. Likewise, the awards they seek and the identity-enhancement techniques available to them are more standardized than those available to the Western mountaineer. Russian mountains are officially graded in difficulty from 1a to 5 b. Mountaineers are similarly graded. Those who have grasped the bare essentials of technique and climbed a mountain rated 1b or more are awarded the badge of "Mountaineer of the USSR." They then may work their way up through Third- and Second- to First-Class Climber. The highest ranks are Master of Sport and Honored Master of Sport. Russian climbers often make considerable efforts to qualify as masters, for the rank carries with it a number of privileges, including the most important one of being allowed to choose one's own climb. In addition, the All-Union Physical Culture and Sport Committee awards bronze, silver, and gold medals to the prizewinners in mountaineering competitions held annually (Keenlyside 1975, 187–88).

2. Through the courtesy and hard work of Katharine Shadell Mitchell and the staff of the Bancroft Library at the University of California, Berkeley, I was able to obtain photocopies of a sample of summit-register entries from ten peaks in the Sierra Nevada. Peaks were selected to represent both easy (Olancha Peak) and difficult (North Palisade) climbing problems, in readily accessible (Mount Ritter) and remote (Mount Goddard) areas, and areas of relative popularity (Mount Ritter) and obscurity (West Tyndall). Other peaks include Mount Sill, University Peak, Dragon Peak, and Middle Palisade. For each peak, the most recent register materials were used as a starting point and then photocopies were made of the thirty preceding pages of register entries or until the material was exhausted, whichever came first. This yielded 270 pages of register copy containing roughly six entries per page for a total of over 1,600 register entries. Because the entries ranged from short, one-line remarks and signatures to multipage messages, and because some of the original register pages were small pocket-notebook size but others were textbook size or even larger, the number of entries per page varied considerably.

Entries began as early as August 1911 (University Peak) and as late as August 1966 (Mount Darwin). The most recent entries were for the July 4, 1970 (Mount Darwin, Mount Sill, North Palisade, Mount Ritter). The longest period of time encompassed by any of the entries from a single sampled peak was fifty-four years for University Peak, from August 1911 to October 1965. The shortest period was four years on Mount Goddard, from July 1966 to August 1969. In general, the more abbreviated the time-spread, the more popular and easily ascended the peak. In addition to these registers that could be examined in detail and at leisure, I examined forty-five summit registers on peaks climbed from 1974 through 1980 in the Sierra Nevada and the Pacific Northwest, dozens of registers on lesser peaks in the Southern California area, and several "record books" in Switzerland. All examples reported here are drawn from the sample for which photocopies were available.

3. Willi Unsold himself was swept to his death in an avalanche on Mount Rainier in March 1979. He was leading a group of twenty students from Evergreen State College in Olympia, Washington, where he was a professor of religion and philosophy. Unsold was one of the first five Americans to reach the summit of Everest in 1963, on the climb discussed more extensively in Chapter 11. (*Summit*, February-March 1979, 34.)

4. For other examples of stylistic limitations and normative change, specifically within the American rock-climbing community, see Lawrence Hamilton's article "Modern American Rock Climbing: Some Aspects of Social Change" (1979, 285–308).

5. Tincture of benzoin is a liquid applied to the fingertips which hardens the skin and

allows more strenuous fingerholds to be accomplished with less pain than when fingers remain untreated.

6. Peter Donnelly (1981b, 28–31) argues that the notion of climbing as being noncompetitive is one of the sports' pervasive fallacies. If this assertion is true, the implications for the future of climbing are serious. In Chapter 14 I will argue that unbridled competition and the attendant shift from intrinsic rewards to extrinsic praises and prizes illustrates the widespread rationalization of sport and other institutionalized leisure.

Personally, I do not believe that a majority of climbers are all that keenly competitive. Contemporary competition in climbing is largely among young, up-and-coming rock-climbing specialists in popular and populous areas. Competition only vaguely describes the motives of mainstream mountaineers. Competition may appear to be increasing because of the high visibility and vociferousness of a small subgroup of the climbing community. For most participants the gratification in mountaineering still lies in the experience itself; external rewards are neither necessary nor appropriate.

Chapter 9

1. For the reader unfamiliar with the books of Erving Goffman, especially his influential first work, *The Presentation of Self in Everyday Life* (1959) some of the terms and expressions used in this chapter may seem confusing or, worse, misleading. Goffman's keen analysis of everyday interaction uses the metaphor of life as drama, the world as a stage, after the perspective of Kenneth Burke (and of course of Jaques in Shakespeare's *As You Like It*). This useful viewpoint draws attention to the action people take to define the social situations in which they participate. Impression management is Goffman's term for this process where social actors offer words, gestures, and other actions that convey their impressions of the goings on and encourage others to define their world similarly. The impressions we provide to others are best interpreted as requests for compliance from others, attempts to get them to see the world as we would like. The child stands straight beside his father's chair at dinner, hair combed, face scrubbed, clothes neat, silent, and beaming. Before the parent is the child's report card, excellent throughout. The child wishes to define this as a time for praise and congratulation and so manages his or her own behavior and the time and place of the interaction to make praise salient and appropriate. To discuss the climber's impression-management efforts is not to imply in some veiled way that mountaineers are hypocrites but to use a model by which behavior may be more clearly understood.

2. For an excellent and comprehensive discussion of the role of souvenirs in the impression-management efforts of tourists, see Dean MacCannell's *The Tourist: A New Theory of the Leisure Class* (New York: Schocken Books), especially chaps. 6 and 8.

3. For an elaboration and refinement of the placement of symbolically meaningful household objects, along with a general discussion of the generation, distribution, and classification of these items, see "The Symbolic Use of Household Objects" by Eugene Rochberg-Halton and Mihaly Csikszentmihalyi (paper presented at the Seventy-third Annual Meeting of the American Sociological Association, San Francisco, September 1978).

4. This is perhaps an unfair illustration, however, for it rarely occurs in contemporary climbing circles. Only a single instance of rope failure uncomplicated by other causes has been reported in the American Alpine Club's summary of accidents in the U.S. and Canada since 1973. Situations approximating this one, on the other hand, do occur. Ropes may be cut by stone-fall or abrasion. These become potential props. Rope used for other purposes, as "prusik" material or "slings" may also be damaged or torn and join the ranks of souvenirs. In the bad old days of weak organic-fiber ropes, before the era of nylon ropes, such failures were more common. When the Matterhorn was climbed for the first time, four of the seven summiteers were killed when the rope joining them together parted in an

accident on the descent. The remaining torn and frayed end was cut off and carried down the mountain by Edward Whymper, the trip's nominal leader. That frayed remnant brought for a time discredit to the guides who accompanied Whymper on his fateful climb and helped focus international attention on the then new "madness of mountaineering." For many years the Matterhorn was considered impossible to climb. It repeatedly repulsed the determined and skilled efforts of Europe's finest alpinists. When this most difficult and coveted objective was achieved and a book chronicling the climb was produced, it was not entitled "The Day the Matterhorn Was Climbed" or something similar. Clark's (1965) account bears another title—*The Day the Rope Broke*. That broken rope-end still can be seen in the climbers' museum in Zermatt, more than a hundred years after the fateful day.

5. The specialized tools used in high-standard technical ice-climbing may be more frequently broken than general-purpose ice axes.

6. Pete Boardman was part of the successful team of British climbers who ascended Everest by the difficult South West Face in 1975. On the summit he posed beside the Chinese tripod left the year before. He was wearing a light T-shirt, hand-lettered with a salutation, over his expedition down jacket (Scott 1976, 31). Similarly, when Tenzing Norkay became the first person to set foot on the world's highest summit he wore a scarf given to him by his friend and former climbing companion, Raymond Lambert. This memento does not show in the famous photo of Tenzing on the top, as it was covered by his outer clothing.

Chapter 10

1. This question is usually put another way. "Why do *men* climb mountains" (emphasis added). With this in mind, a note on sex-specific terms is needed. From time to time throughout this book the reader will come across such phrases as "men do," "men are," "all men desire," and the like, along with single-sex pronouns. Such usage is arbitrary and, if literally interpreted, inaccurate. This is a discussion about mountaineers, a term blessedly free from gender specificity. When a single-sex referent is so used, it should be taken as a statement about all participants regardless of gender. English, the linguists tell us, is one of the world's most highly evolved languages. It also retains considerable vestiges of archaic sexual attitudes. The reader is directed to "Our Sexist Language" by Ethel Strainchamps (1971:347–361) for a more complete discussion of this bias. I feel it is important to recognize this inequity in our common parlance. I have attempted to substitute nonsex-specific terms where I could without undue violation of syntax or continuity.

Climbing engenders an intimacy between people. It is not an intimacy based on vague sentimentality but an honest and profound respect for and trust in the proven skills and judgment of others. It is on that hard, uncompromising ground that we must first judge our companions in the mountains. It is for this reason that this author selected his climbing partner. That that person is a woman is neither surprising nor important. If you are curious about why men climb mountains, I can tell you now it is for essentially the same reasons women do.

2. For examples, see Showell Styles, *On Top of the World*, chaps. 15–20 and James Ramsey Ullman, *The Age of Mountaineering*, pp. 17–23, as histories of mountaineering. See also Woodrow Wilson Sayre, *Four Against Everest*, chap. 15, "Why Men Climb"; Arnold Lunn, *A Century of Mountaineering*, chap. 2, "The Mountain Motive"; Ullman, *the Kingdom of Adventure*; chap. 8, "The Men and the Motives."

3. It is my hope to avoid, in these selections and elsewhere, criticism of the sort John Green directed at the lay writer on mountaineering: "What is it which makes men in Alpine travelbooks write as men never write elsewhere? What is the origin of a style unique in literature, which misses both the sublime and the ridiculous, and constantly hops from tall-talk to a mirth feeble and inane?" (Green, in Lunn 1957, 46).

4. See Freud, *A General Introduction to Psychoanalysis,* pp. 161–62, 313–18, for hints of the origins of these interpretations. Also, Edward Podolsky and Alexandra Alder, *Encyclopedia of Aberrations.*

5. It should be noted that Ryn's sample of subjects roughly approximates the demographic character of Southern California climbers with regard to age, occupational type, education level, and marital status. (See Chapter 12 for a description of the typical Southern California mountaineer.)

6. My thanks to Thomas E. Lasswell and Robert G. Harlow for their constructive criticism. Also my apologies. I have maintained the text in much the form they saw it with the alternative interpretations they proposed only hinted at. The text does, however, reflect what I believe is a consistent and widespread point of view regarding the motives of mountaineers. Even if these members of the mental health profession do not see it that way, it remains my opinion that many others view climbing as the manifestation of some form of mental illness or aberration.

7. These ecstatic reactions come while Herzog is still in the hospital recovering from the exposure and cold injuries that were to require the amputation of most of his fingers and toes and that brought him many times close to death on his retreat from the mountain.

8. This author recalls a forced bivouac on a climb at over 14,000 feet, near the summit of a Sierra Nevada peak. It is true that the stars were brighter than usual up there. Yet I would have gladly foregone such celestial clarity for a cup of hot cocoa and a warm bed in my camp 3,000 feet below. A good night's sleep and pleasant dreams would have more than compensated for the minor loss of astronomical immediacy.

9. The mountaineering reader may be amused by these "offensive" remarks made by Leslie Stephen:

> And what philosophical observations did you make? will be the inquiry of one of those fanatics who, by a reasoning process utterly unscrutable, have somehow irrevocably associated alpine traveling with science. To them I answer that the temperature on the summit of the Zinal Rothorn was approximately (I had no thermometer) 212 (Fahrenheit) below freezing point. As for ozone, if any existed in the atmosphere it was a greater fool than I take it for. (Stephen, in Lunn 1957, 45)

It should be noted that Sir Leslie Stephen, Tyndall's antagonist here and great alpine pioneer in his own right, had somewhat of a reputation for eschewing traditionalism. Although he was descended from evangelical Christians and took Holy Orders himself, he has been described as an "evangelical agnostic stubbornly loyal to Christian morality in spite of his rejection of the Christian creed" (Lunn 1957, 66).

10. Purposeful accounts for climbing are diminished but not gone entirely. During the post-monsoon season of 1981 the American Medical Research Expedition to Mount Everest ascended that peak ostensibly to study the effect of altitude on human physiology, according to Rod Patterson (1981, 11) in his article "Oregon Physician Climbs Everest for Scientific Tests." This climb was cosponsored by the American Alpine Club, the American Physiological Society, and the Explorers Club. Various physiological tests were performed on climbers and Sherpas at points along the climb, and there was a successful summit bid in late October. My guess is that a good time was had by many of those on this climb of the world's highest summit. Science may have benefited, too.

11. When members of the frostbitten, exhausted, and severely dehydrated summit team reached Camp I on their descent from Everest on the 1963 American expedition, there was no water for them to drink except for the melted glacial core samples Maynard Miller had collected painstakingly over the past weeks. These samples were destined to be returned to the U.S. for subsequent analysis. In the face of the parched condition of the descending climbers, however, Miller's entire stock of research materials was quickly

converted into cool drinks for the summiteers, leaving only damp esophagi and a feeling of goodwill in place of considerable scientific data (Ullman 1964b, 278–79).

12. The Snohomish and Quinault tribes on the Pacific coast and Puget Sound areas in the state of Washington have folktales that explain the necessity of rivers flowing in only one direction, from the mountains to the sea, tied to the practical concerns of salmon spawning and the mechanisms of fishing (Clark 1953, 86–87).

Chapter 11

1. Csikszentmihalyi (1975, 1–12) argues for the need to look beyond simple stimulus-response models or others that focus upon strictly extrinsic reward, if enjoyment is to be understood. Similarly, he rejects perspectives which attend only to the function of intrinsically rewarding experience to the exclusion of the experience itself. Such is the case of those who propose the resolution of unconscious dilemmas or the expression of other urges as the prime motives for enjoyment. According to Csikszentmihalyi, people do not dance, play chess, or climb rocks primarily for material gain, social recognition, or to escape the guilt of veiled penis envy. They do these things because they offer a special kind of personal reward in and of themselves.

2. For comparison, 519 persons were killed in automobile accidents during the month of July 1978 in the state of California alone (Radio Broadcast, KNX-AM, August 3, 1978). In addition, 8,300 pedestrians were killed by cars in the U.S. in 1976 (National Safety Council, 1977).

3. This is not to suggest that these activities are not possible occasions for flow but to define more clearly the mountaineer's point of view. The gambler is capable of intense concentration and involvement in the toss of the dice or turn of the wheel. He or she may cling to a hope that "lady luck" or other outside agency will intervene on his or her behalf or that special incantations, body language, lucky talismans, or other sorcery will influence the play. Yet only when attempts are made to influence outcomes physically with weighted dice or controlled wheels do the gambler and the climber come to share a similar involvement with their respective games. Flow is possible for both players but the mountaineers seek to manipulate and control outcomes purposefully while the gambler waits hopefully.

4. See in particular Maddi's (1972, 244–52) discussion and review of empirical findings concerning the role of tension reduction as motive. Also, Fiske and Maddi (1961) for a general collection of articles concerned with stimulus variability in human and animal behavior. Ivan Light (1969) has criticized Berger and Luckman's *The Social Construction of Reality* by arguing that uncertainty as well as certainty is a natural and intentional product of social interaction.

5. The penchant of anxious persons to set themselves very high or very low aspirations has been noted over and over again in the literature on levels of aspiration (see, for instance, Lewin et al. 1944). An intriguing addition to this body of work is contributed by Jay Haley (1971). He discusses the interaction patterns of schizophrenic patients, perhaps the extreme in persons motivated by a desire to avoid failure. He points out that communication between persons defines the roles those interactants will play even when one or both may not wish these situated identities to be defined. Once it is known who one is for the purpose of ongoing interaction, then, one is expected to act upon the basis of that identity and action entails a certain risk of failure, however slim. Haley demonstrates how schizophrenics, in order to avoid having the situation defined, thus running the risk of failure in enactment of some agreed-upon identity, use a system of multilevel negation of all of their communications. Verbal messages are ambiguous and inappropriately articulated through discordant vocal and linguistic patterns. Body movements contradict these messages, and all may be

out of tune with expections of the context in which the communication takes place. Not all persons who seek to avoid failure, however, can be viewed as mentally ill.

6. The "rules" referred to here are not the stylistic or ethical limitations climbers impose on the use of equipment, etc., but the more essential understandings about mutual safeguarding between partners on a rope. Climbers need not share a common view on ethical issues to climb effectively together. Ethics and style are lowland concerns (see Bonnington 1972, 13–17). But no climber, even if he or she is capable, continues to climb with an incompetent, drunk, or absentminded belayer.

Chapter 12

1. One argument which should be put to rest here is that mountaineering appeals only to the affluent and that these differences in avocational choice reflect merely the standard of living within the cited nations. Legions of impoverished American and European youth who take to the mountains each year contradict this belief. Likewise, when sudden wealth comes to those whose prior circumstances were tenuous, they may rejoice in their escape from economic threat but fail to seek control-oriented action in mountaineering and similar sport. Rather, they escalate the level of acceptance-oriented action in which they participate. Shooting craps in the hallway with a few buddies is replaced by high-rolling weekends at the gambling casino, but games of chance remain the central focus. The nouveaux riches may celebrate their newly found solvency by buying yachts and thoroughbred horses, but they do not take up scuba diving or playing polo. Nor is this observed difference at the national level a function of the availability of proximate mountainous terrain. Ugandans have nearby and ready access to Africa's greatest mountains, Kenya and Kilimanjaro, while Britishers have nothing in their native land beyond low and unimpressive training crags and hills. Similarly, the great mountains of the world are to be found in such countries as Peru, Chile, Pakistan, India, and Nepal, yet few climbers hail from these nations.

2. The questionnaire was accompanied by a letter from the chairperson requesting member cooperation. For a mail-out survey of such length and complexity, the response rate was excellent: 108 questionnaires (72 percent) were returned, with four more respondents telephoning to make suggestions and offer apologies for not returning the written form. Apparently the survey was taken seriously and considered important by a large proportion of committee members. When items called for criticisms and new ideas, respondents provided extensive, thoughtful and frequent commentary. Several responded in the margins and in accompanying notes that they were pleased interest was being shown in their background and opinions. While anonymity was ensured in the design of the survey instrument, almost all respondents (95 percent) chose to include their names with their return questionnaires.

3. The noted American author-mountaineer Galen Rowell and I discussed the possibilities of estimating the size and characteristics of the independent climber population, with few constructive results (Field notes, December 1979). To my suggestion that wilderness permits might be used as a way of defining the wilderness-using population, presumably including the independent climber, Rowell remarked, in essence, "I only get a permit if I am absolutely certain I am going to get caught." To the idea of using summit registers as a means of identifying the climbers who reach a particular summit, he retorted that independent climbers do not sign summit registers. (The most famous of solo Sierra Nevada mountaineers was Norman Clyde, and his name appears or has appeared in the summit register of every major peak in the range.) Finally, I suggested a trail-head intercept interview technique of the sort used occasionally with recreational resource use-studies. Rowell dismissed the feasibility of this procedure: "You wouldn't get me that way. I'd be

around the trail head and gone." Apparently the truly independent climber is also the invisible climber whose presence goes undetected at the beginning of his upward journey (the trail head) and at the end (the summit). Undoubtedly there are a few such persons climbing mountains. However, at least on the basis of discussion, I would guess their numbers to be few. The image of mysterious uncounted mountaineers slipping effortlessly past the snares of the law and the social scientist, on their silent, unmarked ways to the peaks is, I believe, more a figment of romantic wishful thinking than a social reality.

4. This impression is supported by data from the Mountaineering Training Committee (MTC) Survey. When the MTC respondents answered the question "How did you first get into mountaineering?" 54 percent ranked "Sierra Club courses" as their first or second most important reason. Of the MTC respondents, 92 percent had taken at least the Sierra Club's Basic Mountaineering Training Course; 59 percent had more advanced club-sponsored training; and 31 percent had sought out and completed mountaineering courses outside those offered by the Sierra Club.

5. The MTC respondents had an average occupational prestige rating of 87. This is a figure based upon the socioeconomic scores for 297 occupational categories with a range from 1 (lowest) to 99 (highest). This is a multiple-item measure derived by averaging scores for the component items of occupation, education, and family income. The data are from males fourteen years old and over in the experienced civilian labor force as of 1950 (Miller 1971, 178–93).

Similar conclusions may be drawn from the results of the Alpine Club of Canada (ACC) survey discussed above. In that poll, information regarding the respondents' income was available in addition to other demographic data. Of the Canadian respondents, 18 percent had incomes below $10,000/year; 14 percent between $15,000 and $20,000; and 29 percent between $20,000 and $30,000. The remainder presumably had incomes of more than $30,000 annually, but due to a typographical error, resulting in the omission of the actual percentage in the published tables, this is only an inference. The major occupational groupings used to describe the Canadian climber include: student, 14 percent; blue-collar, housewife, 7 percent; doctor, lawyer, dentist, 6 percent; engineer, 15 percent; other white-collar occupations, teachers, professors, 34 percent (Bratton et al. 1979, 56). It was noted before that Canadian climbers are similar to their American counterparts in sex distribution, educational level, and marital status. On the basis of the Canadian survey results, a typical ACC climber would most likely be a married male, 30–39 years of age, with a university degree, white-collar employment, and an income between $20,000 and $30,000 per annum. From this description, the image of the mountain climber as a person who enjoys social stability and economic success, with considerable education and occupational prestige, is given further support.

6. Two real-life examples are not too far from these descriptions. A biochemist friend of mine expressed a fervent desire throughout her graduate training to use her skills in support of environmental issues but discovered after months of searching that the only "research" position open to her was as an employee of Tenneco, testing the purity of "Taco," "Swedish Meatball," and other flavored almonds! Another friend with a graduate degree in chemistry now sells gas chromatographs after a fruitless search for advanced medical training or a research position. Both are amply paid for their services and thus, as Festinger (1968) would suggest, are unlikely to change the lowly opinions they have of their work. Both are avid climbers.

Chapter 14

1. It is important to make clear the causal primacy of rationalization. Neither the religious ethic of Protestantism nor the economic organization of capitalism are independently or in combination solely responsible for changes in modern leisure and work life.

Both share a common antecedent: "the same forces that have organized the factory and office have organized leisure as well" (Lasch 1978, 123). The causal independent variable, the classic explanatory factor is rationalization as that term is defined and used here—the urge toward adoption of a scientifically ordered, calculable, quantifiable world view. With regard to play, Guttmann concurs: "The emergence of modern sport represents neither the triumph of capitalism nor the rise of Protestantism but rather the slow development of an empirical, experimental, mathematical *Weltanschauung*" (Guttmann 1978, 85).

Guttmann points out that non-Protestant Japan and noncapitalist Marxist societies have, like the capitalist West, become rationalized in both work and leisure. The alterations in leisure identified here have "less to do with the Protestant ethic and the spirit of capitalism than with the intellectual revolution symbolized by the names of Isaac Newton and John Locke and institutionalized in the Royal Society . . . for the advancement of science" (Guttmann 1978, 85). The form of modern leisure is less the product of capitalist corruption or loss of sacred ritualistic elements in play than it is an effort to infuse scientific understanding and efficient management into all realms of human endeavor. Rationalization, of itself, is sufficient.

The extent to which disenchantment has accompanied rationalization outside Protestant, capitalist societies is a matter of conjecture, awaiting research for confirmation or denial. Gerth and Mills suggest that rationalization and disenchantment are inseparable, the degree of the former indicated by the latter. "The extent and direction of 'rationalization' is thus measured negatively in terms of the degree to which magical elements of thought are displaced, or positively by the extent to which ideas gain in systematic coherence and naturalistic consistency" (Gerth and Mills 1946, 51).

For purposes of discussing Western mountaineering and other leisure activities I assume that rationalization and disenchantment are coincident.

2. Climbers too are constrained by language in trying to articulate their avocation. At the local meeting hall or pub they may gather and discuss endless technical minutia, gadgets, techniques, route details. But if they are called upon to describe the subjective experience of climbing, perhaps by an inquisitive onlooker, the conversationalists are likely to stammer tongue-tied to a halt after a few traditional platitudes about companionship and panoramic views. At times the climber's frustration at his or her inability to externalize through meaningful speech what inwardly is a genuine and profoundly enthralling experience gives rise to displaced anger being expressed toward the questioner. Climbers may retort there is no "need" to discuss motive and sensation, that "you cannot understand it unless you have done it," or that it is simply "natural." Mountaineering writing often reflects a utilitarian bias. Artful and sensitive expressions of the sense of climbing are far less frequent than meticulous, plodding descriptions of preparations, approach travel, equipment, routes, schedules, and other data. The beauty of works like Bob Craig's *Storm and Sorrow* (1977) or Kurt Diemberger's *Summits and Secrets* (1971) is that these fine climbers are able to share the expressive component of their sport with other mountaineers and the lay reader alike.

3. The position taken here is not universal among climbers. In populous and popular rock-climbing areas and areas of heavy mountaineering usage such as the Yosemite Valley in California or the Chamonix region of the Alps intense pressure may brought on individuals to conform to local norms. This external pressure suggests the beginning of rationalization within climbing itself, a movement underscored by increasing concern with competition, records, ratings, and personal recognition to the exclusion of the intrinsic satisfaction of climbing itself. These preoccupations are not yet shared by a majority of climbers but they are to be found among an elite vocal minority.

4. Some may object to this interpretation of Caillois and argue that the intent of segmentation and regulation is to identify those individuals with the greatest skill and to provide each participant with the opportunity for fair play. The underlying assumption of such reasoning is that rationalization serves the interests of participants, not external agencies, and that outcomes hinge on individual skill and will within egalitarian framework.

I suggest that as rationalization progresses the individual dwindles in importance to a position that is no more than equal to, if not actually subservient to, the scientific managers of play, especially when the action has been commercialized or politicized (e.g., NFL football, the Russian Olympic soccer team). The relative importance of managerial style and strategy versus player skill in producing ultimate outcomes is certainly debatable. Clearly the coach/manager is not unimportant. This is obvious in team activities where players enact but do not design much of their own play routines, as in football.

5. Video games may define acts like violent death as inconsequential, even as "fun" if one is on the "winning" side. The extent of this desensitization to human suffering is suggested by the comments of an eyewitness to a real-life tragedy. On May 15, 1982, Gordon Smiley entered turn 3 at the Indianapolis Motor Speedway on his second qualifying lap for the Indianapolis 500 race. He lost control of his car and struck the cement retaining wall head-on. He was traveling over 180 miles per hour when he crashed. His car disintegrated in a roaring ball of high-octane gasoline. The only recognizable piece of wreckage, the front wheels and suspension, rolled out of the flames and flipped almost 500 feet across the asphalt. As the somersaults slowed, Smiley's helmetless body was visible still belted into the remains of his seat. The suspension finally came to rest on top of him. How did one witness see it? What did it remind him of? "It was just like watching one of the Atari games—little explosions all over" (quoted in Duin, 1982: F1).

6. Even experiences as isolated and ephemeral as smelling like a mountain climber are commercially available. In an Avon cosmetic advertisement we learn:

> Every man wants to live life to its fullest. Create excitement. Accept challenges.
> He yearns for experiences that are different. And now there's a fragrance just
> right for him. *Everest*. It's more than a fragrance. It's a statement of masculinity.

Needless to say, Avon's "Everest" fragrance bears no resemblance whatever to the odor of real climbers on an extended trek. The genuine smell is one most climbers are anxious to rid themselves of at the earliest opportunity upon returning home, with the enthusiastic urging of spouses, children, and others downwind.

7. Intrinsically rewarding action focuses on the present; external rewards are based upon differences between the present and either the past or the future. Of course, time in a Newtonian universe is linear and inexorably progressive, but social time can be viewed somewhat differently. When the goal of action is change, creation of new conditions, and the rate of progress is perceived as inadequate, as too slow, persons are alienated. Others may perceive change as undesirable and experience anomie when circumstances alter too rapidly.

8. Only with strong external direction and organizational support do Americans participate in culturally mandated athletics such as baseball, basketball, and football. Although competition and team play may be widely valued, they are not characteristic of American leisure. The National Physical Fitness Survey conducted on behalf of the President's Council on Physical Fitness and Sport collected data on the exercise habits of a representative sample of the U.S. population twenty-two years of age and over. Approximately 62 percent of the males and 45 percent of the females had participated at least once in extra-curricular team sports while attending school, from first grade through college (Opinion Research Corporation 1973, 2). Upon completion of formal education, sport participation dropped sharply. "The only sport with any drawing power in terms of participation on a competitive basis is bowling. . . . The remaining sports show very few people participating in them on a competitive basis" (Opinion Research Corporation 1973, 8). Eight percent of American males had bowled competitively at least once during the year preceding the survey interview. The *combined* participants in baseball, basketball, volleyball, football, handball, gymnastics, soccer, track and field, and wrestling amounted to less than 7 *percent*

during that same period. Women participated still less frequently. (Opinion Research Corporation 1973, 9). The highest participation rates were among high school rather than college students (Opinion Research Corporation 1973, 6).

It is perhaps the case that high school sport is more popular with participants because adolescents are not held to the same standards as adult players and thus avoid some of the criticism older athletes are likely to encounter for less than perfect performance. Additionally, bowling may be popular in part because it receives relatively little publicity and scrutiny from nonparticipants. These data suggest the image of America as a nation of active participants in competitive team sports is largely mythical.

Szalai reports Institute for Social Research data on time use in forty-four American standard metropolitan statistical areas. In the study year 1965–66 Americans spent an average of 6.5 minutes per day in "active sports" (Szalai 1972, 590). In ten years play habits had not apparently changed. Respondents in the 1975–76 survey reported 6.5 minutes of "active sports" participation (Institute for Social Research, n.d., table A 3.1).

Time spent in active sport appears to remain constant, but passive nonparticipant leisure is growing. In 1965–66 Americans watched an average of one hour and thirty minutes of television daily (Szalai 1972, 594). By 1979 this had expanded to four hours and nine minutes per day (Nielsen, in Lane 1981, 413). Already in 1983 the average American watched television every day for six hours and thirty minutes.

The premier leisure event in the United States, during the last decade, the activity involving roughly 45 percent of the nation's population on a single day is not the opening of fishing season, July 4 picnics or New Year's Eve parties. It is the Superbowl; the day more than 90 million people lounge on the sofa or easy chair, drinking and eating snacks and watching their television sets, while sixty or so participants play out a game (Nielsen, in Lane 1981).

Chapter 15

1. Weddings and funerals, awards and demerits, promotions and firings are all stressful yet they call forth different responses. Hans Selye (1956) has suggested two types of stress—distress and eustress. *Distress* connotes suffering, misery, sorrow, impending failure, and the like. Conversely, *eustress* indicates happiness, a sense of fulfillment. It is the latter concept, eustress, that is most frequently associated with successful leisure pursuits.

Neither eustress nor distress is as well defined as flow. Eustress may pehaps be viewed as an appropriate balance between ability and responsibility, i.e., as flow, while distress suggests inadequacy, loss, incapacity, i.e., anomie. It is, however, important to underscore the effortful quality of complete and gratifying leisure. Drawing attention to stress serves that purpose directly.

2. Marx ([1844] 1956) foresaw the mixed blessings of technological advancement. He warned of the alienation to be experienced when pride in one's handiwork and a sense of authorship are stripped away as workers lose control over the means of production. What he could not anticipate was the proportion of persons who would benefit materially under capitalism and, most important, the degree to which materialistic gratifications would be accepted as substitutes for a sense of personal worth and accomplishment in work and other primary roles.

Glossary

Aid climbing: Ascending with the help of mechanical devices such as pitons, chocks, and webbing used directly as handholds and footholds.

Anchor: A firm stance on the mountain created by employing various devices—chocks, pitons, bolts, or slings. Anchors are used to secure the belayer firmly in place and as intermediate protection points placed by the leader through which his or her rope passes in order to limit the potential distance of a fall. Also called "protection points" or "protection."

Belayer: The climber in a roped team who, while securely anchored to a fixed position on the mountain, is responsible for safeguarding those other climbers on the rope who are in motion climbing up or down precarious terrain. Belaying involves rope management aimed at maintaining minimal slack in the rope, thus reducing the maximum distance through which the unanchored climbers might fall. *See also* Leader.

Bergschrund: The gap between a glacier and snow fields on a mountain face; a large crevasse.

Bivouac: An impromptu camp created with minimal equipment, usually in an emergency circumstance.

Bolts: Expansion bolts forced into holes drilled into sections of rock to provide anchors.

Cairn: A pile of stones erected on a mountain summit to mark the presence of first-ascent climbers and to house a summit register. Also used to mark a difficult or confusing route or poor trail.

Carabiner: Strong ovoid metal rings with a gate on one side which is closed by the action of a spring. Carabiners are used for quickly and securely attaching various climbing devices to each other, for example, in attaching the climbing rope to an anchor. Also referred to as "biners" or "snaplinks."

Chocks: Metal wedges which can be fitted or jammed into cracks in rock and which serve as anchors. Also called "nuts," "stoppers," "copperheads." Brand types include Titons, Camlocks, Hexcentrics and Friends.

Cirque: A deep rounded hollow with steep sides and back formed in the mountainside through erosion from glacier ice. Cirques often resemble natural amphitheaters.

Cliff hanger: Small metal hook hung on rock nubbins and used for ascending when aid climbing.

Col: A dip or low point on a mountain ridge, usually between two points.

Cornice: A mass of snow formed by prevailing winds and overhanging the edge of a ridge.

Couloir: A steep gully cutting through a mountain face.

Crampons: Spiked frames which are fitted to the bottom of climbing boots to provide grip on ice and hard snow.

Crevasse: A crack in the surface of a glacier, sometimes very wide and deep, which is caused by movement of the glacier over and around irregular shapes in its bed or around bends.

Deadman: A small alloy metal plate used as an anchor in the snow; it acts like a nautical fluke anchor, digging in deeper the more pressure is applied to the tether line attached to it.

Diamond dust: A type of hoar frost created when airborne water vapor sublimes into solid crystals.

Etrier: Short flexible rope or metal ladders used to support the feet in aid climbing.

Firnspeigel: A thin layer of clear ice observed on snow surfaces in spring or summer, caused by melting below the snow surface as a result of solar radiation while freezing conditions prevail at the surface.

Free climbing: Climbing using only naturally occurring features on the mountain—rock, snow, ice, or vegetation—as handholds and footholds without pulling up on, standing on, or otherwise utilizing any mechanical device attached to the mountain to aid one's progress.

Grade: A measure of the extensiveness of technical difficulties encountered on a climb.

Graupel: A type of soft hail formed when falling snow crystals accumulate free water vapor which freezes, partly obscuring the original crystal structure.

Hoar frost: Ice crystals with distinct shapes such as blades, cups, and scrolls caused by the sublimation of water vapor from the air onto solid objects. When deposited on snow surfaces, this is known as "surface hoar." While still airborne, these particles are called "air hoar" or "diamond dust." When sublimation takes place in the snow pack, it may create a layer of unstable crystals called "depth hoar," a contributor to avalanches.

Ice axe: Multipurpose tool used in snow and ice travel, resembling a lightweight pick adz. Used in maintaining one's balance, in chopping steps in snow and ice, and in arresting a slip on moderate-angled slopes.

Ice fall: Where a glacier falls steeply and creates a series of crevasses and broken ice. Because ice falls are continually moving, albeit slowly, they are unstable and dangerous to travel through.

Ice screws: Metal tubes, spikes, or corkscrews used as anchors in ice.

Jumar: The brand name of a popular kind of mechanical device which allows a rope attached above to be ascended directly. These devices slide upward along the rope when unweighted but lock when a load is applied. Two Jumars are attached with cord, one to each foot, and the rope is climbed in exaggerated stair-step fashion. *See also* Prusik.

Leader: The climber who first advances upward over an unclimbed technical section of a mountain while being safeguarded from below by the belayer. Climbers may exchange the lead during the course of a climb, at the end of a pitch. An expedition leader is the climber responsible for making major strategic and tactical decisions on an expeditionary climb. He or she is not necessarily the first up the mountain.

Marmots: Large rodents similar to woodchucks but frequenting higher altitudes and mountainous terrain.

Moat: The gap between upper snow fields and the mountain rock. Also occurring at the sides of glaciers where the glacier ice meets the adjacent rock.

Neve penitente: Snow pillars produced when suncups become so pronounced that the cups intersect, leaving columns of snow standing between the hollows.

Open book: A rock formation created when two relatively smooth and vertical rock surfaces intersect at an angle like the opposing pages of a partially opened book standing upright. A crack is often found where the two surfaces meet, which facilitates climbing.

Pitch: A unit of measure used to indicate distance traveled up or down a technical portion of a climb. Equivalent to the length of the climbing rope, varying from roughly 100 to 150 feet.

Pitons: Metal spikes that serve as anchor points when pounded into rock cracks. Also called "pins," "pegs"; when large they are called "bongs" and when thin "knife blades." *See also* Rurp.

Porters: Indigenes of some climbing areas, notably the Karakoram and the eastern Himalayas, who are hired to carry loads in nontechnical terrain for expeditions. *See also* Sherpa.

Prusik: To ascend a rope dangling down from above by use of special friction knots and foot loops. Similar to jumaring but using only simple pieces of cord rather than mechanical devices. *See also* Jumar.

Rating: A measure of the maximum degree of technical difficulties encountered on a climb, regardless of the extent of these difficulties. Climbing ratings range from easy walking to the limits of human ability to achieve upward motion. These are expressed by various adjectival and numerical systems which vary from one country to another. *See also* Grade.

Rime: A dull, white dense deposit caused by freezing of airborne liquid water on cold objects exposed to the wind.

Route: The direction followed in ascending the technical portion of a climb.

Rurp: The "Realized Ultimate Reality Piton." A postage-stamp-sized piton used in aid climbing.

Sastrugi: A variety of erosional forms occurring when dry snow is subjected to scouring winds. Most common are wavelike forms with a sharp prow directed toward the prevailing wind.

Serac: Large unstable towers or blocks of ice broken off from the main body of the glacier, usually found in ice falls.

Sherpa: A member of a Tibetan tribe which has migrated to Nepal and northern India. Sherpas often serve expeditions as high-altitude load carriers on technical terrain on climbs in the central and eastern Himalayas. Sherpas are noted for their skill at mountain travel and physical endurance. *See also* Porter.

Sleet: Hollow ice pellets containing unfrozen water, the result of rain falling through air below freezing temperature.

Summit register: A metal box or other container atop a mountain, containing writing materials. Summiteers may record their names and other details of their climb therein.

Suncups: Regular depressions on the surface of summer snow fields caused by differential evaporation and melt across the surface and occurring in dry, warm conditions with some air movement.

Verglas: A layer of thin, clear ice derived from liquid water freezing on a rock surface.

Wind pack: Snow which has been compressed and hardened by wind action.

Several of these definitions were adapted from *Freedom of the Hills* (Manning 1967) and the glossaries in *Everest the Hard Way* (Bonnington 1976) and *Hazards in Mountaineering* (Paulcke and Dumler 1973).

Bibliography

American Alpine Club. 1982. *Accidents in North American Mountaineering*. New York.

Atkinson, John W. 1957. "Motivational Determinants of Risk-taking Behavior." *Psychological Review* 6:359–72.

Babbie, Earl R. 1979. *The Practice of Social Research*. Belmont, Calif.: Wadsworth Publishing.

Ball, Donald. 1972. "What the Action Is: A Cross-Cultural Approach." *Journal for the Theory of Social Behavior* 2 (October):121–43.

Barakat, H. 1969. "Alienation: A Process of Encounter between Utopia and Reality." *British Journal of Sociology* 20:1–20.

Beckey, Fred. 1973. *Cascade Alpine Guide: Columbia River to Stevens Pass*. Seattle: The Mountaineers.

Beer, Gavin R. de. 1967. *Early Travelers in the Alps*. London: Sidgwick and Jackson.

Benuzzi, Felice. 1952. *No Picnic on Mount Kenya*. London: William Kimber.

Berger, Peter L., and Thomas Luckman. 1967. *The Social Construction of Reality*. Garden City, N.Y.: Anchor Books.

Berglund, Peggy. 1978. "The Cussing Scale." *Off Belay* 39 (June):18.

Berlyne, Daniel. 1960. *Conflict, Arousal, and Curiosity*. New York: McGraw-Hill.

Bernstein, Jeremy. 1965. *Ascent: Of the Invention of Mountain Climbing and Its Practice*. New York: Random House.

Biggart, Nicole Woolsey. 1980. "Authentic Experience in a Rationalized World: An Ethnography of Vacation Resorts." Paper presented to the Pacific Sociological Association section on Leisure, Games, and Play, Portland, Oregon.

Blauner, Robert. 1970. "Social Alienation." Pp. 96–198 in Simon Marcson, ed., *Automation, Alienation and Anomie*. New York: Harper and Row.

Blumer, Herbert. 1969. *Symbolic Interactionism*. Englewood Cliffs, N.J.: Prentice-Hall.

Bonnington, Chris. 1971. *Annapurna South Face*. New York: McGraw-Hill.

———. 1972. "Too Cold for Ethics?" *Mountain* 21 (May):13–17.

———. 1976. *Everest the Hard Way*. New York: Random House.

Bowen, Ezra. 1972. *The High Sierra*. New York: Time-Life Books.

Bratton, Robert D., George Kinnear, and Gary Koroluk. 1979. "Reasons for Climbing: A Study of the Calgary Section." *The Canadian Alpine Journal* 62:55–57.

Brink, Jim, and Rob Kelman. 1981. "The Epic Epoch." *Climbing* 66:40–41.

Brniak, Marek. 1980. "Speed Climbing." *Climbing* 61:36–38.

Brown, Bert. 1978. "The Probability Factor." *Off Belay* 39 (June):20.

Brush, Charles F. 1976. "The Perils of Paid Treks." *Backpacker* 15:32–38.

Burdge, Rabel J. 1969. "Levels of Occupational Prestige and Leisure Activity." *Journal of Leisure Research* 3:262–74.

Caillois, Roger. 1961. *Man, Play and Games.* New York: The Free Press.

Camilleri, S. F., J. Berger, and T. L. Conner. 1972. "A Formal Theory of Decision Making." Pp. 21–37 in J. Berger, M. Zeldith, Jr., and B. Anderson, eds., *Sociological Theories in Progress*, vol. 2. Boston: Houghton Mifflin.

Campbell, Robin. 1974. "Climbing Ethics." *Mountain* 35 (May):31–33.

Camphausen, Fred. 1973. "Minus 90°." Stephenson-Warmlite Catalogue:35–47.

Catton, William R., Jr. 1969. "Motivations of Wilderness Users." *Pulp and Paper Magazine of Canada* (December 19):123–26.

Cheney, Michael. 1978. "Korean Mt. Everest Expedition." *American Alpine Journal*:589–90.

Chouinard, Yvon. 1977. "Climbing Ice." *Outside Rolling Stone* (December):31–33.

Clark, Alfred C. 1956. "The Use of Leisure and Its Relation to Occupational Prestige." *American Sociological Review* 21:301–7.

Clark, Donald. 1965. *The Day the Rope Broke.* New York: Harcourt, Brace and World.

Clark, Ella. 1953. *Indian Legends of the Pacific Northwest.* Berkeley: University of California Press.

Cleare, John. 1975. *Mountains.* New York: Crown Publishers.

Cleare, John, and Tony Smythe. 1966. *Rock Climbers in Action in Snowdonia.* London: Secker and Warburg.

Coburn, David. 1975. "Job-Worker Incongruence: Consequences for Health." *Journal of Health and Social Behavior* 16(2):213–25.

Cooley, Charles Horton. 1912. *Social Organization: A Study of the Larger Mind.* New York: Charles Scribner's Sons.

———. 1972. "Looking-glass Self." Pp. 231–33 in Jerome G. Manis and Bernard N. Meltzer, eds., *Symbolic Interaction*, 2d ed. Boston: Allyn and Bacon.

Coser, Lewis A., and Bernard Rosenberg, eds. 1969. *Sociological Theory* London: Macmillan.

Coser, Rose Laub, and Gerald Rokoff. 1974. "Women in the Occupational World: Social Disruption and Conflict." Pp. 490–511 in Rose Laub Coser, ed., *The Family: Its Structures and Functions.* New York: St. Martin's Press.

Craig, Robert W. 1977. *Storm and Sorrow in the High Pamirs.* Seattle: The Mountaineers.

Csikszentmihalyi, Mihaly. 1974. *Flow: Studies in Enjoyment.* PHS Grant Report N. RO1HM 22883–02.

———. 1975. *Beyond Boredom and Anxiety.* San Francisco: Jossey-Bass.

———. 1978. "Intrinsic Rewards and Emergent Motivation." Pp. 205–216 in Mark R. Lepper and David Greene, eds., *The Hidden Costs of Reward.* New York: John Wiley and Sons.

———. 1981. "Leisure and Socialization." *Social Forces* 60:332–40.

Csikszentmihalyi, Mihaly, and Eugene Rochberg-Halton. 1981. *The Meaning of Things*. Cambridge: Cambridge University Press.

Diemberger, Kurt. 1971. *Summits and Secrets*. London: George Allen and Unwin.

Dodge, Nicholas A. 1975. *A Climbing Guide to Oregon*. Beaverton, Ore.: Touchstone Press.

Donnelly, Peter. 1981a. "Four Fallacies." *Mountain* 80:38–40.

———. 1981b. "Climbing Is Non-competitive." *Mountain* 81:28–31.

Drasdo, Harold. 1974. "Climbing as Art." *Ascent*:78–79.

Duin, Steve. 1982. "Gordon Smiley 36th Crash Victim of Indy 500." *Portland Oregonian*, May 16, 1982:F1.

Durkheim, Emile. [1893] 1947. *The Division of Labor in Society*. New York: The Free Press.

———. [1895] 1938. *The Rules of Sociological Method*. New York: The Free Press.

———. [1897] 1951. *Suicide*. New York: The Free Press.

Dyhrenfurth, Norman. 1980. "Everest." *Mountain* 76:30–39.

———. 1980. "Everest Historical Summary." *Mountain* 76:42–43.

Edwards, R. H. T. 1975. "Physiology of Fitness and Fatigue." Pp. 107–10 in Charles Clarke, Michael Ward, and Edward Williams, eds., *Mountain Medicine and Physiology*. London: British Alpine Club.

Ewert, Alan. 1978. "Planning an Expedition." *Off Belay* 41 (October):2–7.

Fabiano Shoe Company. 1978. Advertisement. *Backpacker* 25, 1 (February):58.

Farquhar, Francis P. 1965. *History of the Sierra Nevada*. Berkeley: University of California Press.

Ferber, Peggy, ed. 1974. *Mountaineering: The Freedom of the Hills*, 3d ed. Seattle: The Mountaineers. (For 2d ed., see Manning.)

Festinger, Leon. 1954. "A Theory of Social Comparison Process." *Human Relations* 7: 117–40.

———. 1968. *A Theory of Cognitive Dissonance*. Stanford, Calif.: University of Stanford Press.

Feuer, Lewis. 1963. "What is Alienation?" Pp. 127–47 in Maurice Stein and Arthur Vidich, eds., *Sociology on Trial*. Englewood Cliffs, N.J.: Prentice-Hall.

Fiske, Donald W., and Salvatore R. Maddi. 1961. *Functions of Varied Experience*. Homewood, Ill.: The Dorsey Press.

Fontana, Andrea. 1978. "Over the Edge: A Return to Primitive Sensations in Play and Games." *Urban Life* 2 (July):213–29.

Ford, Daniel. 1983 "Tracking the Trails of Yesteryear." *Cross-Country Skier* February:38–43.

Ford, Dennis. 1978. "The Mountaineering Experience." *Summit* 3 (June–July):12–13.

French, J.R.P., and R.L. Kahn. 1962. "A Programmatic Approach to Studying the Industrial Environment and Mental Health." *Journal of Social Issues* 18 (January):1–47.

Freud, Sigmund. 1969. *A General Introduction to Psychoanalysis*. New York: Pocket Books.

Freund, Julien. 1969. *The Sociology of Max Weber*. New York: Vintage Books.

Frostline, Inc. 1976. Frostline Catalogue. Fall/Winter.

Gastorf, J., and J. Sols. 1978. "Performance Evaluation via Social Comparison: Performance Similarity versus Related-Attribute Similarity." *Social Psychology* 4:297–305.

Gerth, H.H., and C. Wright Mills, eds. 1946. *From Max Weber*. New York: Oxford University Press.

Giddens, Anthony. 1971. *Capitalism and Modern Social Theory*. London: Cambridge University Press.

Glaser, Barney G., and Anselm L. Strauss. 1972. "Awareness Contexts and Social Interaction." Pp. 442–62 in Jerome G. Manis and Bernard N. Meltzer, eds., *Symbolic Interaction*, 2d ed. Boston: Allyn and Bacon.

Glaser, Daniel. 1972. "Criminality Theories and Behavioral Images." Pp. 482–97 in Jerome G. Manis and Bernard N. Meltzer, eds., *Symbolic Interaction*, 2d ed. Boston: Allyn and Bacon.

———. 1978. *Crime in Our Changing Society*. New York: Holt, Rinehart and Winston.

———. 1981. Personal communication.

Godfrey, Bob. 1975. "An Englishman in the Court of King Royal." *Climbing* (May–June):2–7.

Goethals, G., and J. Darley. 1977. "Social Comparison Theory: An Attribution Approach." In J. M. Sols and R. L. Miller, eds., *Social Comparison Process: Theoretical and Empirical Perspectives*. Washington, D.C.: Hemisphere/Halsted.

Goffman, Erving. 1959. *The Presentation of Self in Everyday Life*. New York: Doubleday Anchor Books.

———. 1967. "Where the Action Is." Pp. 149–270 in *Interaction Ritual*. New York: Doubleday Anchor Books.

Grauer, John Foerste. 1975. *Mt. Hood: A Complete History*. Gresham, Ore.: Grauer.

Grazia, Sebastian de. 1962. *Of Time, Work, and Leisure*. Garden City, N.Y.: Doubleday.

Grey, Dennis. 1976. "Olympic Mountaineering." *Mountain* 51 (September/October):42.

Gross, Edward, and Gregory P. Stone. 1970. "Embarrassment and the Analysis of Role Requirements." Pp. 174–89 in Gregory P. Stone and Harvey A. Farberman, eds., *Social Psychology through Symbolic Interaction*. Waltham, Mass.: Ginn-Blaisdell.

Guttmann, Allen. 1978. *From Ritual to Record*. New York: Columbia University Press.

Haley, Jay. 1971. "Communication and Therapy: Blocking Metaphors." *American Journal of Psychotherapy* 2 (April): 214–27.

Hamilton, Lawrence. 1979. "Modern American Rock Climbing." *Pacific Sociological Review* 3 (July):285–308.

Harris, Dorothy V. 1972. "Stress-seeking and Sport Involvement." Pp. 71–89 in Dorothy V. Harris, ed., *Women and Sport: A National Research Conference*. Pennsylvania State University. Penn State HPER series 2.

Hebb, Donald O. 1955. "Drive and the CNS." *Psychological Review* (July):243–52.

Herzog, Maurice. 1953. *Annapurna*. New York. E. P. Dutton.

Hillary, Edmund. 1955. *High Adventure*. New York: E. P. Dutton.

Huizinga, Johan. 1950. *Homo Ludens: A Study of the Play Element in Culture*. Boston: Beacon Press.

Hunt, John. 1954. *The Conquest of Everest*. New York: E. P. Dutton.

Hunt, Joseph M. 1965. "Intrinsic Motivation and Its Role in Psychological Development." Nebraska Symposium on Motivation. Lincoln: University of Nebraska Press.

Hyman, Herbert H., and Eleanor Singer, eds. 1968. *Readings in Reference Group Theory and Research*. New York: The Free Press.

Institute of Social Research. N.d. "Patterns of Adult Time Use Based on the 1975–76 Time Use Data." Survey Research Center, Institute of Social Research, University of Michigan.

Israel, J. 1971. *Alienation: From Marx to Modern Sociology*. Boston: Allyn and Bacon.

Jenkins, Thomas M. 1979. "Perfume in the Ozone." *Summit* (June–July):20–21, 24–25, 29–30.

Johnson, Frank, ed. 1973. *Alienation*. New York: Seminar Press.

Jones, Chris. 1976. *Climbing in North America*. Berkeley: University of California.

Josephson, E., and M. Josephson. 1962. *Man Alone*. New York: Dell.

Kando, Thomas M., and Worth C. Summers. 1971. "The Impact of Work on Leisure." *Pacific Sociological Review* 14 (July):310–27.

Karrimor International, Ltd. 1976. Advertisement. *Mountain* 50 (July–August):55.

Kaufmann, Walter. 1970. "The Inevitability of Alienation." Pp. xiii-lvi in Richard Schacht, ed., *Alienation*. Garden City, N.Y.: Doubleday.

Keenlyside, Francis. 1975. *Peaks and Pioneers*. London: Paul Elek.

Kelly, John. 1981. "Leisure Interaction and the Social Dialectic." *Social Forces* 60:301–22.

King, Clarence. [1872] 1970. *Mountaineering in the Sierra Nevada*. Lincoln: University of Nebraska Press.

Kidder, Tracy. 1982. *The Soul of a New Machine*. New York: Avon Books.

Kingsley, Norman. 1975. *Icecraft*. Glendale, Calif.: La Siesta Press.

Kuhn, Manford H., and Thomas S. McPartland. 1954. "Empirical Investigation of Self Attitudes." *American Sociological Review* 60 (February):68–76.

Kuhn, Thomas S. 1962. *The Structure of Scientific Revolutions*. Chicago: The University of Chicago Press.

Kuypers, Joseph A., and Vern L. Bengtson. N.d. "Social Breakdown and Competence: A Model of Normal Aging." Revised version of paper prepared for the Community Mental Health and Aging Summer Institute, University of Southern California.

La Chapelle, E. R. 1970. *The ABC of Avalanche Safety*. Denver: Colorado Outdoor Sports Co.

Lasch, Christopher. 1978. *The Culture of Narcssism*. New York: W.W. Norton.

Lasswell, Thomas. 1979. Personal communication.

Lathrop, Theodore G. 1975. *Hypothermia*. Portland, Ore.: Mazamas.

Levin, Steven. 1978. "Lotus Flower Tower, Free Ascent." *American Alpine Journal*: 545, 547.

Lewin, K., T. Dembo, L. Festinger, and P. S. Sears. 1944. "Level of Aspiration." In J. Mc V. Hunt, ed., *Personality and the Behavior Disorders*, vol. 1. New York: Ronald Press.

Light, Ivan H. 1969. "The Social Construction of Uncertainty." *Journal of Sociology* 14:189–99.

Lunn, Arnold. 1957. *A Century of Mountaineering*. London: George Allen and Unwin.

Lyman, Stanford M., and Marvin B. Scott. 1970. "Accounts." Pp. 111–43 in Stanford M. Lyman and Marvin B. Scott, *A Sociology of the Absurd*. New York: Appleton-Century-Crofts.

MacAloon, John J., and Mihaly Csikszentmihalyi. 1974. "Structure and Experience in Rock-Climbing." Pp. 119–59 in M. Csikszentmihalyi, *Flow: Studies in Enjoyment*. PHS Grant Report N.R01HM 22883-02.

———. 1975. "Deep Play and the Flow Experience in Rock Climbing." Pp. 74–101 in M. Csikszentmihalyi, *Beyond Boredom and Anxiety*. San Francisco: Jossey-Bass.

MacCannell, Dean. 1976. *The Tourist: A New Theory of the Leisure Class*. New York: Shocken Books.

Maddi, Salvatore R. 1972. *Personality Theories*. Homewood, Ill.: The Dorsey Press.

Manning, Harvey, ed. 1967. *Mountaineering: The Freedom of the Hills*, 2d ed. Seattle: The Mountaineers. (For 3d ed., see Ferber.)

Marx, Karl. [1844] 1956. *Karl Marx: Selected Writings in Sociology and Social Philosophy*. T. B. Bottomore and Maximilien Rubel, eds. London: Watts.

Maslow, A. H. 1963. "The Need to Know and the Fear of Knowing." *Journal of General Psychology* 68:111–25.

Matous, Ron. 1980. "*Étranger* in a Strange Land." *Summit* 1 (February–March): 6–7, 32, 34, 36.

Mead, George Herbert. [1934] 1970. *Mind, Self and Society*. Charles W. Morris, ed. Chicago: University of Chicago Press.

———. 1938. *The Philosophy of the Act*. Charles W. Morris, ed. Chicago: University of Chicago Press.

———. 1964. *On Social Psychology*. Anselm Strauss, ed. Chicago: University of Chicago Press.

Mehan, Hugh, and Houston Wood. 1975. *The Reality of Ethnomethodology*. New York: John Wiley and Sons.

Mendenhall, Ruth. 1979. Personal communication.

Merton, Robert K. 1938. "Social Structure and Anomie." *American Sociological Review* 3 (October):672–82.

———. 1957. *Social Theory and Social Structure*. Glencoe, Ill.: The Free Press, 131–94.

Messner, Reinhold. 1974. *The Seventh Grade*. New York: Oxford University Press.

Metcalf, Peter. 1976. "A McKinley Traverse via Reality Ridge." *American Alpine Journal*:313–19.

Miller, Delbert C. 1971. *Handbook of Research Design and Social Measurement*, 2d ed. New York: David Mckay.

Mountain Magazine, Ltd. 1973. "International Grading Comparisons." *Mountain* 28 (July):14.

———. 1979. "Karakoram Opens Up." *Mountain* (May–June):18.

Mountain Travel, Inc. 1976. Mountain Travel Catalogue.

The Mountaineers. 1979. *Climber's Guide to the Olympic Mountains*, 2d ed. Seattle.

Murdock, George Peter. 1967. *Ethnographic Atlas*. Pittsburgh: University of Pittsburgh Press.

National Safety Council. 1977. "Motor Vehicle Deaths by Type of Accident, 1937–1976." P. 780 in Theodore B. Dolmatch, ed., *Information Please Almanac, 1978*. New York: Information Please Publishers.

Nelson, Marc. 1981. "Psychological Testing at High Altitudes." *Summit* 27(1):22–25.

Nielsen, A. C. 1981. "All-time Television Programs." P. 414 in Hana V. Lane, ed. *The World Almanac and Book of Facts*. New York: Newspaper Enterprise Association.

Noyce, Wilfrid. 1950. *Scholar Mountaineers*. New York: Roy Publishers.

O'Brien, Bart. 1978. "Climbing Half Dome—Twenty Years After." *American Alpine Journal*:466–70.

Opinion Research Corporation. 1973. *National Physical Fitness Survey.* Princeton, N.J.

Parker, Stanley. 1971. *The Future of Work and Leisure*. New York: Praeger.

Parsons, Talcott. 1951. *The Social System*. Glencoe, Ill.: The Free Press.

Patterson, Rod. 1981. "Oregon Physician Climbs Everest for Scientific Tests." *Portland Oregonian*, December 13, 1981:11.

Paulcke, Wilheim, and Helmut Dumler. 1973. *Hazards in Mountaineering*. London: Fakenham and Reading.

Pearson, Grant H. 1962. *My Life of High Adventure*. Englewood Cliffs, N.J.: Prentice-Hall.

Phillips, Derek L. 1971. *Knowledge from What?* Chicago: Rand McNally.

Podolsky, Edward, and Alexandra Alder. 1965. *Encyclopedia of Aberrations*. New York: Citadel Press.

Price, Tom. 1974. "Adventure by the Numbers." *Mountain* 38 (September):17–19.

Prochazka, Vladimir. 1981. "Czech Rock." *Climbing* (May–June) 66:16–19.

Putnam, William L., and Glen W. Boles. 1973. *Climber's Guide to the Rocky Mountains of Canada-South*. Springfield, Mass.: American Alpine Club.

Rebuffat, Gaston. 1957. *Starlight and Storm*. New York: E. P. Dutton.

Rebuffat, Gaston, and Pierre Tairraz. 1970. *Between Heaven and Earth*. New York: Oxford University Press.

Recreational Equipment, Inc. 1975. Summer Catalogue 1. Seattle.

Ridgeway, Rick. 1978. *The Last Step: The American Ascent of K2*. Seattle: The Mountaineers.

Robbins, Royal. 1973. *Advanced Rockcraft*. Glendale, Calif.: La Siesta Press.

Rochberg-Halton, Eugene, and Mihaly Csikszentmihalyi. 1978. "The Symbolic Use of Household Objects." Paper presented at the 73rd Annual Meeting of the American Sociological Association, San Francisco.

Roper, Steve. 1976. *The Climber's Guide to the High Sierra*. San Francisco: Sierra Club Books.

Rouse, Alan. 1972. "Two's a Crowd." *Mountain* 21 (May):28–31.

———. 1975. "Grading Systems." *Mountain* 43 (May–June):35–36).

Rowell, Galen. 1977a. *In the Throne Room of the Mountain Gods*. San Francisco: Sierra Club Books.

———. 1977b. "Hot Tuna Tower, Open Book Route." *American Alpine Journal*:182.

Ryn, Z. 1971. "Psychopathology in Alpinism." *Acta Medica Polona* 3: 453–67.

Sayre, Woodrow Wilson. 1964. *Four Against Everest*. Englewood Cliffs, N.J.: Prentice-Hall.

Schacht, Richard, ed. 1970. *Alienation*. Garden City, N.Y.: Doubleday.

Schlucter, Wolfgang. 1979. "The Paradox of Rationalization: On the Relation of Ethics and the World." Pp. 11–64 in G. Roth and W. Schlucter, eds., *Max Weber's Vision of History*. Berkeley: University of California Press.

Schutz, Alfred. 1962. *Collected Papers*: I. *The Problem of Social Reality*. Maurice Nelson, ed. The Hague: Martinus Nijhoff.

Scott, Doug. 1976. "Everest South West Face Climbed." *Mountain* 47:31.

Scott, M. D. 1965. "The Social Sources of Alienation." Pp. 239–52 in I. Horowitz, ed., *The New Sociology*. New York: Oxford University Press.

Seeman, Melvin. 1959. "On the Meaning of Alienation." *American Sociological Review* 24:783–91.

Selye, Hans. 1956. *The Stress of Life*. New York: McGraw-Hill.

Sherman, Paddy. 1965. *Cloud Walkers*. New York: St. Martin's Press.

Sierra Club. Annual. *Ascent*. San Francisco.

Sierra Club, Angeles Chapter—Ski Mountaineering and Rock Climbing Section. 1977. *Mugelnoos* 530 (February 16). Los Angeles.

Simmel, Georg. 1971. *On Individuality and Social Forms*. Donald N. Levine, ed. Chicago: University of Chicago Press.

Smith, Adam. [1776] 1980. *An Inquiry into the Wealth of Nations*. London: Methuen.

Snyder, Howard. 1973. *The Hall of the Mountain King*. New York: Charles Scribner's Sons.

Stephenson-Warmlite, Inc. 1974. "1973 Vagmarken Mount McKinley Expedition." Warmlite Catalogue:35–47.

Strainchamps, Ethel. 1971. "Our Sexist Language." Pp. 347–361 in Vivian Gornick and Barbara K. Moran, eds., *Woman in Sexist Society*. New York: Basic Books.

Stuck, Hudson. 1977. *The Ascent of Denali*. Seattle: The Mountaineers.

Styles, Showell. 1967. *On the Top of the World*. New York: Macmillan.

Summit, Inc. 1979. "Scree." *Summit* 1 (February–March):34.

Sykes, Gresham M., and David Matza. 1957. "Techniques of Neutralization: A Theory of Delinquency." *American Journal of Sociology* 22 (December):664–70.

Szalai, Alexander. 1972. *The Use of Time*. The Hague: Mouton.

Taylor, Frederick Winslow. 1923. *Principles of Scientific Management*. New York: Harper.

Tejada-Flores, Lito. 1967. "Games Climbers Play." *Ascent*:23–25.

———. 1974. "The Guidebook Problem." *Ascent*:80–85.

Terray, Lionel. 1963. *The Borders of the Impossible*. Garden City, N.Y.: Doubleday.

Textor, Robert B. 1967. *A Cross-Cultural Summary*. New Haven, Conn.: Human Relations Area Files Press.

Thomas, William I., and Dorothy Swain Thomas. 1928. *The Child in America*. New York: Alfred A. Knopf.

Thompson, Mike. 1979. "Sahibs and Sherpas." *Mountain* 48 (July–August):45–49.

Tillman, H. W. 1975. "Practical Problems of Nutrition." Pp. 62–66 in Charles Clarke, Michael Ward, and Edward Williams, eds., *Mountain Medicine and Physiology*. London: British Alpine Club.

Tobias, Michael. 1975. "The Anthropology of Ascent." *Mountain* 44 (July–August): 31–36.

Turner, Ralph H. 1956. "Role-taking, Role Standpoint, and Reference Group Behavior." *American Journal of Sociology* 61 (January):316–28.

Ullman, James Ramsey. 1947. *The Kingdom of Adventure: Everest*. Toronto: George B. McLeod.

———. 1964a. *The Age of Mountaineering*. New York: Lippincott.

———. 1964b. *Americans on Everest*. New York: Lippincott.

U.S. Department of Commerce, Bureau of the Census. 1973. *Census of the Population 1970*. Vol. 2, *Subject Reports. Occupational Characteristics*. Washington, D.C.: U.S. Government Printing Office.

———. 1977. *Social Indicators 1976*. Washington, D.C.: U.S. Government Printing Office.

Unsold, Willi, and Louis F. Reichardt. 1977. "Nanda Devi from the North." *American Alpine Journal*: 1–23.

Voge, Harvey H., and Andrew I. Smatko, eds. 1972. *Mountaineer's Guide to the High Sierra*. San Francisco: Sierra Club Books.

Weber, Max. 1958. *The Protestant Ethic and the Spirit of Capitalism*. New York: Charles Scribner.

Webster, Murray, and Barbara Sobieszek. 1974. *Sources of Self-Evaluation*. New York: John Wiley and Sons.

Whorf, Benjamin Lee. 1970. "Science and Linguistics." Pp. 112–21 in Gregory P. Stone and Harvey A. Farberman, eds., *Social Psychology through Symbolic Interaction*. Waltham, Mass.: Ginn-Blaisdell.

White, R.C. 1955. "Social Class Differences in the Use of Leisure." *American Journal of Sociology* 61:145–50.

Whymper, Edward. 1891. *Scrambles Amongst the Alps*. Cleveland, Ohio: The Burrows Brothers Co.

Wilder, Thornton. 1956. "The Matchmaker." P. 237 in Louis Kronenberger, ed., *The Best Plays of 1955–56*. New York: Dodd, Mead.

Wilensky, Harold L., 1960. "Work Careers and Social Integration." *International Social Science Journal* 12 (Fall):543–60.

Wilson, Robert N. 1981. "The Courage to Be Leisured." *Social Forces* 60:282–303.

Young, Geoffrey Winthrop. 1926. *On High Hills*. New York: E. P. Dutton.

Zanna, M., G. Goethals, and J. Hill. 1975. "Evaluating a Sex-related Ability: Social Comparison with Similar Others and Standard-Setters." *Journal of Experimental Social Psychology* 11:86–93.

Index